C-2212 CAREER EXAMINATION SERIES

This is your
PASSBOOK for...

Highway Maintenance Supervisor

Test Preparation Study Guide
Questions & Answers

NATIONAL LEARNING CORPORATION®

COPYRIGHT NOTICE

This book is SOLELY intended for, is sold ONLY to, and its use is RESTRICTED to individual, bona fide applicants or candidates who qualify by virtue of having seriously filed applications for appropriate license, certificate, professional and/or promotional advancement, higher school matriculation, scholarship, or other legitimate requirements of education and/or governmental authorities.

This book is NOT intended for use, class instruction, tutoring, training, duplication, copying, reprinting, excerption, or adaptation, etc., by:

1) Other publishers
2) Proprietors and/or Instructors of "Coaching" and/or Preparatory Courses
3) Personnel and/or Training Divisions of commercial, industrial, and governmental organizations
4) Schools, colleges, or universities and/or their departments and staffs, including teachers and other personnel
5) Testing Agencies or Bureaus
6) Study groups which seek by the purchase of a single volume to copy and/or duplicate and/or adapt this material for use by the group as a whole without having purchased individual volumes for each of the members of the group
7) Et al.

Such persons would be in violation of appropriate Federal and State statutes.

PROVISION OF LICENSING AGREEMENTS – Recognized educational, commercial, industrial, and governmental institutions and organizations, and others legitimately engaged in educational pursuits, including training, testing, and measurement activities, may address request for a licensing agreement to the copyright owners, who will determine whether, and under what conditions, including fees and charges, the materials in this book may be used them. In other words, a licensing facility exists for the legitimate use of the material in this book on other than an individual basis. However, it is asseverated and affirmed here that the material in this book CANNOT be used without the receipt of the express permission of such a licensing agreement from the Publishers. Inquiries re licensing should be addressed to the company, attention rights and permissions department.

All rights reserved, including the right of reproduction in whole or in part, in any form or by any means, electronic or mechanical, including photocopying, recording, or by any information storage and retrieval system, without permission in writing from the Publisher.

Copyright © 2024 by
National Learning Corporation

212 Michael Drive, Syosset, NY 11791
(516) 921-8888 • www.passbooks.com
E-mail: info@passbooks.com

PUBLISHED IN THE UNITED STATES OF AMERICA

PASSBOOK® SERIES

THE *PASSBOOK® SERIES* has been created to prepare applicants and candidates for the ultimate academic battlefield – the examination room.

At some time in our lives, each and every one of us may be required to take an examination – for validation, matriculation, admission, qualification, registration, certification, or licensure.

Based on the assumption that every applicant or candidate has met the basic formal educational standards, has taken the required number of courses, and read the necessary texts, the *PASSBOOK® SERIES* furnishes the one special preparation which may assure passing with confidence, instead of failing with insecurity. Examination questions – together with answers – are furnished as the basic vehicle for study so that the mysteries of the examination and its compounding difficulties may be eliminated or diminished by a sure method.

This book is meant to help you pass your examination provided that you qualify and are serious in your objective.

The entire field is reviewed through the huge store of content information which is succinctly presented through a provocative and challenging approach – the question-and-answer method.

A climate of success is established by furnishing the correct answers at the end of each test.

You soon learn to recognize types of questions, forms of questions, and patterns of questioning. You may even begin to anticipate expected outcomes.

You perceive that many questions are repeated or adapted so that you can gain acute insights, which may enable you to score many sure points.

You learn how to confront new questions, or types of questions, and to attack them confidently and work out the correct answers.

You note objectives and emphases, and recognize pitfalls and dangers, so that you may make positive educational adjustments.

Moreover, you are kept fully informed in relation to new concepts, methods, practices, and directions in the field.

You discover that you are actually taking the examination all the time: you are preparing for the examination by "taking" an examination, not by reading extraneous and/or supererogatory textbooks.

In short, this PASSBOOK®, used directedly, should be an important factor in helping you to pass your test.

HIGHWAY MAINTENANCE SUPERVISOR

DUTIES:

Highway Maintenance Supervisors are employed by the department of transportation at various locations throughout the State. They supervise and work with a force of laborers and operators of various-sized equipment involved in maintenance and repair projects on highways or some structural unit. These projects may include patching pavements and filling holes; cleaning ditches and culverts; cutting grass; painting and repairing guide rails and signs; and plowing roads and sanding icy pavements in winter.

As a Highway Maintenance Supervisor I, you would be a working supervisor for a highway maintenance crew assigned to the operation of various-sized equipment involved in maintenance and repair projects on or adjacent to state highways or structural units. These projects may include, but are not limited to, patching pavements and filling holes; cleaning and repairing ditches and culverts and other drainage structures; cutting grass and other right-of-way maintenance; repairing guide rails and signs; and snow and ice control. On large maintenance projects, you may supervise a phase of the project under the general direction of a Highway Maintenance Supervisor II. You would operate light trucks and may operate heavy dump trucks, perform one-person snow plowing, and operate other highway equipment. You would be required to answer emergency calls outside of your regular hours of work, perform related work as required, and maintain electronic work records.

As a Highway Maintenance Supervisor II, you would supervise several subordinate Maintenance Supervisors and their crews in maintenance and repair projects on or adjacent to state highways or structural units. Such projects may include any of the following: widening, surfacing, and resurfacing highways; extending or building shoulders; installing curbing; erecting signs; removing trees; erecting guide rails; building and repairing culverts; repairing drainage systems; erecting cribbing; doing major excavation work; cleaning stream beds; and plowing snow and treating icy pavement. You would plan and schedule work and maintain electronic work records. You would be required to answer emergency calls outside of your regular hours of work. You may be required to operate heavy dump trucks, perform one-person snow plowing, and operate other highway equipment.

SUBJECT OF EXAMINATION

The written test is designed to test for knowledge, skills, and/or abilities in such areas as:

1. **Highways, drainage facilities, related structures, and snow and ice control** - These questions test for knowledge of practices and materials used in the maintenance and repair of highway-related structures and may include such areas as roadway surfaces, shoulders, embankments, drainage materials, guide rails, highway maintenance equipment, and ice and snow removal control.

2. **Safety practices** - These questions test for knowledge of and the ability to apply safety principles related to construction and maintenance work zones, including traffic control, the safe use of equipment, and the overall safety of workers, the traveling public, and the work environment.

3. **Supervision** - These questions test for knowledge of the principles and practices employed in planning, organizing, and controlling the activities of a work unit toward predetermined objectives. The concepts covered, usually in a situational question format, include such topics as assigning and reviewing work; evaluating performance; maintaining work standards; motivating and developing subordinates; implementing procedural change; increasing efficiency; and dealing with problems of absenteeism, morale, and discipline.

4. **Scheduling work and equipment** - These questions test for knowledge of work scheduling principles and for the ability to arrange work and equipment assignments in a manner that will achieve work goals while staying within scheduling criteria. This may include setting up vacation or work schedules taking into consideration such factors as seniority, work skills, duty hours, and shift coverage.
5. **Administrative supervision** - These questions test for knowledge of the principles and practices involved in directing the activities of a large subordinate staff, including subordinate supervisors. Questions relate to the personal interactions between an upper level supervisor and his/her subordinate supervisors in the accomplishment of objectives. These questions cover such areas as assigning work to and coordinating the activities of several units, establishing and guiding staff development programs, evaluating the performance of subordinate supervisors, and maintaining relationships with other organizational sections.

HOW TO TAKE A TEST

I. YOU MUST PASS AN EXAMINATION

A. WHAT EVERY CANDIDATE SHOULD KNOW

Examination applicants often ask us for help in preparing for the written test. What can I study in advance? What kinds of questions will be asked? How will the test be given? How will the papers be graded?

As an applicant for a civil service examination, you may be wondering about some of these things. Our purpose here is to suggest effective methods of advance study and to describe civil service examinations.

Your chances for success on this examination can be increased if you know how to prepare. Those "pre-examination jitters" can be reduced if you know what to expect. You can even experience an adventure in good citizenship if you know why civil service exams are given.

B. WHY ARE CIVIL SERVICE EXAMINATIONS GIVEN?

Civil service examinations are important to you in two ways. As a citizen, you want public jobs filled by employees who know how to do their work. As a job seeker, you want a fair chance to compete for that job on an equal footing with other candidates. The best-known means of accomplishing this two-fold goal is the competitive examination.

Exams are widely publicized throughout the nation. They may be administered for jobs in federal, state, city, municipal, town or village governments or agencies.

Any citizen may apply, with some limitations, such as the age or residence of applicants. Your experience and education may be reviewed to see whether you meet the requirements for the particular examination. When these requirements exist, they are reasonable and applied consistently to all applicants. Thus, a competitive examination may cause you some uneasiness now, but it is your privilege and safeguard.

C. HOW ARE CIVIL SERVICE EXAMS DEVELOPED?

Examinations are carefully written by trained technicians who are specialists in the field known as "psychological measurement," in consultation with recognized authorities in the field of work that the test will cover. These experts recommend the subject matter areas or skills to be tested; only those knowledges or skills important to your success on the job are included. The most reliable books and source materials available are used as references. Together, the experts and technicians judge the difficulty level of the questions.

Test technicians know how to phrase questions so that the problem is clearly stated. Their ethics do not permit "trick" or "catch" questions. Questions may have been tried out on sample groups, or subjected to statistical analysis, to determine their usefulness.

Written tests are often used in combination with performance tests, ratings of training and experience, and oral interviews. All of these measures combine to form the best-known means of finding the right person for the right job.

II. HOW TO PASS THE WRITTEN TEST

A. NATURE OF THE EXAMINATION

To prepare intelligently for civil service examinations, you should know how they differ from school examinations you have taken. In school you were assigned certain definite pages to read or subjects to cover. The examination questions were quite detailed and usually emphasized memory. Civil service exams, on the other hand, try to discover your present ability to perform the duties of a position, plus your potentiality to learn these duties. In other words, a civil service exam attempts to predict how successful you will be. Questions cover such a broad area that they cannot be as minute and detailed as school exam questions.

In the public service similar kinds of work, or positions, are grouped together in one "class." This process is known as *position-classification*. All the positions in a class are paid according to the salary range for that class. One class title covers all of these positions, and they are all tested by the same examination.

B. FOUR BASIC STEPS

1) Study the announcement

How, then, can you know what subjects to study? Our best answer is: "Learn as much as possible about the class of positions for which you've applied." The exam will test the knowledge, skills and abilities needed to do the work.

Your most valuable source of information about the position you want is the official exam announcement. This announcement lists the training and experience qualifications. Check these standards and apply only if you come reasonably close to meeting them.

The brief description of the position in the examination announcement offers some clues to the subjects which will be tested. Think about the job itself. Review the duties in your mind. Can you perform them, or are there some in which you are rusty? Fill in the blank spots in your preparation.

Many jurisdictions preview the written test in the exam announcement by including a section called "Knowledge and Abilities Required," "Scope of the Examination," or some similar heading. Here you will find out specifically what fields will be tested.

2) Review your own background

Once you learn in general what the position is all about, and what you need to know to do the work, ask yourself which subjects you already know fairly well and which need improvement. You may wonder whether to concentrate on improving your strong areas or on building some background in your fields of weakness. When the announcement has specified "some knowledge" or "considerable knowledge," or has used adjectives like "beginning principles of..." or "advanced ... methods," you can get a clue as to the number and difficulty of questions to be asked in any given field. More questions, and hence broader coverage, would be included for those subjects which are more important in the work. Now weigh your strengths and weaknesses against the job requirements and prepare accordingly.

3) Determine the level of the position

Another way to tell how intensively you should prepare is to understand the level of the job for which you are applying. Is it the entering level? In other words, is this the position in which beginners in a field of work are hired? Or is it an intermediate or advanced level? Sometimes this is indicated by such words as "Junior" or "Senior" in the class title. Other jurisdictions use Roman numerals to designate the level – Clerk I, Clerk II, for example. The word "Supervisor" sometimes appears in the title. If the level is not indicated by the title, check the description of duties. Will you be working under very close supervision, or will you have responsibility for independent decisions in this work?

4) Choose appropriate study materials

Now that you know the subjects to be examined and the relative amount of each subject to be covered, you can choose suitable study materials. For beginning level jobs, or even advanced ones, if you have a pronounced weakness in some aspect of your training, read a modern, standard textbook in that field. Be sure it is up to date and has general coverage. Such books are normally available at your library, and the librarian will be glad to help you locate one. For entry-level positions, questions of appropriate difficulty are chosen -- neither highly advanced questions, nor those too simple. Such questions require careful thought but not advanced training.

If the position for which you are applying is technical or advanced, you will read more advanced, specialized material. If you are already familiar with the basic principles of your field, elementary textbooks would waste your time. Concentrate on advanced textbooks and technical periodicals. Think through the concepts and review difficult problems in your field.

These are all general sources. You can get more ideas on your own initiative, following these leads. For example, training manuals and publications of the government agency which employs workers in your field can be useful, particularly for technical and professional positions. A letter or visit to the government department involved may result in more specific study suggestions, and certainly will provide you with a more definite idea of the exact nature of the position you are seeking.

III. KINDS OF TESTS

Tests are used for purposes other than measuring knowledge and ability to perform specified duties. For some positions, it is equally important to test ability to make adjustments to new situations or to profit from training. In others, basic mental abilities not dependent on information are essential. Questions which test these things may not appear as pertinent to the duties of the position as those which test for knowledge and information. Yet they are often highly important parts of a fair examination. For very general questions, it is almost impossible to help you direct your study efforts. What we can do is to point out some of the more common of these general abilities needed in public service positions and describe some typical questions.

1) General information

Broad, general information has been found useful for predicting job success in some kinds of work. This is tested in a variety of ways, from vocabulary lists to questions about current events. Basic background in some field of work, such as sociology or economics, may be sampled in a group of questions. Often these are principles which have become familiar to most persons through exposure rather than through formal training. It is difficult to advise you how to study for these questions; being alert to the world around you is our best suggestion.

2) Verbal ability

An example of an ability needed in many positions is verbal or language ability. Verbal ability is, in brief, the ability to use and understand words. Vocabulary and grammar tests are typical measures of this ability. Reading comprehension or paragraph interpretation questions are common in many kinds of civil service tests. You are given a paragraph of written material and asked to find its central meaning.

3) Numerical ability

Number skills can be tested by the familiar arithmetic problem, by checking paired lists of numbers to see which are alike and which are different, or by interpreting charts and graphs. In the latter test, a graph may be printed in the test booklet which you are asked to use as the basis for answering questions.

4) Observation

A popular test for law-enforcement positions is the observation test. A picture is shown to you for several minutes, then taken away. Questions about the picture test your ability to observe both details and larger elements.

5) Following directions

In many positions in the public service, the employee must be able to carry out written instructions dependably and accurately. You may be given a chart with several columns, each column listing a variety of information. The questions require you to carry out directions involving the information given in the chart.

6) Skills and aptitudes

Performance tests effectively measure some manual skills and aptitudes. When the skill is one in which you are trained, such as typing or shorthand, you can practice. These tests are often very much like those given in business school or high school courses. For many of the other skills and aptitudes, however, no short-time preparation can be made. Skills and abilities natural to you or that you have developed throughout your lifetime are being tested.

Many of the general questions just described provide all the data needed to answer the questions and ask you to use your reasoning ability to find the answers. Your best preparation for these tests, as well as for tests of facts and ideas, is to be at your physical and mental best. You, no doubt, have your own methods of getting into an exam-taking mood and keeping "in shape." The next section lists some ideas on this subject.

IV. KINDS OF QUESTIONS

Only rarely is the "essay" question, which you answer in narrative form, used in civil service tests. Civil service tests are usually of the short-answer type. Full instructions for answering these questions will be given to you at the examination. But in case this is your first experience with short-answer questions and separate answer sheets, here is what you need to know:

1) **Multiple-choice Questions**

Most popular of the short-answer questions is the "multiple choice" or "best answer" question. It can be used, for example, to test for factual knowledge, ability to solve problems or judgment in meeting situations found at work.

A multiple-choice question is normally one of three types—
- It can begin with an incomplete statement followed by several possible endings. You are to find the one ending which *best* completes the statement, although some of the others may not be entirely wrong.
- It can also be a complete statement in the form of a question which is answered by choosing one of the statements listed.

- It can be in the form of a problem – again you select the best answer.

Here is an example of a multiple-choice question with a discussion which should give you some clues as to the method for choosing the right answer:

When an employee has a complaint about his assignment, the action which will *best* help him overcome his difficulty is to
- A. discuss his difficulty with his coworkers
- B. take the problem to the head of the organization
- C. take the problem to the person who gave him the assignment
- D. say nothing to anyone about his complaint

In answering this question, you should study each of the choices to find which is best. Consider choice "A" – Certainly an employee may discuss his complaint with fellow employees, but no change or improvement can result, and the complaint remains unresolved. Choice "B" is a poor choice since the head of the organization probably does not know what assignment you have been given, and taking your problem to him is known as "going over the head" of the supervisor. The supervisor, or person who made the assignment, is the person who can clarify it or correct any injustice. Choice "C" is, therefore, correct. To say nothing, as in choice "D," is unwise. Supervisors have and interest in knowing the problems employees are facing, and the employee is seeking a solution to his problem.

2) True/False Questions

The "true/false" or "right/wrong" form of question is sometimes used. Here a complete statement is given. Your job is to decide whether the statement is right or wrong.

SAMPLE: A roaming cell-phone call to a nearby city costs less than a non-roaming call to a distant city.

This statement is wrong, or false, since roaming calls are more expensive.

This is not a complete list of all possible question forms, although most of the others are variations of these common types. You will always get complete directions for answering questions. Be sure you understand *how* to mark your answers – ask questions until you do.

V. RECORDING YOUR ANSWERS

Computer terminals are used more and more today for many different kinds of exams.
For an examination with very few applicants, you may be told to record your answers in the test booklet itself. Separate answer sheets are much more common. If this separate answer sheet is to be scored by machine – and this is often the case – it is highly important that you mark your answers correctly in order to get credit.

An electronic scoring machine is often used in civil service offices because of the speed with which papers can be scored. Machine-scored answer sheets must be marked with a pencil, which will be given to you. This pencil has a high graphite content which responds to the electronic scoring machine. As a matter of fact, stray dots may register as answers, so do not let your pencil rest on the answer sheet while you are pondering the correct answer. Also, if your pencil lead breaks or is otherwise defective, ask for another.

Since the answer sheet will be dropped in a slot in the scoring machine, be careful not to bend the corners or get the paper crumpled.

The answer sheet normally has five vertical columns of numbers, with 30 numbers to a column. These numbers correspond to the question numbers in your test booklet. After each number, going across the page are four or five pairs of dotted lines. These short dotted lines have small letters or numbers above them. The first two pairs may also have a "T" or "F" above the letters. This indicates that the first two pairs only are to be used if the questions are of the true-false type. If the questions are multiple choice, disregard the "T" and "F" and pay attention only to the small letters or numbers.

Answer your questions in the manner of the sample that follows:

32. The largest city in the United States is
    A. Washington, D.C.
    B. New York City
    C. Chicago
    D. Detroit
    E. San Francisco

1) Choose the answer you think is best. (New York City is the largest, so "B" is correct.)
2) Find the row of dotted lines numbered the same as the question you are answering. (Find row number 32)
3) Find the pair of dotted lines corresponding to the answer. (Find the pair of lines under the mark "B.")
4) Make a solid black mark between the dotted lines.

VI. BEFORE THE TEST

Common sense will help you find procedures to follow to get ready for an examination. Too many of us, however, overlook these sensible measures. Indeed, nervousness and fatigue have been found to be the most serious reasons why applicants fail to do their best on civil service tests. Here is a list of reminders:

- Begin your preparation early – Don't wait until the last minute to go scurrying around for books and materials or to find out what the position is all about.
- Prepare continuously – An hour a night for a week is better than an all-night cram session. This has been definitely established. What is more, a night a week for a month will return better dividends than crowding your study into a shorter period of time.
- Locate the place of the exam – You have been sent a notice telling you when and where to report for the examination. If the location is in a different town or otherwise unfamiliar to you, it would be well to inquire the best route and learn something about the building.
- Relax the night before the test – Allow your mind to rest. Do not study at all that night. Plan some mild recreation or diversion; then go to bed early and get a good night's sleep.
- Get up early enough to make a leisurely trip to the place for the test – This way unforeseen events, traffic snarls, unfamiliar buildings, etc. will not upset you.
- Dress comfortably – A written test is not a fashion show. You will be known by number and not by name, so wear something comfortable.

- Leave excess paraphernalia at home – Shopping bags and odd bundles will get in your way. You need bring only the items mentioned in the official notice you received; usually everything you need is provided. Do not bring reference books to the exam. They will only confuse those last minutes and be taken away from you when in the test room.
- Arrive somewhat ahead of time – If because of transportation schedules you must get there very early, bring a newspaper or magazine to take your mind off yourself while waiting.
- Locate the examination room – When you have found the proper room, you will be directed to the seat or part of the room where you will sit. Sometimes you are given a sheet of instructions to read while you are waiting. Do not fill out any forms until you are told to do so; just read them and be prepared.
- Relax and prepare to listen to the instructions
- If you have any physical problem that may keep you from doing your best, be sure to tell the test administrator. If you are sick or in poor health, you really cannot do your best on the exam. You can come back and take the test some other time.

VII. AT THE TEST

The day of the test is here and you have the test booklet in your hand. The temptation to get going is very strong. Caution! There is more to success than knowing the right answers. You must know how to identify your papers and understand variations in the type of short-answer question used in this particular examination. Follow these suggestions for maximum results from your efforts:

1) Cooperate with the monitor

The test administrator has a duty to create a situation in which you can be as much at ease as possible. He will give instructions, tell you when to begin, check to see that you are marking your answer sheet correctly, and so on. He is not there to guard you, although he will see that your competitors do not take unfair advantage. He wants to help you do your best.

2) Listen to all instructions

Don't jump the gun! Wait until you understand all directions. In most civil service tests you get more time than you need to answer the questions. So don't be in a hurry. Read each word of instructions until you clearly understand the meaning. Study the examples, listen to all announcements and follow directions. Ask questions if you do not understand what to do.

3) Identify your papers

Civil service exams are usually identified by number only. You will be assigned a number; you must not put your name on your test papers. Be sure to copy your number correctly. Since more than one exam may be given, copy your exact examination title.

4) Plan your time

Unless you are told that a test is a "speed" or "rate of work" test, speed itself is usually not important. Time enough to answer all the questions will be provided, but this does not mean that you have all day. An overall time limit has been set. Divide the total time (in minutes) by the number of questions to determine the approximate time you have for each question.

5) Do not linger over difficult questions

If you come across a difficult question, mark it with a paper clip (useful to have along) and come back to it when you have been through the booklet. One caution if you do this – be sure to skip a number on your answer sheet as well. Check often to be sure that you have not lost your place and that you are marking in the row numbered the same as the question you are answering.

6) Read the questions

Be sure you know what the question asks! Many capable people are unsuccessful because they failed to *read* the questions correctly.

7) Answer all questions

Unless you have been instructed that a penalty will be deducted for incorrect answers, it is better to guess than to omit a question.

8) Speed tests

It is often better NOT to guess on speed tests. It has been found that on timed tests people are tempted to spend the last few seconds before time is called in marking answers at random – without even reading them – in the hope of picking up a few extra points. To discourage this practice, the instructions may warn you that your score will be "corrected" for guessing. That is, a penalty will be applied. The incorrect answers will be deducted from the correct ones, or some other penalty formula will be used.

9) Review your answers

If you finish before time is called, go back to the questions you guessed or omitted to give them further thought. Review other answers if you have time.

10) Return your test materials

If you are ready to leave before others have finished or time is called, take ALL your materials to the monitor and leave quietly. Never take any test material with you. The monitor can discover whose papers are not complete, and taking a test booklet may be grounds for disqualification.

VIII. EXAMINATION TECHNIQUES

1) Read the general instructions carefully. These are usually printed on the first page of the exam booklet. As a rule, these instructions refer to the timing of the examination; the fact that you should not start work until the signal and must stop work at a signal, etc. If there are any *special* instructions, such as a choice of questions to be answered, make sure that you note this instruction carefully.

2) When you are ready to start work on the examination, that is as soon as the signal has been given, read the instructions to each question booklet, underline any key words or phrases, such as *least, best, outline, describe* and the like. In this way you will tend to answer as requested rather than discover on reviewing your paper that you *listed without describing*, that you selected the *worst* choice rather than the *best* choice, etc.

3) If the examination is of the objective or multiple-choice type – that is, each question will also give a series of possible answers: A, B, C or D, and you are called upon to select the best answer and write the letter next to that answer on your answer paper – it is advisable to start answering each question in turn. There may be anywhere from 50 to 100 such questions in the three or four hours allotted and you can see how much time would be taken if you read through all the questions before beginning to answer any. Furthermore, if you come across a question or group of questions which you know would be difficult to answer, it would undoubtedly affect your handling of all the other questions.

4) If the examination is of the essay type and contains but a few questions, it is a moot point as to whether you should read all the questions before starting to answer any one. Of course, if you are given a choice – say five out of seven and the like – then it is essential to read all the questions so you can eliminate the two that are most difficult. If, however, you are asked to answer all the questions, there may be danger in trying to answer the easiest one first because you may find that you will spend too much time on it. The best technique is to answer the first question, then proceed to the second, etc.

5) Time your answers. Before the exam begins, write down the time it started, then add the time allowed for the examination and write down the time it must be completed, then divide the time available somewhat as follows:
    - If 3-1/2 hours are allowed, that would be 210 minutes. If you have 80 objective-type questions, that would be an average of 2-1/2 minutes per question. Allow yourself no more than 2 minutes per question, or a total of 160 minutes, which will permit about 50 minutes to review.
    - If for the time allotment of 210 minutes there are 7 essay questions to answer, that would average about 30 minutes a question. Give yourself only 25 minutes per question so that you have about 35 minutes to review.

6) The most important instruction is to *read each question* and make sure you know what is wanted. The second most important instruction is to *time yourself properly* so that you answer every question. The third most important instruction is to *answer every question*. Guess if you have to but include something for each question. Remember that you will receive no credit for a blank and will probably receive some credit if you write something in answer to an essay question. If you guess a letter – say "B" for a multiple-choice question – you may have guessed right. If you leave a blank as an answer to a multiple-choice question, the examiners may respect your feelings but it will not add a point to your score. Some exams may penalize you for wrong answers, so in such cases *only*, you may not want to guess unless you have some basis for your answer.

7) Suggestions
    a. Objective-type questions
        1. Examine the question booklet for proper sequence of pages and questions
        2. Read all instructions carefully
        3. Skip any question which seems too difficult; return to it after all other questions have been answered
        4. Apportion your time properly; do not spend too much time on any single question or group of questions

5. Note and underline key words – *all, most, fewest, least, best, worst, same, opposite,* etc.
6. Pay particular attention to negatives
7. Note unusual option, e.g., unduly long, short, complex, different or similar in content to the body of the question
8. Observe the use of "hedging" words – *probably, may, most likely,* etc.
9. Make sure that your answer is put next to the same number as the question
10. Do not second-guess unless you have good reason to believe the second answer is definitely more correct
11. Cross out original answer if you decide another answer is more accurate; do not erase until you are ready to hand your paper in
12. Answer all questions; guess unless instructed otherwise
13. Leave time for review

b. Essay questions
1. Read each question carefully
2. Determine exactly what is wanted. Underline key words or phrases.
3. Decide on outline or paragraph answer
4. Include many different points and elements unless asked to develop any one or two points or elements
5. Show impartiality by giving pros and cons unless directed to select one side only
6. Make and write down any assumptions you find necessary to answer the questions
7. Watch your English, grammar, punctuation and choice of words
8. Time your answers; don't crowd material

8) Answering the essay question

Most essay questions can be answered by framing the specific response around several key words or ideas. Here are a few such key words or ideas:

M's: manpower, materials, methods, money, management
P's: purpose, program, policy, plan, procedure, practice, problems, pitfalls, personnel, public relations

a. Six basic steps in handling problems:
1. Preliminary plan and background development
2. Collect information, data and facts
3. Analyze and interpret information, data and facts
4. Analyze and develop solutions as well as make recommendations
5. Prepare report and sell recommendations
6. Install recommendations and follow up effectiveness

b. Pitfalls to avoid
1. *Taking things for granted* – A statement of the situation does not necessarily imply that each of the elements is necessarily true; for example, a complaint may be invalid and biased so that all that can be taken for granted is that a complaint has been registered

2. *Considering only one side of a situation* – Wherever possible, indicate several alternatives and then point out the reasons you selected the best one
3. *Failing to indicate follow up* – Whenever your answer indicates action on your part, make certain that you will take proper follow-up action to see how successful your recommendations, procedures or actions turn out to be
4. *Taking too long in answering any single question* – Remember to time your answers properly

IX. AFTER THE TEST

Scoring procedures differ in detail among civil service jurisdictions although the general principles are the same. Whether the papers are hand-scored or graded by machine we have described, they are nearly always graded by number. That is, the person who marks the paper knows only the number – never the name – of the applicant. Not until all the papers have been graded will they be matched with names. If other tests, such as training and experience or oral interview ratings have been given, scores will be combined. Different parts of the examination usually have different weights. For example, the written test might count 60 percent of the final grade, and a rating of training and experience 40 percent. In many jurisdictions, veterans will have a certain number of points added to their grades.

After the final grade has been determined, the names are placed in grade order and an eligible list is established. There are various methods for resolving ties between those who get the same final grade – probably the most common is to place first the name of the person whose application was received first. Job offers are made from the eligible list in the order the names appear on it. You will be notified of your grade and your rank as soon as all these computations have been made. This will be done as rapidly as possible.

People who are found to meet the requirements in the announcement are called "eligibles." Their names are put on a list of eligible candidates. An eligible's chances of getting a job depend on how high he stands on this list and how fast agencies are filling jobs from the list.

When a job is to be filled from a list of eligibles, the agency asks for the names of people on the list of eligibles for that job. When the civil service commission receives this request, it sends to the agency the names of the three people highest on this list. Or, if the job to be filled has specialized requirements, the office sends the agency the names of the top three persons who meet these requirements from the general list.

The appointing officer makes a choice from among the three people whose names were sent to him. If the selected person accepts the appointment, the names of the others are put back on the list to be considered for future openings.

That is the rule in hiring from all kinds of eligible lists, whether they are for typist, carpenter, chemist, or something else. For every vacancy, the appointing officer has his choice of any one of the top three eligibles on the list. This explains why the person whose name is on top of the list sometimes does not get an appointment when some of the persons lower on the list do. If the appointing officer chooses the second or third eligible, the No. 1 eligible does not get a job at once, but stays on the list until he is appointed or the list is terminated.

X. HOW TO PASS THE INTERVIEW TEST

The examination for which you applied requires an oral interview test. You have already taken the written test and you are now being called for the interview test – the final part of the formal examination.

You may think that it is not possible to prepare for an interview test and that there are no procedures to follow during an interview. Our purpose is to point out some things you can do in advance that will help you and some good rules to follow and pitfalls to avoid while you are being interviewed.

What is an interview supposed to test?

The written examination is designed to test the technical knowledge and competence of the candidate; the oral is designed to evaluate intangible qualities, not readily measured otherwise, and to establish a list showing the relative fitness of each candidate – as measured against his competitors – for the position sought. Scoring is not on the basis of "right" and "wrong," but on a sliding scale of values ranging from "not passable" to "outstanding." As a matter of fact, it is possible to achieve a relatively low score without a single "incorrect" answer because of evident weakness in the qualities being measured.

Occasionally, an examination may consist entirely of an oral test – either an individual or a group oral. In such cases, information is sought concerning the technical knowledges and abilities of the candidate, since there has been no written examination for this purpose. More commonly, however, an oral test is used to supplement a written examination.

Who conducts interviews?

The composition of oral boards varies among different jurisdictions. In nearly all, a representative of the personnel department serves as chairman. One of the members of the board may be a representative of the department in which the candidate would work. In some cases, "outside experts" are used, and, frequently, a businessman or some other representative of the general public is asked to serve. Labor and management or other special groups may be represented. The aim is to secure the services of experts in the appropriate field.

However the board is composed, it is a good idea (and not at all improper or unethical) to ascertain in advance of the interview who the members are and what groups they represent. When you are introduced to them, you will have some idea of their backgrounds and interests, and at least you will not stutter and stammer over their names.

What should be done before the interview?

While knowledge about the board members is useful and takes some of the surprise element out of the interview, there is other preparation which is more substantive. It *is* possible to prepare for an oral interview – in several ways:

1) Keep a copy of your application and review it carefully before the interview

This may be the only document before the oral board, and the starting point of the interview. Know what education and experience you have listed there, and the sequence and dates of all of it. Sometimes the board will ask you to review the highlights of your experience for them; you should not have to hem and haw doing it.

2) Study the class specification and the examination announcement

Usually, the oral board has one or both of these to guide them. The qualities, characteristics or knowledges required by the position sought are stated in these documents. They offer valuable clues as to the nature of the oral interview. For example, if the job involves supervisory responsibilities, the announcement will usually indicate that knowledge of modern supervisory methods and the qualifications of the candidate as a supervisor will be tested. If so, you can expect such questions, frequently in the form of a hypothetical situation which you are expected to solve. NEVER go into an oral without knowledge of the duties and responsibilities of the job you seek.

3) Think through each qualification required

Try to visualize the kind of questions you would ask if you were a board member. How well could you answer them? Try especially to appraise your own knowledge and background in each area, *measured against the job sought*, and identify any areas in which you are weak. Be critical and realistic – do not flatter yourself.

4) Do some general reading in areas in which you feel you may be weak

For example, if the job involves supervision and your past experience has NOT, some general reading in supervisory methods and practices, particularly in the field of human relations, might be useful. Do NOT study agency procedures or detailed manuals. The oral board will be testing your understanding and capacity, not your memory.

5) Get a good night's sleep and watch your general health and mental attitude

You will want a clear head at the interview. Take care of a cold or any other minor ailment, and of course, no hangovers.

What should be done on the day of the interview?

Now comes the day of the interview itself. Give yourself plenty of time to get there. Plan to arrive somewhat ahead of the scheduled time, particularly if your appointment is in the fore part of the day. If a previous candidate fails to appear, the board might be ready for you a bit early. By early afternoon an oral board is almost invariably behind schedule if there are many candidates, and you may have to wait. Take along a book or magazine to read, or your application to review, but leave any extraneous material in the waiting room when you go in for your interview. In any event, relax and compose yourself.

The matter of dress is important. The board is forming impressions about you – from your experience, your manners, your attitude, and your appearance. Give your personal appearance careful attention. Dress your best, but not your flashiest. Choose conservative, appropriate clothing, and be sure it is immaculate. This is a business interview, and your appearance should indicate that you regard it as such. Besides, being well groomed and properly dressed will help boost your confidence.

Sooner or later, someone will call your name and escort you into the interview room. *This is it.* From here on you are on your own. It is too late for any more preparation. But remember, you asked for this opportunity to prove your fitness, and you are here because your request was granted.

What happens when you go in?

The usual sequence of events will be as follows: The clerk (who is often the board stenographer) will introduce you to the chairman of the oral board, who will introduce you to the other members of the board. Acknowledge the introductions before you sit down. Do not be surprised if you find a microphone facing you or a stenotypist sitting by. Oral interviews are usually recorded in the event of an appeal or other review.

Usually the chairman of the board will open the interview by reviewing the highlights of your education and work experience from your application – primarily for the benefit of the other members of the board, as well as to get the material into the record. Do not interrupt or comment unless there is an error or significant misinterpretation; if that is the case, do not hesitate. But do not quibble about insignificant matters. Also, he will usually ask you some question about your education, experience or your present job – partly to get you to start talking and to establish the interviewing "rapport." He may start the actual questioning, or turn it over to one of the other members. Frequently, each member undertakes the questioning on a particular area, one in which he is perhaps most competent, so you can expect each member to participate in the examination. Because time is limited, you may also expect some rather abrupt switches in the direction the questioning takes, so do not be upset by it. Normally, a board member will not pursue a single line of questioning unless he discovers a particular strength or weakness.

After each member has participated, the chairman will usually ask whether any member has any further questions, then will ask you if you have anything you wish to add. Unless you are expecting this question, it may floor you. Worse, it may start you off on an extended, extemporaneous speech. The board is not usually seeking more information. The question is principally to offer you a last opportunity to present further qualifications or to indicate that you have nothing to add. So, if you feel that a significant qualification or characteristic has been overlooked, it is proper to point it out in a sentence or so. Do not compliment the board on the thoroughness of their examination – they have been sketchy, and you know it. If you wish, merely say, "No thank you, I have nothing further to add." This is a point where you can "talk yourself out" of a good impression or fail to present an important bit of information. Remember, *you close the interview yourself.*

The chairman will then say, "That is all, Mr. _____, thank you." Do not be startled; the interview is over, and quicker than you think. Thank him, gather your belongings and take your leave. Save your sigh of relief for the other side of the door.

How to put your best foot forward
Throughout this entire process, you may feel that the board individually and collectively is trying to pierce your defenses, seek out your hidden weaknesses and embarrass and confuse you. Actually, this is not true. They are obliged to make an appraisal of your qualifications for the job you are seeking, and they want to see you in your best light. Remember, they must interview all candidates and a non-cooperative candidate may become a failure in spite of their best efforts to bring out his qualifications. Here are 15 suggestions that will help you:

1) Be natural – Keep your attitude confident, not cocky
If you are not confident that you can do the job, do not expect the board to be. Do not apologize for your weaknesses, try to bring out your strong points. The board is interested in a positive, not negative, presentation. Cockiness will antagonize any board member and make him wonder if you are covering up a weakness by a false show of strength.

2) Get comfortable, but don't lounge or sprawl
Sit erectly but not stiffly. A careless posture may lead the board to conclude that you are careless in other things, or at least that you are not impressed by the importance of the occasion. Either conclusion is natural, even if incorrect. Do not fuss with your clothing, a pencil or an ashtray. Your hands may occasionally be useful to emphasize a point; do not let them become a point of distraction.

3) Do not wisecrack or make small talk
This is a serious situation, and your attitude should show that you consider it as such. Further, the time of the board is limited – they do not want to waste it, and neither should you.

4) Do not exaggerate your experience or abilities

In the first place, from information in the application or other interviews and sources, the board may know more about you than you think. Secondly, you probably will not get away with it. An experienced board is rather adept at spotting such a situation, so do not take the chance.

5) If you know a board member, do not make a point of it, yet do not hide it

Certainly you are not fooling him, and probably not the other members of the board. Do not try to take advantage of your acquaintanceship – it will probably do you little good.

6) Do not dominate the interview

Let the board do that. They will give you the clues – do not assume that you have to do all the talking. Realize that the board has a number of questions to ask you, and do not try to take up all the interview time by showing off your extensive knowledge of the answer to the first one.

7) Be attentive

You only have 20 minutes or so, and you should keep your attention at its sharpest throughout. When a member is addressing a problem or question to you, give him your undivided attention. Address your reply principally to him, but do not exclude the other board members.

8) Do not interrupt

A board member may be stating a problem for you to analyze. He will ask you a question when the time comes. Let him state the problem, and wait for the question.

9) Make sure you understand the question

Do not try to answer until you are sure what the question is. If it is not clear, restate it in your own words or ask the board member to clarify it for you. However, do not haggle about minor elements.

10) Reply promptly but not hastily

A common entry on oral board rating sheets is "candidate responded readily," or "candidate hesitated in replies." Respond as promptly and quickly as you can, but do not jump to a hasty, ill-considered answer.

11) Do not be peremptory in your answers

A brief answer is proper – but do not fire your answer back. That is a losing game from your point of view. The board member can probably ask questions much faster than you can answer them.

12) Do not try to create the answer you think the board member wants

He is interested in what kind of mind you have and how it works – not in playing games. Furthermore, he can usually spot this practice and will actually grade you down on it.

13) Do not switch sides in your reply merely to agree with a board member

Frequently, a member will take a contrary position merely to draw you out and to see if you are willing and able to defend your point of view. Do not start a debate, yet do not surrender a good position. If a position is worth taking, it is worth defending.

14) Do not be afraid to admit an error in judgment if you are shown to be wrong

The board knows that you are forced to reply without any opportunity for careful consideration. Your answer may be demonstrably wrong. If so, admit it and get on with the interview.

15) Do not dwell at length on your present job

The opening question may relate to your present assignment. Answer the question but do not go into an extended discussion. You are being examined for a *new* job, not your present one. As a matter of fact, try to phrase ALL your answers in terms of the job for which you are being examined.

Basis of Rating

Probably you will forget most of these "do's" and "don'ts" when you walk into the oral interview room. Even remembering them all will not ensure you a passing grade. Perhaps you did not have the qualifications in the first place. But remembering them will help you to put your best foot forward, without treading on the toes of the board members.

Rumor and popular opinion to the contrary notwithstanding, an oral board wants you to make the best appearance possible. They know you are under pressure – but they also want to see how you respond to it as a guide to what your reaction would be under the pressures of the job you seek. They will be influenced by the degree of poise you display, the personal traits you show and the manner in which you respond.

ABOUT THIS BOOK

This book contains tests divided into Examination Sections. Go through each test, answering every question in the margin. We have also attached a sample answer sheet at the back of the book that can be removed and used. At the end of each test look at the answer key and check your answers. On the ones you got wrong, look at the right answer choice and learn. Do not fill in the answers first. Do not memorize the questions and answers, but understand the answer and principles involved. On your test, the questions will likely be different from the samples. Questions are changed and new ones added. If you understand these past questions you should have success with any changes that arise. Tests may consist of several types of questions. We have additional books on each subject should more study be advisable or necessary for you. Finally, the more you study, the better prepared you will be. This book is intended to be the last thing you study before you walk into the examination room. Prior study of relevant texts is also recommended. NLC publishes some of these in our Fundamental Series. Knowledge and good sense are important factors in passing your exam. Good luck also helps. So now study this Passbook, absorb the material contained within and take that knowledge into the examination. Then do your best to pass that exam.

EXAMINATION SECTION

EXAMINATION SECTION
TEST 1

DIRECTIONS: Each question or incomplete statement is followed by several suggested answers or completions. Select the one that BEST answers the question or completes the statement. *PRINT THE LETTER OF THE CORRECT ANSWER IN THE SPACE AT THE RIGHT.*

1. On the monthly report of the amount of work completed, the units used to measure the amount of work completed on guardrails and beam barriers installed on arterial highways is

    A. square feet
    B. square yards
    C. linear feet
    D. linear yards

2. On the daily work report for the sidewalk concrete gang is a formula, M = [G - (D + U)], where G = total man-hours worked, D = total man-hours delays, U = total man-hours unmeasured work, and M = total man-hours measured work.
If G = 98, D = 42, U = 21, then M is equal to

    A. 35   B. 56   C. 77   D. 119

3. When a plumber *opens a street*, he is responsible for restoring the pavement. After completion of the permanent restoration, the plumber is responsible for maintaining the restored area for a total period of

    A. six months
    B. one year
    C. one year and 6 months
    D. two years

4. A permit for a street opening may be issued for a single permit activity for one block length up to a MAXIMUM length of _____ feet.

    A. 50   B. 100   C. 200   D. 300

5. A street obstruction bond taken out by a contractor working in the street is to insure the city if

    A. a pedestrian is injured by material stored on the sidewalk
    B. an automobile is damaged by material stored in the street
    C. curbs, sidewalks, and pavements are damaged
    D. obstructions, illegally placed in the street, must be removed

6. On the daily work report for the sidewalk concrete gang is an item *curb*.
The different types of curb listed on the report are: bluestone or granite, concrete-steel face, concrete-regular face, and

    A. drop
    B. paving block
    C. concrete block
    D. prefabricated

7. On the monthly report of work output under time (manhours) is a column headed MSO, which refers to manhours

    A. of mechanical services operator other than MVO
    B. of operation time lost while waiting
    C. of operation time lost due to the weather
    D. spent operating mechanical equipment by the MVO

8. In the city, concrete sidewalks are required to have a minimum thickness of concrete of _____ inches.

   A. 3   B. 4   C. 5   D. 6

9. Asphalt was laid for a length of 210 feet on the entire width of a street whose curb-to-curb distance is 30 feet. The number of square yards covered with asphalt is MOST NEARLY

   A. 210   B. 700   C. 2100   D. 6300

10. A layer of cinders is used as a base for a concrete sidewalk.
    The MAIN purpose of the cinders is to

    A. act as an air entraining agent for the concrete in the sidewalk
    B. replace poor soil under the sidewalk
    C. provide drainage under the sidewalk
    D. cushion the sidewalk when heavy loads are placed on the sidewalk

11. The unit used on the daily gang report to report the amount of measurement of debris removed is

    A. square foot   B. square yard
    C. cubic foot   D. cubic yard

12. 627 cubic feet contains MOST NEARLY _____ cubic yards.

    A. 21   B. 22   C. 23   D. 24

13. Of the following, the one that is INCORRECT curb construction is a curb made

    A. with a height of 5 inches
    B. with a steel angle for the face
    C. without a steel face
    D. monolithically with the sidewalk

14. Where feasible, concrete sidewalk panels should be made in squares of _____ feet by _____ feet.

    A. 3; 3   B. 5; 5   C. 6; 6   D. 7; 7

15. The steel facing for concrete curbs are splayed

    A. at an expansion joint
    B. where it butts against an adjacent steel plate
    C. at a drop curb
    D. at a radius bend

16. Expansion joints in steel curb facing shall be 1/4 inch wide and shall be filled with

    A. sand   B. premolded filler
    C. poured asphalt D. dry pack

17. One inch is MOST NEARLY equal to _____ feet.

    A. 0.8   B. 0.08   C. 0.008   D. 0.0008

18. Of the following, the *final* finish on a sidewalk is MOST frequently made with a   18._____

    A. wood float   B. screed
    C. steel trowel   D. darby

19. An air entraining compound would be added to concrete MAINLY to   19._____

    A. make the concrete lighter
    B. make the concrete cure faster
    C. improve the resistance of the concrete to frost action
    D. increase the tensile strength of the concrete

20. *ASTM*, as used in specifications for concrete, is an abbreviation for the   20._____

    A. American Society for Testing Materials
    B. American Standard Training Manual
    C. American Standard Testing Materials
    D. Association of Scientists for Testing Materials

21. A 15-foot-wide sidewalk has a pitch of 1/4 inch per foot. The difference in elevation from the curb to 15 feet from the curb in the direction of the pitch is _____ inches.   21._____

    A. 3   B. 3 3/4   C. 4   D. 4 1/2

22. A liquid asphalt is designated *RC70*.   22._____
    The letters RC stand for

    A. Rough Course   B. Rubber Cement
    C. Rapid Curing   D. Reinforced Concrete

23. Unless otherwise specified, steel faced concrete curb shall consist of the steel curb facing in _____-foot lengths.   23._____

    A. 5   B. 10   C. 15   D. 20

24. The difference between sheet asphalt and asphaltic concrete is that sheet asphalt   24._____

    A. contains no sand while asphaltic concrete contains sand
    B. contains no coarse aggregate while asphaltic concrete contains coarse aggregate
    C. contains no mineral filler while asphaltic concrete contains mineral filler
    D. has no flux while asphaltic concrete has flux

25. An approved roller shall weigh not less than 225 pounds per inch width of main roll. If the main roll width is 60 inches, the MINIMUM roller weight shall be equal to or greater than _____ lbs.   25._____

    A. 12,000   B. 12,500   C. 13,000   D. 13,500

KEY (CORRECT ANSWERS)

1. C
2. A
3. D
4. D
5. C

6. A
7. A
8. B
9. B
10. C

11. D
12. C
13. D
14. B
15. C

16. B
17. B
18. A
19. C
20. A

21. B
22. C
23. D
24. B
25. D

TEST 2

DIRECTIONS: Each question or incomplete statement is followed by several suggested answers or completions. Select the one that BEST answers the question or completes the statement. *PRINT THE LETTER OF THE CORRECT ANSWER IN THE SPACE AT THE RIGHT.*

1. A specification states that the rate of application of asphalt cement shall be 1 1/2 gallons per square yard with a tolerance of 1/10 of a gallon.
   Of the following, the rate of application that would be acceptable is _____ gallons per square yard.

   A. 1.2   B. 1.3   C. 1.6   D. 1.7

2. Of the following, the BEST reason for compacting backfill is to

   A. prevent settlement
   B. crush oversized rocks
   C. facilitate drainage
   D. make the soil uniform

3. Asphalt block is hexagonal tile block.
   The number of vertical sides of each block in place is

   A. 4   B. 6   C. 8   D. 10

4. Concrete driveways shall have a MINIMUM thickness of concrete of _____ inches.

   A. 5   B. 6   C. 7   D. 8

5. When the tops of manholes must be raised because of repaving, the MOST practical of the following methods to use is to

   A. break out the manhole frame and replace it with a deeper frame
   B. remove the manhole frame, build up the top of the manhole with bricks, and reset the frame
   C. use a thicker manhole cover
   D. place a metal collar on top of the existing frame

6. In a 1:2:4 concrete mix, the 2 indicates the quantity of

   A. water   B. sand   C. cement   D. aggregate

7. A tree pit shall be located in the area immediately in back of the curb.
   The MAXIMUM size of the tree pit shall be

   A. 3' x 3'   B. 4' x 4'   C. 5' x 5'   D. 6' x 6'

8. A temporary asphaltic pavement is placed over an excavation in the street by a private contractor.
   The MINIMUM required thickness of the finish course of the temporary asphaltic pavement is _____ inch(es).

   A. 1   B. 2   C. 3   D. 4

9. When a vault is abandoned, it must be filled in with clean incombustible materials, well-tamped.
   Where such structures adjoin the curb of a street, the roof must be removed and the enclosing walls cut down below the curb to a depth of _____ feet.

   A. 2   B. 4   C. 6   D. 8

10. Granite curbs are required to be set on a cradle. The MAIN purpose of the cradle is to

    A. prevent cracking of the curb
    B. prevent settling of the curb
    C. help keep the curb in line while it is being set
    D. separate the curb from the adjacent sidewalk

11. Paving was installed on a street from Station 3+15 to Station 4+90. The length of street that was paved is _____ feet.

    A. 75   B. 115   C. 175   D. 215

12. A district foreman uses an engineer's tape and measures a distance of 26.50 feet. This distance is equal to _____ feet _____ inch(es).

    A. 26; 5   B. 26; 6   C. 26; 1/2   D. 26; 0.6

13. Written on a can containing material delivered from a manufacturer is the notation *Approved by the B.S. & A.*
    The B.S. & A. is an abbreviation for the

    A. Bureau of Shipping and Allocation
    B. Board of Standards and Appeals
    C. Board of Supervision and Approval
    D. Bureau of Supervision and Assistance

14. An asphalt macadam pavement consists of a base course and a wearing course. The purpose of the base course is to

    A. provide drainage
    B. provide a level surface for the wearing course
    C. spread the load from the surface when it reaches the soil
    D. replace defective soil

15. Of the following, the MOST important recent advancement in power-driven equipment and tools is

    A. reduction in weight of the equipment
    B. improved surface finish
    C. higher operating speed
    D. lower noise levels

16. A wooden horse, used to warn traffic away, should be placed in front of which of the following defects in the street?
    A

    A. broken curb
    B. piece of roadway pavement that is very thin and the pavement whose base is starting to show through
    C. very badly broken manhole cover in the center of the street
    D. catch basin filled to the surface with debris

17. When a street is to be paved, the roller should

    A. start at the curb, go the length of the street and then move toward the center
    B. move from curb to curb transversely across the street
    C. start at the center, go the length of the street, and then move toward the curb
    D. roll at all the manhole covers first and then start rolling the length of the street

18. The use of long chutes to place concrete for a road base is usually prohibited.
    The BEST of the following reasons for prohibiting long chutes in this case is that

    A. the concrete will set by the time it is in place
    B. the water will evaporate from the mix
    C. segregation of the aggregate will occur
    D. the stone will be broken down into smaller particles

19. When sheet asphalt is spread by hand, the speed of the rolling should NOT exceed _____ square yards per hour.

    A. 100   B. 300   C. 500   D. 700

20. Of the following, the BEST way to insure long trouble-free operation of mechanical equipment is by periodic inspection and

    A. use   B. servicing
    C. painting   D. rotation of operators

21. Of the following maintenance work, the one type that is LEAST likely to be done by your agency on mechanical equipment is

    A. tune-up   B. repairing
    C. overhauling   D. rebuilding

22. Of the following, the MOST important equipment needed to lay sheet asphalt pavement is truck, roller, fire wagon, and

    A. grader   B. distributor
    C. planer   D. spreader

23. Of the following, the BEST reason why deep potholes should be repaired *immediately* is that

    A. they look bad
    B. they are a safety hazard
    C. they present a drainage problem
    D. people complaining about unfilled potholes cause unfavorable publicity

24. Of the following, the MOST serious safety hazard on highway and street maintenance work is

    A. injury from flying debris during pavement breaking
    B. motor traffic
    C. working close to trucks, bulldozers, and rollers
    D. cave-ins

25. Of the following, the BEST way a laborer can avoid accidents is to 25.____

    A. work slowly B. be alert
    C. wear safety shoes D. wear glasses

26. Of the following, the BEST first aid treatment for a second degree burn is to cover the 26.____
    burn with a _____ sterile dressing.

    A. thin, wet B. thin, dry
    C. thick, wet D. thick, dry

27. One of the laborers on the job feels unusually tired, has a headache and nausea, is per- 27.____
    spiring heavily, and the skin is pale and clammy.
    He is probably suffering from

    A. epilepsy B. food poisoning
    C. heat exhaustion D. sunstroke

28. If a laborer feels faint, the BEST advice to give him is to advise him to 28.____

    A. lie flat with his head low
    B. walk around till he revives
    C. run around till he revives
    D. drink a glass of cold water

29. Of the following types of fire extinguisher, the one to use on an electrical fire is 29.____

    A. soda acid B. carbon dioxide
    C. water pump tank D. pyrene

30. The GREATEST number of injuries from equipment used in construction work result from 30.____

    A. carelessness of the operator
    B. poor maintenance of the equipment
    C. overloading of the equipment
    D. poor inspection of the equipment

KEY (CORRECT ANSWERS)

1.	C	16.	C
2.	A	17.	A
3.	B	18.	C
4.	C	19.	B
5.	D	20.	B
6.	B	21.	D
7.	C	22.	D
8.	C	23.	B
9.	A	24.	B
10.	B	25.	B
11.	C	26.	D
12.	B	27.	C
13.	B	28.	A
14.	C	29.	B
15.	D	30.	A

EXAMINATION SECTION
TEST 1

DIRECTIONS: Each question or incomplete statement is followed by several suggested answers or completions. Select the one that BEST answers the question or completes the statement. *PRINT THE LETTER OF THE CORRECT ANSWER IN THE SPACE AT THE RIGHT.*

1. Before placing asphalt block for a pavement on the concrete base, the concrete base should be

    A. wet down with water
    B. painted with hot asphaltic cement
    C. covered with a bitumen-sand bed
    D. covered with broken stone

    1.____

2. Of the following ingredients, the one which is present in asphaltic concrete but not in a sheet asphalt mix is

    A. asphaltic cement   B. sand
    C. mineral dust   D. broken stone

    2.____

3. Of the following materials, the one which would make the BEST macadam base course is

    A. freshly broken rock consisting of angular pieces
    B. broken rock which had weathered for a long time
    C. gravel consisting of smooth round rock
    D. freshly crushed gravel

    3.____

4. The one of the following in which a surface heater would be MOST useful is

    A. new concrete construction
    B. new asphalt construction
    C. repair work on concrete
    D. repair work on asphalt

    4.____

5. A pneumatic jack hammer is powered by

    A. compressed air   B. electricity
    C. steam   D. water pressure

    5.____

6. A mattock could be BEST used in place of a

    A. hammer   B. pick-axe   C. rake   D. shovel

    6.____

7. The one of the following tools that is used to finish concrete so that a very smooth surface is obtained is

    A. template   B. trowel
    C. vibrator   D. wooden float

    7.____

8. The type of cement used in MOST concrete work is called

    A. asbestos   B. natural   C. Portland   D. rock

    8.____

11

9. Cement brought on the job in bags should be

    A. piled in criss-cross stacks on the ground near the work
    B. piled in stacks 10 bags high in a convenient place on the ground
    C. put on a platform and covered with waterproof covering
    D. put under a tree or awning where the sun's rays can't reach it

10. In the concrete trade, sand is called

    A. binder   B. coarse aggregate
    C. filler   D. fine aggregate

11. A 1:2:4 concrete mix means one part _____, two parts _____, four parts _____.

    A. cement; gravel; sand   B. cement; sand; gravel
    C. gravel; sand; cement   D. sand; gravel; cement

12. A slump test is used in concrete to determine

    A. consistency   B. construction
    C. expansion   D. slope

13. After mixing, the *initial* set of concrete will take place in about _____ hour(s).

    A. 3/4 of an   B. 2 1/4
    C. 4 3/4   D. 8

14. Concrete that has become partly set in the mixer should be

    A. covered with water for about 24 hours to soften it before using
    B. discarded and not used at all
    C. mixed in with another regular batch of concrete before using
    D. re-tempered by adding more cement and mixed again before using

15. In hot weather, newly-placed concrete will set better when it is

    A. covered with wet burlap
    B. dried by exposure to the sun
    C. mixed with grout
    D. shaded from the sun's rays

16. A 1:2:4 concrete mix is prepared on the job with 10 gallons of water. This concrete mix is

    A. *desirable,* because it will require less tamping
    B. *desirable,* because it will set faster
    C. *undesirable,* because its strength is reduced by excess water
    D. *undesirable,* because it will show less honeycomb

17. Of the following, the one which will lengthen the setting time of concrete is a(n)

    A. higher water temperature
    B. increase in proportion of water used
    C. less humid atmosphere
    D. shorter mixing period

18. Of the following, quick drying of concrete will MOST likely cause 18.____

    A. air bubbles   B. bumps
    C. cracks   D. swelling

19. Of the following, the BEST way to prepare an old concrete surface for a new layer of concrete is to 19.____

    A. clean it and apply a rich cement mortar
    B. cover it with wet sand
    C. steam and dry it
    D. wash it thoroughly and leave it wet

20. Grout is used MAINLY to 20.____

    A. fill surface impressions and imperfections
    B. lower the freezing point of the concrete mix
    C. make the base harden faster
    D. provide a wearing surface layer

21. The usual method of repairing cracks in concrete roadways is to fill with 21.____

    A. limestone   B. mineral filler
    C. sand   D. tar

22. Joints are placed in concrete sidewalks to take care of 22.____

    A. bumps   B. cracks
    C. drainage   D. expansion and contraction

23. To take care of surface drainage, concrete sidewalks usually have slopes of _____ inch(es) to the foot. 23.____

    A. 1/4   B. 1   C. 2   D. 3

24. The grade of a street is the 24.____

    A. AAA rating of the street's riding qualities
    B. difference in height between the crown and berm
    C. slope of a cut or fill
    D. variation in elevation per 100 feet

25. If a street rises 2' in 400', the grade is 25.____

    A. 0.2%   B. 0.5%   C. 2.0%   D. 5.0%

4 (#1)

KEY (CORRECT ANSWERS)

1.	C	11.	B
2.	D	12.	A
3.	A	13.	A
4.	D	14.	B
5.	A	15.	A
6.	B	16.	C
7.	B	17.	B
8.	C	18.	C
9.	C	19.	A
10.	D	20.	A

21. D
22. D
23. A
24. D
25. B

———

TEST 2

DIRECTIONS: Each question or incomplete statement is followed by several suggested answers or completions. Select the one that BEST answers the question or completes the statement. *PRINT THE LETTER OF THE CORRECT ANSWER IN THE SPACE AT THE RIGHT.*

1. The top course of an asphalt pavement is known as the _____ course.

    A. aggregate B. base C. binder D. wearing

2. In paving terms, a two-course concrete sidewalk is one which is

    A. composed of concrete both hand and machine mixed
    B. composed of two layers, a base and a wearing surface
    C. wide enough for traffic going in opposite directions
    D. wide enough for two pedestrians to walk side by side

3. The foundations for asphalt surface should be

    A. clean and damp
    B. clean and dry
    C. damp and sprinkled with sand
    D. dry and sprinkled with sand

4. A catch basin is used to

    A. detain floating rubbish which might clog a sewer
    B. hold water used in flushing sewers
    C. record and measure the depth of flow of sewage
    D. regulate the flow of sewage to a treatment plant

5. A sewer built to carry the flows in excess of the capacity of an existing sewer is called a _____ sewer.

    A. lateral B. main C. relief D. trunk

6. A sewer designed to carry domestic sewage, industrial waste, and storm sewage is called a

    A. combined sewer B. house connection
    C. sanitary sewer D. storm sewer

7. A pipe conveying sewage from a single building to a common sewer is called a

    A. catch basin B. grease trap
    C. house connection D. relief sewer

8. The PRINCIPAL effort in maintaining sewers is to keep them

    A. clean and unobstructed
    B. free from poisonous gases
    C. free of illegal connections
    D. properly backfilled

2 (#2)

9. Catch basins in unpaved streets should be cleaned

   A. daily in winter, weekly in summer
   B. once a year
   C. every six months
   D. after every large storm

10. In using a flexible sewer rod to clean a sewer, the work is usually begun at the

    A. chimney between manholes
    B. nearest catch basin
    C. top of the flooded manhole
    D. nearest house connection

11. In flushing sewers, the MOST important of the following qualities of the water used is its

    A. cleanliness   B. quantity
    C. temperature   D. velocity

12. Grease can be prevented from entering a sewer by the

    A. addition of copper sulfate
    B. installation of a copper ring in pipe joints
    C. installation of a separator
    D. coating of the outside of the pipe with tar

13. Manholes are used CHIEFLY as a(n)

    A. access for cleaning sewers
    B. outlet for sewer gas
    C. run-off for storm water
    D. support for sewer pipes

14. If the sewage at a manhole is backed up, it indicates MOST probably that, with respect to this manhole, there is an obstruction in the

    A. nearest catch basin   B. nearest house connection
    C. upstream sewer   D. downstream sewer

15. The one of the following at which a manhole in a sewer line is NOT necessary is wherever there is a

    A. change in direction
    B. change in pipe size
    C. considerable change in grade
    D. house connection

16. Manholes are usually placed at intervals of _____ to _____ feet.

    A. 50; 75   B. 100; 200   C. 700; 900   D. 1200; 1400

17. Of the following, the STRONGEST method for sheeting a trench is

    A. box sheeting   B. poling boards
    C. stay bracing   D. vertical sheeting

18. The one of the following that would be MOST commonly used to join a house sewer to a common sewer is a(n) 18._____

    A. increaser
    B. reducer
    C. running trap
    D. Y branch

19. After making joints in sewer pipe, the minimum safe length of time to allow before they should be exposed to running water is _____ hour(s). 19._____

    A. 1 B. 8 C. 24 D. 48

20. The one of the following that is the LEAST important health precaution for a sewer worker to take is 20._____

    A. frequent washing
    B. shading his eyes from reflected light
    C. using an antiseptic in cuts
    D. wearing rubber gloves

Questions 21-25.

DIRECTIONS: Column I below contains pictures of pipe connections used in sewer lines. Column II lists the names of these fittings. For each picture, indicate the capital letter preceding its correct name in Column II.

COLUMN II
A. Elbow
B. Reducer
C. Running trap
D. T branch
E. Y branch

21. 21._____

22. 22._____

23. 23._____

4 (#2)

24. 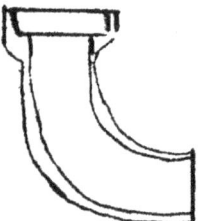   24.____

25.    25.____

KEY (CORRECT ANSWERS)

1. D   11. D
2. B   12. C
3. B   13. A
4. A   14. D
5. C   15. D

6. A   16. A
7. C   17. D
8. A   18. D
9. D   19. C
10. C 20. B

21. E
22. D
23. C
24. A
25. B

EXAMINATION SECTION
TEST 1

DIRECTIONS: Each question consists of a statement. You are to indicate whether the statement is TRUE (T) or FALSE (F). *PRINT THE LETTER OF THE CORRECT ANSWER IN THE SPACE AT THE RIGHT.*

1. A stillson wrench may properly be used on wrought iron pipe. 1.____

2. A pneumatic hammer is run by electricity. 2.____

3. A pneumatic drill, when not in use, should be left standing on its rod. 3.____

4. A cubic yard contains 27 cubic feet. 4.____

5. A tarpaulin is a lubricating oil for air compressors. 5.____

6. In working in manholes or pits, it is advisable to have one or two of the crew outside in case of emergency. 6.____

7. Men should be cautioned against entering manholes or vaults without first testing the air inside. 7.____

8. An air compressor is best used to yarn a joint. 8.____

9. To dig a trench, it is best to use a square-pointed shovel. 9.____

10. A street or road which rises at a uniform grade of 5 feet in 100 feet has a 5% grade. 10.____

11. If a candle will burn at the bottom of a manhole, it is a sign of gas and men should keep out. 11.____

12. It is good practice to wait until a sewer has been ventilated before going down into it. 12.____

13. It is good practice to drop lighted matches down a manhole to see if gas is present. 13.____

14. Workmen handling tar or asphalt should have their trousers fastened tightly around their ankles. 14.____

15. Cement brought to a job in bags should be piled neatly in criss-cross stacks on the ground. 15.____

16. Bagged cement should be piled about 25 bags high. 16.____

17. Men placing cement and concrete should have sleeves rolled up since they can work faster that way. 17.____

18. When mixing concrete, workmen should not stand so the wind blows in their faces. 18.____

19. Manholes are provided at suitable intervals along a sewer so that it may be inspected and cleaned. 19.____

20. The operator of a pneumatic drill should grasp it very loosely to prevent fatigue from constant vibration. 20.____

21. A catch basin's main use is to prevent storm water from entering a combined sewer. 21._____

22. Catch basins are generally built of brick or concrete. 22._____

23. Catch basins in New York City are generally cleaned by the use of orange peel type buckets. 23._____

24. A flexible rod is a tool often used in cleaning sewers. 24._____

25. Sewer obstructions can be removed by running scrapers and brushes through the sewer pipe. 25._____

KEY (CORRECT ANSWERS)

1.	T	11.	F
2.	F	12.	T
3.	F	13.	F
4.	T	14.	T
5.	F	15.	F
6.	T	16.	F
7.	T	17.	F
8.	F	18.	T
9.	F	19.	T
10.	T	20.	F

21.	F
22.	T
23.	T
24.	T
25.	T

TEST 2

DIRECTIONS: Each question consists of a statement. You are to indicate whether the statement is TRUE (T) or FALSE (F). *PRINT THE LETTER OF THE CORRECT ANSWER IN THE SPACE AT THE RIGHT.*

1. In flushing sewers, the amount of water used is more important than the speed at which the water is played into the sewer. 1._____
2. Many pavement failures can be traced to the action of water or moisture. 2._____
3. A pot hole in paving is a device for heating tar. 3._____
4. A surface heater is usually used to heat the binder course. 4._____
5. Tampers are used to compact a pavement in places where rollers cannot reach. 5._____
6. A straight edge is used to determine the smoothness of a finished pavement. 6._____
7. Concrete is a mixture of cement, sand, gravel and water in the proper proportions. 7._____
8. To clean a concrete mixer, you should operate it with water and small stones in the drum. 8._____
9. A concrete mixture will do a satisfactory job if it is allowed to stand one hour before placing. 9._____
10. Rapid drying of concrete adds to its strength. 10._____
11. In mixing concrete, the quantity of water used makes no difference. 11._____
12. Cracks in concrete open wider in cold weather. 12._____
13. A 1:2:4 concrete mix means one part cement, two parts sand, and four parts gravel. 13._____
14. Coarse aggregate consists of clean crushed rock or gravel. 14._____
15. A good way to prevent concrete from sticking to forms is to wet the forms with oil. 15._____
16. Concrete that has partly set in the mixer can be broken up and used with another batch of concrete. 16._____
17. Wings of a roadway are at the same elevation as center line. 17._____
18. The crown of a street is the fall from the center to edges. 18._____
19. A cold patch mixture when ready to be deposited usually contains wire mesh. 19._____
20. Grout is used to fill cracks in asphalt pavement. 20._____
21. In pouring cracks, just enough material should be used to fill the opening. 21._____
22. In hot weather, a pavement will contract. 22._____
23. Streets should usually be patched with the same material used in their construction. 23._____

24. Expansion joints are used in paving to provide for changes in temperature. 24.____

25. The main purpose of a seal coat in paving is to water-proof a surface. 25.____

KEY (CORRECT ANSWERS)

1.	F	11.	F
2.	T	12.	T
3.	F	13.	T
4.	F	14.	T
5.	T	15.	T
6.	T	16.	F
7.	T	17.	F
8.	T	18.	T
9.	F	19.	F
10.	F	20.	F

21. T
22. F
23. T
24. T
25. T

EXAMINATION SECTION
TEST 1

DIRECTIONS: Each question or incomplete statement is followed by several suggested answers or completions. Select the one that BEST answers the question or completes the statement. *PRINT THE LETTER OF THE CORRECT ANSWER IN THE SPACE AT THE RIGHT.*

1. Asphalt is derived mainly

    A. as a byproduct from the production of coke
    B. from asphalt deposits seeping to the surface of the earth
    C. from the refining of crude oil
    D. from bituminous coal

    1._____

2. Cutback liquid asphalts are prepared by blending asphalt with a volatile solvent. The one of the following that is NOT used as an asphalt solvent is

    A. naphtha   B. gasoline   C. kerosene   D. toluene

    2._____

3. The primary purpose of the solvent in cutback asphalt is to allow the

    A. use of a larger size aggregate in the mix
    B. application of the asphalt at a relatively low temperature
    C. application of asphalt in wet weather
    D. application of asphalt in hot weather

    3._____

4. The thickness of the sheet asphalt on a sheet asphalt pavement is usually _____ inch(es).

    A. 1/2 inch to 3/4   B. 1 inch to 1 1/2
    C. 1 5/8 inches to 2   D. 2 1/4 inches to 3

    4._____

5. The grade of an asphalt cement is designated as AR4000.
The AR is an abbreviation for

    A. asphalt rating   B. acid resistance
    C. aged residue   D. aging resistance

    5._____

6. An asphaltic emulsion is a suspension of asphalt in

    A. kerosene   B. gasoline   C. toluene   D. water

    6._____

7. A very light application of asphalt on an existing paved surface will promote bond between this surface and the subsequent course is known as a(n) _____ coat.

    A. prime   B. adhesion
    C. tack   D. penetrating

    7._____

8. Of the following, payment is usually made for asphalt pavements at the contract price per

    A. square inch   B. square foot
    C. square yard   D. 100 square feet

    8._____

23

9. The grade of an asphalt cement is designated AR4000. The 4000 is a measure of

   A. strength B. viscosity C. ductility D. density

10. Of the following, the geometric shape of a horizontal curve on a highway is

    A. parabolic
    B. hyperbolic
    C. circular
    D. elliptical

11. A borrow pit in highway construction is used

    A. for storing stormwater in a heavy rain
    B. for coarse aggregate in Portland cement concrete
    C. for coarse aggregate in asphalt concrete
    D. to obtain fill for embankments

12. Overhaul in highway construction is usually measured and paid for by the

    A. yard - cubic foot
    B. yard - cubic yard
    C. station - cubic foot
    D. station - cubic yard

13. A Benkelman beam is used in highway work

    A. as an indicator of the ability of a pavement to withstand loading
    B. to measure the roughness of an asphalt concrete pavement
    C. to measure the uniformity of an asphalt concrete pavement
    D. to measure the ability of an asphalt concrete pavement to remain serviceable if the subgrade is undermined

14. When surfacing over an existing pavement, of the following, the MOST practical way to insure that the required thickness of new pavement is met is

    A. expansion of clay when exposed to water
    B. expansion of soil when excavated
    C. waviness in a soil embankment when being compacted with a roller
    D. expansion of loamy soil when exposed to water

15. When surfacing over an existing pavement, of the following, the MOST practical way to insure that the required thickness of new pavement is met is

    A. have wood blocks of the thickness of the new pavement temporarily placed on the existing pavement to insure that the thickness requirements will be met at the time of paving
    B. make a survey of the existing pavement elevations and a survey of the final pavement elevations and check that the thickness requirements are met
    C. check that the amount of asphalt delivered is adequate to meet the depth requirements of the area to be paved
    D. take core borings to determine if the thickness meets specifications

16. The maximum roller speed for steel tired rollers paving asphalt concrete is a maximum of _____ mile(s) per hour.

    A. 7 B. 5 C. 3 D. 1

17. The weathered or dry surface appearing on a relatively new pavement can generally be attributed to

    A. inadequate rolling
    B. oversized coarse aggregate in the mix
    C. excessive amount of fine aggregate
    D. insufficient asphalt in the mix

17._____

18. Construction contracts for highways have items paid either by unit price or lump sum. The one of the following that is usually a lump sum item on a highway contract is

    A. excavation   B. paving
    C. fencing   D. demolition

18._____

19. Highway roadway subgrades are usually required to have a relative density of _____ percent.

    A. 80 to 84   B. 85 to 89   C. 90 to 95   D. 100

19._____

20. A *profile* of a highway is

    A. the section taken along the centerline of the highway
    B. an aesthetic landscape sketch of the highway
    C. used to determine the line of the highway
    D. used to locate overpasses

20._____

21. A culvert as used under a highway is usually installed

    A. as a relief sewer
    B. as a bypass for a stream
    C. in a stream bed
    D. to carry sanitary and storm flow

21._____

22. A mass diagram as related to highway construction work is used to

    A. minimize traffic congestion
    B. compute payment for hauling excavation and fill
    C. find the largest feasible radius of curvature for a horizontal curve
    D. help determine the depth of an asphalt concrete pavement

22._____

23. The geometric shape of a vertical curve on a highway is a(n)

    A. parabola   B. hyperbola   C. circle   D. ellipse

23._____

24. When cast iron bell and spigot pipe is used in sewer construction, the joint is usually sealed with

    A. lead   B. tin
    C. cement mortar   D. oakum

24._____

25. A planimeter is used to measure

    A. location   B. area   C. elevation   D. angles

25._____

KEY (CORRECT ANSWERS)

1.	C	11.	D
2.	D	12.	D
3.	B	13.	A
4.	B	14.	B
5.	C	15.	A
6.	D	16.	C
7.	C	17.	D
8.	B	18.	D
9.	B	19.	C
10.	C	20.	A

21. C
22. B
23. A
24. A
25. B

TEST 2

DIRECTIONS: Each question or incomplete statement is followed by several suggested answers or completions. Select the one that BEST answers the question or completes the statement. *PRINT THE LETTER OF THE CORRECT ANSWER IN THE SPACE AT THE RIGHT.*

1. A witness stake is usually used in surveying primarily as 1.____

   A. proof that a given location has been surveyed
   B. an aid in locating a surveying stake
   C. a marker to prevent a stake being disturbed
   D. an offset stake

2. Before the contractor begins work on a sewer or highway project, a detailed survey is made of all existing structures that may be affected by the construction in order to 2.____

   A. protect against false claims for damage
   B. insure that the contractor causes no damage to property
   C. insure that existing elevations conform to elevations on the contract drawings
   D. uncover potential weaknesses in structures

3. The optimum moisture content of a given soil will result in the 3.____

   A. plastic limit of the soil is reached
   B. liquid limit of the soil is reached
   C. porosity of the soil is at its maximum
   D. soil is compacted to its maximum dry density

4. The letters SC for soil means 4.____

   A. silty clay   B. clayey sand
   C. sandy clay   D. clayey silt

5. A cradle is used under a large precast circular concrete pipe sewer. The purpose of the cradle is mainly to 5.____

   A. minimize the settlement of the earth on the sides of the sewer
   B. minimize the settlement under the pipe
   C. strengthen the pipe against collapse
   D. resist side pressure against the pipe

6. The joints on laid precast concrete pipe were poorly made. The consequence of this poor workmanship is most likely 6.____

   A. the pipe will settle
   B. the pipe may collapse
   C. the water table may be adversely affected
   D. there will be excessive infiltration

7. An existing sewer is to connect into a new deep manhole for a new sewer. According to old plans for the existing sewer, the elevation of the existing sewer is 1/2 inch lower than shown on the plan.
Of the following, the BEST action that the inspector can take is 7.____

A. call his superior for instructions
B. do nothing
C. have the contractor relay the existing pipe to the theoretical elevation shown on the old plan
D. have an adjustable connection placed between the old pipe and the new manhole

8. The contractor proposes using a cement-lime mix for cement mortar to be used in building a manhole.
This is

   A. *good* practice as this is a more workable mortar
   B. *good* practice as the mortar is slow setting
   C. *poor* practice because the mortar weakens in a wet environment
   D. *poor* practice as a cement-lime mortar is more porous than a cement mortar

9. Most serious claims for extra payment on large sewer contracts result from

   A. soil conditions that are markedly different from those that were presented by the owner
   B. the inspectors being unreasonable in their demands
   C. delay in making the areas available for work
   D. the fact that the method of construction required by the owner proved to be unworkable

10. Unconsolidated fill is at pipe laying depth. Of the following, the BEST action that an inspector can take is to

    A. have the unconsolidated fill removed and replaced with concrete
    B. have the unconsolidated fill removed and replaced with sound fill
    C. report this matter to your supervisor for his consideration
    D. ask the contractor to consolidate the fill

11. Buried debris not shown on the borings is uncovered near the surface of an excavation for a deep sewer. Of the following, the BEST action for an inspector to take is to

    A. record the depth and extent of the debris in the event of a claim
    B. do nothing as this has no effect on the final product
    C. notify the contractor that there is no valid claim for the extra work required
    D. be certain that the debris is not used in the backfill

12. A come-along or deadman is sometimes used in the laying of large precast concrete pipe to insure

    A. the pipe is at proper grade
    B. the pipe is on proper line
    C. that the pipe will not subsequently settle
    D. that the pipe is properly seated

13. In laying sewers,

    A. accuracy in the line of the sewer is more important than accuracy in the grade of the sewer
    B. accuracy in the grade of the sewer is more important than accuracy in the line of the sewer

C. accuracy in the line and grade of the sewer are equally important
D. since the sewer is underground, accuracy is not required either for line or grade

14. A sewer contract is given out with a price per foot of sewer for different diameter sewers. After the contract is let, the low bidder is required to give a breakdown of his price per foot of sewer to include excavation, sewer in place, backfill, and restoration. The purpose of this breakdown is to

    A. facilitate partial payments
    B. insure the bid is not unbalanced
    C. enable the agency to gather up-to-date cost data for future projects
    D. make it easier to price extra work

14.____

15. The house sewer runs from the house to the main line sewer. The size of this sewer is most frequently _____ inches.

    A. 4 B. 5 C. 6 D. 8

15.____

16. A line on centerline at the inside bottom of a pipe or conduit is known as the

    A. convert B. invert C. subvert D. exvert

16.____

17. One of the most important elements of excavating for sewer construction is to maintain the specified width of the trench at the top of the pipe. If the width at the top of the pipe is too great,

    A. this may cause excessive settlement of the pipe
    B. this may cause excessive settlement of the backfill damaging the final pavement
    C. this may place excessive load on the pipe
    D. it may undermine utilities adjacent to the pipe

17.____

18. Wellpoints are used in sewer construction mainly to

    A. keep water out of the trench due to a heavy rainstorm
    B. keep water out of the excavation and subsoil to avoid excessive pressure on the sheeting
    C. prevent a boil from forming in the trench
    D. lower the water table to facilitate construction of the sewer

18.____

19. When a trench excavation uses soldier beams and horizontal sheeting for support, the minimum number of braces for each soldier beam is

    A. 1 B. 2 C. 3 D. 4

19.____

20. Bell and spigot pipe should be laid _____ with the bell end pointed _____.

    A. downstream; upstream   B. downstream; downstream
    C. upstream; upstream   D. upstream; downstream

20.____

21. The specifications state that house sewers should be laid at a grade of not less than 2%. In 40 feet of house sewer, the change in grade for 40 feet should be most nearly _____ inches.

    A. 8 B. 8 1/2 C. 9 D. 9 1/2

21.____

22. Two percent grade on a house sewer is equal to most nearly _____ inch per foot.

    A. 1/8 B. 3/16 C. 1/4 D. 5/16

23. When working underground in spaces that are closed and confined, such as manholes, the gas that is dangerous and most likely of the following to be present is

    A. carbon monoxide B. carbon dioxide
    C. ammonia D. methane

24. Of the following, air entrained cement would most likely be used in

    A. concrete roadways
    B. precast concrete pipe
    C. precast concrete manholes
    D. the cradle for precast concrete pipe

25. A slump cone is filled to overflowing in _____ layer(s).

    A. one B. two separate
    C. three separate D. four separate

KEY (CORRECT ANSWERS)

1. B		11. A
2. A		12. D
3. D		13. B
4. B		14. A
5. B		15. C
6. D		16. B
7. B		17. C
8. C		18. D
9. A		19. B
10. C		20. C

21. D
22. C
23. D
24. A
25. C

EXAMINATION SECTION
TEST 1

DIRECTIONS: Each question or incomplete statement is followed by several suggested answers or completions. Select the one that BEST answers the question or completes the statement. *PRINT THE LETTER OF THE CORRECT ANSWER IN THE SPACE AT THE RIGHT.*

1. The top course of an asphalt pavement is called the _____ course.

    A. base
    B. binder
    C. water-proofing
    D. wearing

    1._____

2. The MAIN reason for heating materials used in asphalt paving is that

    A. the impurities can be burned out
    B. the poor quality asphalt can be separated out
    C. their wearing qualities can be increased
    D. they can be mixed and handled properly

    2._____

3. In laying an asphalt wearing surface, the finished surface is USUALLY bonded to the concrete base by a(n)

    A. asphaltic cement and stone binder
    B. coat of tar
    C. layer of plain asphalt
    D. Portland cement grout

    3._____

4. The surface of an asphalt which is being heated is foaming.
    The temperature of the asphalt is 200° F.
    The foaming indicates that

    A. there is water present in the asphalt
    B. the asphalt is overheated
    C. asphalt is not hot enough
    D. vessel in which asphalt is being heated is too small

    4._____

5. Traffic should NOT be allowed on a completed asphaltic concrete pavement

    A. until the mixture has cooled
    B. for 2 days
    C. for 7 days
    D. for 30 days

    5._____

6. A penetration test has been performed with a standard needle on an asphaltic material.
    In reporting the test, it is NOT necessary to specify

    A. loading of needle
    B. time required for penetration
    C. thickness of sample
    D. temperature of sample

    6._____

7. Water-cement ratio is USUALLY expressed in

    A. cubic feet per cubic foot
    B. gallons per sack
    C. pounds per cubic foot
    D. gallons per pound

    7._____

8. Surface moisture is all water

   A. carried by the aggregate
   B. absorbed by the aggregate particles
   C. carried by the aggregate other than that absorbed by the aggregate particles
   D. except that carried by the aggregate

9. A quick-setting emulsified asphalt would MOST likely be used for

   A. coarse aggregate mixes   B. retread mixes
   C. heavy premix   D. joint filler

10. Asphaltic cement for asphaltic concrete should be heated, before mixing with aggregate, to a temperature of

    A. 150°F   B. 225°F   C. 300°F   D. 375°F

11. The temperature of sand to be used in ordinary asphaltic concrete, when delivered to the weighing box, should NOT exceed

    A. 1250°F   B. 225°F   C. 325°F   D. 525°F

12. The temperature of an ordinary sheet asphalt mix, when delivered on the street, should NOT be less than

    A. 325°F   B. 275°F   C. 225°F   D. 175°F

13. When a sheet asphalt pavement is being constructed, contact surfaces should be painted

    A. *before* the binder course is laid
    B. *before* the surface course is laid
    C. *before* the surface course is rolled
    D. *after* the surface course is rolled

14. The use of smoothing irons on the surface of sheet asphalt pavements is usually NOT permitted

    A. at joints
    B. to smooth irregularities in the surface
    C. at contact surfaces
    D. to iron in hot asphaltic cement on a strip adjacent to the curb

15. Rolling of the surface mixture of a sheet asphalt pavement should be continued until all but one of the following conditions are met.
    The condition which need NOT be met is the one wherein

    A. the mixture has cooled
    B. no marks show under the roller
    C. the pavement is free from waves
    D. the surface has been tested with an approved straight edge or surface testing machine

16. In determining the area of pavement to be paid for, the areas of the spaces occupied by column bases, manhole heads, gate boxes, and similar structures are

    A. not deducted from the gross area
    B. deducted from the gross area
    C. deducted only if the area occupied by a structure exceeds one square foot
    D. deducted only if the area occupied by a structure is less than one square foot

17. Concrete base for pavement is specified to be ten inches thick.
    Around manhole heads and similar structures, this base should have a depth, in inches, of

    A. 12   B. 10   C. 8   D. 6

18. Cores taken from a concrete base for pavement 40 ft. wide by 250 ft. long have the following thicknesses: 8 1/8", 8 3/8", 7 3/4", and 8 1/4".

    The volume of concrete to be paid for is, in cubic yards, MOST NEARLY

    A. 251   B. 255   C. 259   D. 263

19. The slump of concrete to be used for a pavement base should be, in inches, about

    A. 7   B. 8 ¼   C. 4   D. 2 ½

20. Adhesion of asphaltic material to the rolls of a roller is prevented by spraying the rolls with

    A. water   B. heavy oil   C. gasoline   D. naphtha

21. Of the following, the one which would NOT normally be used for a base or binder course is

    A. water-bound macadam   B. asphalt macadam
    C. asphaltic concrete   D. sheet asphalt

22. Some specifications require that the roller weigh not less than 225 lbs. per inch width of main roll while others require the roller weigh not less than ten tons.
    It is CORRECT to say that the first type of specification

    A. permits the use of rollers too light for the job
    B. will probably obtain more uniform compaction by a group of contractors
    C. may result in the use of rollers which are too wide
    D. may result in the use of rollers which are too heavy

23. The MOST stable macadam base course will probably result if the material used consists of

    A. angular pieces of freshly broken rock
    B. angular pieces of rock which has weathered after breaking
    C. bank-run gravel
    D. rounded pieces of freshly broken gravel

24. A pavement 40 feet wide between curbs which are at the same elevation has a crown of 5 inches. One end of a straight board 10 ft. long is placed on the pavement at the center line of the pavement. The board is leveled and runs perpendicular to the curb.
The vertical space between the board and the pavement at the other end is, in inches, about

   A. 5   B. 3 ¾   C. 2 ½   D. 1 ¼

25. A sheet asphalt pavement has been cut for a water connection. The width of cut in the asphalt is the same as that in the concrete base.
The FIRST thing to do after the concrete base has been repaired and has hardened is to

   A. paint the edges of the asphalt
   B. cut the asphalt back several inches from the edges of the concrete patch
   C. soften the edges of the asphalt with a surface heater
   D. heat the edges of the asphalt with a smoothing iron

KEY (CORRECT ANSWERS)

1. D		11. C	
2. D		12. B	
3. A		13. B	
4. A		14. B	
5. A		15. D	
6. C		16. C	
7. B		17. A	
8. C		18. A	
9. D		19. D	
10. C		20. A	

21. D
22. B
23. A
24. D
25. B

EXAMINATION SECTION
TEST 1

DIRECTIONS: Each question or incomplete statement is followed by several suggested answers or completions. Select the one that BEST answers the question or completes the statement. *PRINT THE LETTER OF THE CORRECT ANSWER IN THE SPACE AT THE RIGHT.*

Question 1.

DIRECTIONS: Question 1 refers to the cross-sections shown in the sketch below.

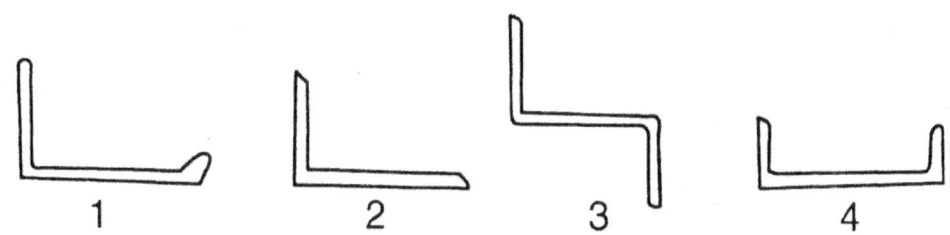

1. A steel curb angle has a cross-section similar to that marked

   A. 1 B. 2 C. 3 D. 4

2. Steel mesh is used in highway work to reinforce

   A. asphalt macadam   B. cold-patch mixes
   C. sheet asphalt   D. concrete

3. While raking out a sheet asphalt mixture, it is discovered that it is very lumpy. The BEST thing to do is

   A. to break up the lumps
   B. to force the lumps below the surface
   C. not use the mixture
   D. to allow it to cool before raking

4. Before a new portion of sheet asphalt on a street is laid, the cold edge of the sheet asphalt which was laid the day before should be

   A. heated   B. painted
   C. tamped   D. cut back and painted

5. If asphalt sticks to the roller,

   A. the roller should be mopped or sprayed with kerosene and water
   B. nothing has to be done
   C. the roller should be heated
   D. the mixture is not hot enough

6. If the sheet asphalt is to be 2 inches thick after rolling, it should USUALLY be raked out to a thickness of _____ inches.

   A. 4 B. 3.25 C. 3 D. 2.25

35

2 (#1)

7. The length of the teeth on an asphalt rake to be used for sheet asphalt which is to have a final thickness of two inches should be AT LEAST _____ inches.   7.____

   A. 1.5 B. 2 C. 2.5 D. 3

8. A surface heater is USUALLY used   8.____

   A. in fixing small surface defects
   B. to heat the base
   C. to heat the binder course
   D. to heat the mixture

9. Cracks less than one-eighth of an inch wide in sheet asphalt pavements are GENERALLY   9.____

   A. filled with hot asphaltic cement
   B. filled with a mixture of hot asphaltic cement and sand
   C. filled with cut-back asphalt
   D. left alone

10. When a pavement has been cut through for a water connection in a street which has sheet asphalt directly on a concrete base, the sheet asphalt patch should be   10.____

    A. the same size as the opening in the concrete
    B. larger than the opening in the concrete, the original surface being cut back around the opening in the concrete
    C. lower than the surrounding surface
    D. placed on a black-base

11. An automobile traveling rapidly strikes one of the men on a patching job and does not stop. The man is badly hurt. There is a taxicab nearby.
    You should   11.____

    A. put the man in the taxicab and rush him to the nearest hospital
    B. get in the taxicab and chase the automobile
    C. take the man to the nearest house and telephone for a doctor
    D. send for an ambulance and let the man lie in the street until the ambulance arrives

12. One truck is loaded with sand, a second with one-half-inch stones, and a third with one inch stones. A box is to be filled from the trucks.
    The box will be HEAVIEST when the material is taken from   12.____

    A. the second truck
    B. the third truck
    C. the second and third trucks and mixed
    D. all three trucks and mixed in equal proportion

13. Tampers and smoothers are used MOSTLY　　　　　　　　　　　　　　　　　　　　　　13.____

    A. where streets cross
    B. along curbs and at manholes
    C. when small steam rollers are used
    D. at the highest part of the street

14. Around a manhole, the asphaltic top should be loosely raked to a height above the man-　14.____
    hole casting of about _____ inch(es).

    A. .25　　　　　　B. .75　　　　　　C. 1.5　　　　　　D. 2

15. The BEST way to handle the smoothing iron is to push with heel　　　　　　　　　　　15.____

    A. down and pull with toe down
    B. up and pull with toe up
    C. down and pull with toe up
    D. up and pull with toe down

16. In the construction of sheet asphalt roadways, the asphalt mixture for the top layer　　　16.____
    should be delivered to the site, in degrees Fahrenheit, of between

    A. 100 to 250　　　　　　　　　　　B. 250 to 350
    C. 350 to 450　　　　　　　　　　　D. 450 to 550

17. The front wheels of a cart are 24 inches in diameter, and the rear wheels are 48 inches in　17.____
    diameter.
    When the cart is traveling at 10 miles per hour and there is no skidding, the

    A. rear wheels turn faster than the front wheels
    B. rear wheels turn the same number of times per minute as the front wheels
    C. front wheels turn faster than the rear wheels
    D. front wheels may turn faster or slower than the rear wheels, depending on the
       speed of the cart

18. Concrete is a mixture of water and　　　　　　　　　　　　　　　　　　　　　　　　　18.____

    A. lime and cement
    B. sand and cement
    C. broken stones and cement
    D. broken stones, sand, and cement

19. Shovels used in the construction of asphalt roadways should NOT be put into the firebox　19.____
    for cleaning because this may

    A. waste fuel unnecessarily
    B. change the temper of the steel
    C. put out the fire
    D. cause delay in the work

20. The edges of manholes where asphalt is to be placed should be 20.____

   A. coated with cement grout
   B. coated with hot asphaltic cement
   C. left as they are
   D. coated with oil paint

Questions 21-22.

DIRECTIONS: Questions 21 and 22 refer to the sketch shown below.

21. Using all five blocks shown above, to arrange them so that they will all fit each other in a tongue and groove fashion, 21.____

   A. is impossible
   B. the order is 1-2-5-4-3
   C. the order is 2-1-3-5-4
   D. the order is 4-2-1-3-5

22. Using only blocks numbered 1, 2, 4, 5 in the sketch above, to arrange them so that they will all fit each other in a tongue and groove fashion, 22.____

   A. is impossible   B. the order is 5-2-1-4
   C. the order is 4-2-1-5   D. the order is 1-2-4-5

23. A cold patch mixture when ready to be deposited GENERALLY contains 23.____

   A. cement   B. stones   C. plaster   D. wire mesh

24. On asphalt roadway construction work, the name *Buffalo Springfield* is GENERALLY connected with 24.____

   A. a brand of asphalt   B. steel curbing
   C. rollers   D. manhole covers

25. When the asphalt rake needs repairs, it should be 25.____

   A. sent to the plant or shop
   B. thrown away, handle and all
   C. put aside for minor repair work
   D. put aside for emergency work

KEY (CORRECT ANSWERS)

1. A
2. D
3. C
4. D
5. A

6. D
7. D
8. A
9. D
10. B

11. D
12. D
13. B
14. B
15. A

16. B
17. C
18. D
19. B
20. B

21. D
22. A
23. B
24. C
25. A

TEST 2

DIRECTIONS: Each question or incomplete statement is followed by several suggested answers or completions. Select the one that BEST answers the question or completes the statement. *PRINT THE LETTER OF THE CORRECT ANSWER IN THE SPACE AT THE RIGHT.*

1. Texaco Cold Patch GENERALLY comes in

    A. sacks   B. kegs   C. barrels   D. drums

2. The fuel in a fire wagon used to heat tools is

    A. always charcoal
    B. usually oil or coal
    C. always Consolidated gas
    D. superheated steam from the roller

3. Of the following, the one which has been MOST used for curbs in the city is

    A. terra-cotta   B. asbestos
    C. granite   D. marble

4. A tarpaulin is a

    A. tool for raking   B. cover
    C. fuel oil   D. special wrench

5. The USUAL unit for measuring sheet asphalt paving is

    A. tons   B. cubic feet
    C. square yards   D. square inches

6. A barricade is used

    A. as fuel for the roller
    B. to mix sheet asphalt
    C. to close off a street
    D. to break up the concrete base of a roadway

7. When first rolling new asphalt, it should GENERALLY be rolled

    A. first along the sides and gradually toward the center
    B. first along the center and gradually toward the sides
    C. cross-wise from curb to curb
    D. with a hand roller

8. The white powder used on the surface of a newly laid asphalt road is GENERALLY

    A. Portland cement or powdered stone
    B. very hot powdered asphalt
    C. talcum powder
    D. bleached flour

9. The valve that *blows* in case of excessive pressure in a steam roller is called a _____ valve.

    A. cut-off   B. blower   C. superheat   D. safety

10. The number of cubic yards in a bin 3 feet x 27 feet x 9 feet is

    A. 729　　　　B. 72　　　　C. 27　　　　D. 792

11. A scarifier is USUALLY used to

    A. break up an old road surface
    B. mix Portland cement
    C. smooth out asphalt
    D. reheat asphaltic cement on the job

12. The correct way to clean a rake is FIRST to

    A. rub it with gasoline
    B. scrape it with a dull knife
    C. soak it in naphtha oil
    D. put it into a tool heater

13. If a steam roller cannot go over a rain water catch basin on the roadway, the asphalt worker should

    A. lay planking each side of the catch basin for the roller to ride on
    B. see that the catch basin cover is supported by heavy timber
    C. tamp the asphalt top to grade and then finish with the smoothing iron
    D. ask for a lighter steam roller

14. A good way to prepare a joint between new and old asphalt is to cut all sides of the old asphalt

    A. to a feather edge and paint with hot asphaltic cement
    B. on a slope and heat them
    C. to a square edge and paint with hot asphaltic cement
    D. on a slope and paint with kerosene

15. The MAIN reason why asphalt cement should not be spilled on the surface during construction of a roadway is that it

    A. will stick to the drums of the roller and cause them to pick up the newly spread asphalt
    B. is a waste of expensive material
    C. will make the drums of the roller skid
    D. will burn the leather of the workers' shoes

16. To prevent honeycombing of the surface asphalt mixture, the raker should

    A. first tamp it into place before the roller goes to work
    B. see that it is run through a heater to prevent cold lumps
    C. comb through it with the rake and remove all cold lumps
    D. see to it that the mixture is not burned

17. If you do not understand the instructions of your foreman, you should   17._____

    A. ask him to put it in writing
    B. tell him that you understand, then think and use your own judgment
    C. ask him to explain again
    D. ask a fellow worker

18. Water will freeze at   18._____

    A. 32° F   B. 32° C   C. 100° F   D. 218° F

19. Assuming that you happen to be alone with one of your fellow workers and he accidentally cuts an artery in his wrist, the FIRST thing you should do is to   19._____

    A. run to inform your foreman
    B. run to the nearest telephone and ask for an ambulance
    C. tie a cord tightly on his arm above the cut to stop the flow of blood
    D. help the man to the nearest first aid station

20. The MAIN reason for heating some asphalt working tools is to   20._____

    A. help them keep their temper
    B. make them harder
    C. make them more useful for working the asphalt
    D. prevent rusting

21. The shovelers should not distribute the asphalt faster than it can be properly handled by the rakers.   21._____
    As used above, *distribute* means, MOST NEARLY,

    A. dump   B. pick-up   C. spread   D. heat

22. Any defective places should be cut out.   22._____
    As used, *defective* means, MOST NEARLY,

    A. low   B. hard   C. soft   D. faulty

23. It is more economical to use available local aggregate rather than to bring in aggregate from far distant sources. This statement means that local aggregate is _____ than other aggregate.   23._____

    A. better   B. worse
    C. cheaper   D. more expensive

24. The term *pneumatic,* when applied to rollers, refers to   24._____

    A. steel wheels   B. three axles
    C. adjustable weight   D. rubber tires

25. Rollers are made in several sizes.   25._____
    As used above, *several* means, MOST NEARLY,

    A. large   B. heavy   C. standard   D. different

KEY (CORRECT ANSWERS)

1.	D	11.	A
2.	B	12.	D
3.	C	13.	C
4.	B	14.	C
5.	C	15.	A
6.	C	16.	C
7.	A	17.	C
8.	A	18.	A
9.	D	19.	C
10.	C	20.	C

21. C
22. D
23. C
24. D
25. D

EXAMINATION SECTION
TEST 1

DIRECTIONS: Each question or incomplete statement is followed by several suggested answers or completions. Select the one that BEST answers the question or completes the statement. *PRINT THE LETTER OF THE CORRECT ANSWER IN THE SPACE AT THE RIGHT.*

1. One of your men is doing a new job incorrectly.
   The BEST action for you to take is to

   A. criticize him in the presence of the other men
   B. criticize him in private
   C. bring him up on charges
   D. show him how to do it correctly

2. Of the following, the BEST reason why it is unacceptable policy for you to become too friendly with the men you supervise is that the men may

   A. try to take advantage of your friendship
   B. resent your familiarity
   C. wish to borrow money from you
   D. be transferred to another unit

3. Of the following, the attitude for you to have toward your men in order to accomplish your job BEST is to be

   A. harsh and uncompromising
   B. firm and fair
   C. easygoing and forgiving
   D. aloof and unsocial

4. A man in your gang complains that the work is dirty.
   Of the following, the BEST action for you to take is to

   A. give the man only the clean jobs
   B. tell the man that the dirt is part of the working conditions
   C. tell the man to quit if he does not like the working conditions
   D. bring the man up on charges

5. Although you estimate that you will need 4 men to do a certain job, you bring 6 men to do the job.
   This practice is considered by authorities to be

   A. *good,* since you will be sure to get the job done on time
   B. *good,* since some men may get sick on the job and may be unable to work
   C. *poor,* since men may stand around doing nothing
   D. *poor,* since the work will not be divided evenly

6. One of your men tends to *goof off* whenever he has the chance.
   Of the following, the BEST procedure to follow first with respect to this man is to

   A. have him transferred to another unit
   B. deduct the estimated wasted time from his time off
   C. give him the hardest jobs
   D. watch him closely

45

7. If four men work seven hours during the day, the number of man-hours of work done is

   A. 4 B. 7 C. 11 D. 28

8. You should check that you have all the equipment and material you need for the day before work is started. Of the following, the BEST reason for personally making this check is that

   A. the men under your supervision cannot be trusted
   B. the men are usually too busy to check the material and equipment
   C. it is your responsibility to see that everything is in order
   D. it is very difficult to get help for checking once you are in the field

9. One of your men is injured on the job.
   The FIRST thing you should do is to

   A. assist the injured man
   B. find out the circumstances of the accident
   C. call the office to notify your supervisor of the accident
   D. fill out the paperwork relating to the accident

10. When investigating a complaint by a home owner of sewage backing up in a house, you find that the house trap in the basement is blocked.
    Of the following, the PROPER action for you to take is to

    A. call in a plumber for the home owner
    B. clean out the house trap
    C. tell the home owner to call in a plumber
    D. disconnect the house trap from the piping, clean it out, and reinstall the trap

11. If it takes four men fourteen days to do a certain job, seven men, working at the same rate, should be able to do the same job in _____ days.

    A. 8 B. 7 C. 6 D. 5

12. The men you supervise suggest that work be started an hour earlier so that they can leave an hour earlier at the end of the day.
    Of the following, the BEST action for you to take is to

    A. ignore the request
    B. start work an hour earlier
    C. tell them you will forward their suggestion to your superior
    D. report the men for insubordination

13. One of the men under your supervision tells you he is ill and would like to leave the job.
    Of the following, the BEST action for you to take is to

    A. grant the request
    B. report the man for trying to goof off
    C. take the man personally to the department doctor
    D. tell the man he has to work the rest of the day or he will lose a day's pay

14. One of your men scheduled to arrive at 8 A.M. calls you at noon to inform you that he will not be in because of personal business.
Of the following, the BEST action for you to take FIRST is to

    A. tell him to take it off sick leave
    B. call the office and ask for a replacement
    C. tell the man he should have called in on or about 8 A.M.
    D. tell him to charge the absence to lateness

14.____

15. Assume that you are in the field and have completed your work 2 hours before quitting time. The men spend the remaining 2 hours sitting in a restaurant.
This practice is considered by authorities to be

    A. *good,* as the men put in a full day
    B. *good,* as make–work is a poor policy
    C. *poor,* because it creates a bad public image
    D. *poor,* as it disrupts the restaurant's business

15.____

16. As a foreman, you insist that all mechanical equipment you use be PROPERLY serviced and maintained by your men. This policy is

    A. *poor,* since you may be pressuring the men
    B. *poor,* since the men may not cooperate
    C. *good,* since it helps prevent breakdown in equipment which can cause work to stop
    D. *good,* since the equipment is serviced on the men's time so that you get more work out of the men

16.____

17. Assume that the men you supervise are cleaning out a catchbasin and uncover a gun.
Of the following, the BEST action to take is to

    A. notify the police department of the discovery
    B. throw the gun away because it probably does not work
    C. keep the gun since you may be able to repair it
    D. dismantle the gun before disposing of it because it may be loaded

17.____

18. While your crew is working, a passer–by stops and asks you what they are doing.
Of the following, the BEST action to take is to

    A. tell him to mind his own business
    B. briefly explain your operation
    C. tell him to write a letter to the sewer department
    D. ignore the man and call the police if he persists

18.____

19. Your men should be careful not to break manhole covers. Of the following, the BEST reason for taking this precaution is that

    A. the cost of the manhole cover will be taken out of your paycheck
    B. the manhole cover can't be replaced
    C. manhole covers cost money to replace
    D. broken manhole covers are difficult to get rid of

19.____

20. While on the job, you teach your duties to one of the laborers. 20.____
    This practice is considered by authorities to be

    A. *poor,* because it shows favoritism
    B. *poor,* because this laborer may undermine your authority
    C. *good,* because the laborer will then be able to pass a promotion examination
    D. *good,* because the laborer can replace you in an emergency

KEY (CORRECT ANSWERS)

1.	D	11.	A
2.	A	12.	C
3.	B	13.	A
4.	B	14.	C
5.	C	15.	C
6.	D	16.	C
7.	D	17.	A
8.	C	18.	B
9.	A	19.	C
10.	C	20.	D

TEST 2

DIRECTIONS: Each question or incomplete statement is followed by several suggested answers or completions. Select the one that BEST answers the question or completes the statement. *PRINT THE LETTER OF THE CORRECT ANSWER IN THE SPACE AT THE RIGHT.*

1. The BEST reason for you to advise your men to be alert at all times while working in the street is that

    A. working in the street could be dangerous
    B. they may see some criminal activity
    C. somebody from the main office may be observing your men
    D. they may create a bad public image if they are not always alert

2. It is GOOD practice to complete a report on an accident as soon as possible after the accident occurs MAINLY because

    A. paperwork should be submitted to the office on the same day an accident occurs
    B. if you do not you may forget some of the necessary details
    C. this gives you more time to change the report if this should be necessary
    D. the department can then immediately prepare its defense

3. Official directives state that you are to report immediately by telephone if a manhole cover or basin grate is missing.
   Of the following, the BEST reason for having this requirement is to

    A. permit the cover or grate to be ordered if it is not on hand
    B. be able to assess the responsibility for this condition
    C. prevent an accident
    D. enable the sanitation department to clean the street

4. A complainant is a

    A. city agency that responds to a complaint
    B. person filing a complaint
    C. crew member that responds to a complaint
    D. lawyer who defends a client against a complaint

5. In filling out an accident form, there is a section entitled *Accident Type*.
   Of the following, the one that is an accident type is

    A. struck by falling object
    B. operated without authority
    C. worked too slowly
    D. engaged in horseplay

6. On an accident report, there is an item labeled *Nature of Injury*.
   Of the following, the one that belongs in this category is

    A. fracture
    B. carelessness
    C. defective equipment
    D. loose clothing

7. Of the following, the LEAST serious of the defects filed in a sewer report is

    A. broken casting
    B. missing casting
    C. noisy manhole cover
    D. backed up sewer

8. When signing a time sheet, the employee must sign his name and his number. The BEST of the following reasons for requiring his number in addition to his name is

    A. to be sure the employee has not entered the wrong time on the time sheet
    B. to make it easier to contact the employee
    C. his signature may be difficult to read
    D. the employee is paid based on his number which is fed into the IBM machine

9. One of the men in your unit states that he will take off the next day to attend his father-in-law's funeral and wants to know if he can change the absence to sick leave. Of the following, the BEST answer you can give him is that

    A. he can charge half the time to sick leave and half to annual leave
    B. the rules do not permit this to be done
    C. this can only be done if his father-in-law had lived with him
    D. sick leave can be used this way only if he had 10 years or more in service

10. In addition to the Department of Water Resources, the Environmental Protection Administration consists of the

    A. Board of Water Supply, the Department of Sanitation, and the Department of Air Resources
    B. Department of Sanitation, the Department of Municipal Services, and the Department of Air Resources
    C. Department of Sanitation and the Department of Municipal Services
    D. Department of Sanitation and the Department of Air Resources

11. The government calendar year starts on _____ 1.

    A. June   B. July   C. May   D. January

12. A truck leaves the garage at 9:26 A.M. and returns the same day at 3:43 P.M. The period of time that the truck was away from the garage is MOST NEARLY _____ hours _____ minutes.

    A. 5; 17   B. 5; 43   C. 6; 17   D. 6; 26

13. Of the following, the BEST method for a foreman to use to teach a man how to lift a manhole cover safely is to

    A. tell him how to do it
    B. make a sketch showing the correct method to use
    C. actually lift a cover with the man watching
    D. let the man try to lift the cover and correct any mistakes

14. Assume that one of the laborers you supervise is unable to read well and that you have advised him to go evenings to school to learn to read and write English. According to good supervisory practice, the advice is considered to be

    A. *poor,* because it is none of your business
    B. *poor,* because a laborer does not have to know how to read
    C. *good,* because he can then go on to get a high school diploma
    D. *good,* because he will be able to read signs and avoid danger on the job

15. Assume that a new piece of mechanical equipment is brought to the job.
    Of the following, the BEST way for the men to learn the proper use of the equipment is to

    A. have a representative of the company that manufactures the equipment come to the job and demonstrate its use
    B. let the men try out the equipment and learn the operation of the equipment by using it
    C. let the men read the instruction manual carefully before trying out the equipment
    D. deliver a lecture to the men that have to use the equipment on the proper use of the equipment

16. Assume that you are training a group of men on the adjustment of a high-pressure relief valve.
    Of the following, the FIRST topic you should discuss with the men is

    A. the conditions under which it is necessary to adjust the relief valve
    B. how to order parts for the relief valve
    C. how the springs in the relief valve work
    D. how to take apart the relief valve

17. Assume that a new man is assigned to your unit and you explain to him exactly what is expected of him.
    This procedure is

    A. *poor,* because the new man will feel that you are threatening him
    B. *poor,* because this leaves the new man with no freedom to do the job as he feels best
    C. *good,* because then the new man can quit if he does not like the foreman
    D. *good,* because the new man will know what is required of him

18. A foreman explains to a man a way of doing a particular job and the man says he does not understand.
    Of the following, the BEST action for the foreman to take is to

    A. repeat the explanation
    B. let the man remain ignorant
    C. transfer the man to another unit
    D. tell the man he may understand the procedure at a later time

19. A new piece of equipment is ordered and the men who will use it are trained in its use before the equipment arrives on the job.
    This practice is

    A. *poor,* because the order may be cancelled and time wasted
    B. *poor,* because it takes longer to train men when the equipment is not present
    C. *good,* because it keeps the men busy when they do not have anything to do
    D. *good,* because the equipment can immediately be put to use

20. You observe a man using a piece of equipment incorrectly. Of the following, the BEST action for you to take is to 20.____

   A. have somebody else work with the equipment
   B. transfer the man to another unit
   C. bring the man up on charges
   D. show him how to use the equipment correctly

KEY (CORRECT ANSWERS)

1.	A	11.	D
2.	B	12.	C
3.	C	13.	C
4.	B	14.	D
5.	A	15.	A
6.	A	16.	A
7.	C	17.	D
8.	C	18.	A
9.	B	19.	D
10.	D	20.	D

EXAMINATION SECTION
TEST 1

DIRECTIONS: Each question or incomplete statement is followed by several suggested answers or completions. Select the one that BEST answers the question or completes the statement. *PRINT THE LETTER OF THE CORRECT ANSWER IN THE SPACE AT THE RIGHT.*

1. Of the following, the one MOST important quality required of a good supervisor is
   A. ambition   B. leadership   C. friendliness   D. popularity

   1.____

2. It is often said that a supervisor can delegate authority but never responsibility. This means MOST NEARLY that
   A. a supervisor must do his own work if he expects it to be done properly
   B. a supervisor can assign someone else to do his work, but in the last analysis, the supervisor himself must take the blame for any actions followed
   C. authority and responsibility are two separate things that cannot be borne by the same person
   D. it is better for a supervisor never to delegate his authority

   2.____

3. One of your men who is a habitual complainer asks you to grant him a minor privilege.
   Before granting or denying such a request, you should consider
   A. the merits of the case
   B. that it is good for group morale to grant a request of this nature
   C. the man's seniority
   D. that to deny such a request will lower your standing with the men

   3.____

4. A supervisory practice on the part of a foreman which is MOST likely to lead to confusion and inefficiency is for him to
   A. give orders verbally directly to the man assigned to the job
   B. issue orders only in writing
   C. follow up his orders after issuing them
   D. relay his orders to the men through co-workers

   4.____

5. It would be POOR supervision on a foreman's part if he
   A. asked an experienced maintainer for his opinion on the method of doing a special job
   B. make it a policy to avoid criticizing a man in front of his co-workers
   C. consulted his assistant supervisor on unusual problems
   D. allowed a cooling-off period of several days before giving one of his men a deserved reprimand

   5.____

6. Of the following behavior characteristics of a supervisor, the one that is MOST likely to lower the morale of the men he supervises is
   A. diligence
   B. favoritism
   C. punctuality
   D. thoroughness

7. Of the following, the BEST method of getting an employee who is not working up to his capacity to produce more work is to
   A. have another employee criticize his production
   B. privately criticize his production but encourage him to produce more
   C. criticize his production before his associates
   D. criticize his production and threaten to fire him

8. Of the following, the BEST thing for a supervisor to do when a subordinate has done a very good job is to
   A. tell him to take it easy
   B. praise his work
   C. reduce his workload
   D. say nothing because he may become conceited

9. Your orders to your crew are MOST likely to be followed if you
   A. explain the reasons for these orders
   B. warn that all violators will be punished
   C. promise easy assignments to those who follow these orders best
   D. say that they are for the good of the department

10. In order to be a good supervisor, you should
    A. impress upon your men that you demand perfection in their work at all times
    B. avoid being blamed for your crew's mistakes
    C. impress your superior with your ability
    D. see to it that your men get what they are entitled to

11. In giving instructions to a crew, you should
    A. speak in as loud a tone as possible
    B. speak in a coaxing, persuasive manner
    C. speak quietly, clearly, and courteously
    D. always use the word *please* when giving instructions

12. Of the following factors, the one which is LEAST important in evaluating an employee and his work is his
    A. dependability
    B. quantity of work done
    C. quality of work done
    D. education and training

13. When a District Superintendent first assumes his command, it is LEAST important for him at the beginning to observe
    A. how his equipment is designed and its adaptability
    B. how to reorganize the district for greater efficiency
    C. the capabilities of the men in the district
    D. the methods of operation being employed

14. When making an inspection of one of the buildings under your supervision, the BEST procedure to follow in making a record of the inspection is to
    A. return immediately to the office and write a report from memory
    B. write down all the important facts during or as soon as you complete the inspection
    C. fix in your mind all important facts so that you can repeat them from memory if necessary
    D. fix in your mind all important facts so that you can make out your report at the end of the day

15. Assume that your superior has directed you to make certain changes in your established procedure. After using this modified procedure on several occasions, you find that the original procedure was distinctly superior and you wish to return to it.
    You should
    A. let your superior find this out for himself
    B. simply change back to the original procedure
    C. compile definite data and information to prove your case to your superior
    D. persuade one of the more experienced workers to take this matter up with your superior

16. An inspector visited a large building under construction. He inspected the soil lines at 9 A.M., water lines at 10 A.M., fixtures at 11 A.M., and did his office work in the afternoon. He followed the same pattern daily for weeks.
    This procedure was
    A. *good*, because it was methodical and he did not miss anything
    B. *good*, because it gave equal time to all phases of the plumbing
    C. *bad*, because not enough time was devoted to fixtures
    D. *bad*, because the tradesmen knew when the inspection would occur

17. Assume that one of the foremen in a training course, which you are conducting, proposes a poor solution for a maintenance problem.
    Of the following, the BEST course of action for you to take is to
    A. accept the solution tentatively and correct it during the next class meeting
    B. point out all the defects of this proposed solution and wait until somebody thinks of a better solution
    C. try to get the class to reject this proposed solution and develop a better solution
    D. let the matter pass since somebody will present a better solution as the class work proceeds

18. As a supervisor, you should be seeking ways to improve the efficiency of shop operations by means such as changing established work procedures.
    The following are offered as possible actions that you should consider in changing established work procedures:
    I. Make changes only when your foremen agree to them
    II. Discuss changes with your supervisor before putting them into practice

III. Standardize any operation which is performed on a continuing basis
IV. Make changes quickly and quietly in order to avoid dissent
V. Secure expert guidance before instituting unfamiliar procedures
Of the following suggested answers, the one that describes the actions to be taken to change established work procedures is
A. I, IV, V   B. II, III, V   C. III, IV, V   D. All of the above

19. A supervisor determined that a foreman, without informing his superior, delegated responsibility for checking time cards to a member of his gang. The supervisor then called the foreman into his office where he reprimanded the foreman.
This action of the supervisor in reprimanding the foreman was
    A. *proper*, because the checking of time cards is the foreman's responsibility and should not be delegated
    B. *proper*, because the foreman did not ask the supervisor for permission to delegate responsibility
    C. *improper*, because the foreman may no longer take the initiative in solving future problems
    D. *improper*, because the supervisor is interfering in a function which is not his responsibility

19.____

20. A capable supervisor should check all operations under his control.
Of the following, the LEAST important reason for doing this is to make sure that
    A. operations are being performed as scheduled
    B. he personally observes all operations at all times
    C. all the operations are still needed
    D. his manpower is being utilized efficiently

20.____

21. A supervisor makes it a practice to apply fair and firm discipline in all cases of rule infractions, including those of a minor nature.
This practice should PRIMARILY be considered
    A. *bad*, since applying discipline for minor violations is a waste of time
    B. *good*, because not applying discipline for minor infractions can lead to a more serious erosion of discipline
    C. *bad*, because employees do not like to be disciplined for minor violations of the rules
    D. *good*, because violating any rule can cause a dangerous situation to occur

21.____

22. A maintainer would PROPERLY consider it poor supervisory practice for a foreman to consult with him on
    A. which of several repair jobs should be scheduled first
    B. how to cope with personal problems at home
    C. whether the neatness of his headquarters can be improved
    D. how to express a suggestion which the maintainer plans to submit formally

22.____

5 (#1)

23. Assume that you have determined that the work of one of your foremen and the men he supervises is consistently behind schedule. When you discuss this situation with the foreman, he tells you that his men are poor workers and then complains that he must spend all of his time checking on their work.
The following actions are offered for your consideration as possible ways of solving the problem of poor performance of the foreman and his men:
I. Review the work standards with the foreman and determine whether they are realistic.
II. Tell the foreman that you will recommend him for the foreman's training course for retraining.
III. Ask the foreman for the names of the maintainers and then replace them as soon as possible.
IV. Tell the foreman that you expect him to meet a satisfactory level of performance.
V. Tell the foreman to insist that his men work overtime to catch up to the schedule.
VI. Tell the foreman to review the type and amount of training he has given the maintainers.
VII. Tell the foreman that he will be out of a job if he does not produce on schedule.
VIII. Avoid all criticism of the foreman and his methods.
Which of the following suggested answers CORRECTLY lists the proper actions to be taken to solve the problem of poor performance of the foreman and his men?
A. I, II, IV, VI   B. I, III, V, VII   C. II, III, VI, VIII   D. IV, V, VI, VIII

23.____

24. When a conference or a group discussion is tending to turn into a *bull session* without constructive purpose, the BEST action to take is to
A. reprimand the leader of the bull session
B. redirect the discussion to the business at hand
C. dismiss the meeting and reschedule it for another day
D. allow the bull session to continue

24.____

25. Assume that you have been assigned responsibility for a program in which a high production rate is mandatory. From past experience, you know that your foremen do not perform equally well in the various types of jobs given to them. Which of the following methods should you use in selecting foremen for the specific types of work involved in the program?
A. Leave the method of selecting foremen to your supervisor
B. Assign each foreman to the work he does best
C. Allow each foreman to choose his own job
D. Assign each foreman to a job which will permit him to improve his own abilities

25.____

KEY (CORRECT ANSWERS)

1.	B	11.	C
2.	B	12.	D
3.	A	13.	B
4.	D	14.	B
5.	D	15.	C
6.	B	16.	D
7.	B	17.	C
8.	B	18.	B
9.	A	19.	A
10.	D	20.	B

21.	B
22.	A
23.	A
24.	B
25.	B

TEST 2

DIRECTIONS: Each question or incomplete statement is followed by several suggested answers or completions. Select the one that BEST answers the question or completes the statement. *PRINT THE LETTER OF THE CORRECT ANSWER IN THE SPACE AT THE RIGHT.*

1. A foreman who is familiar with modern management principles should know that the one of the following requirements of an administrator which is LEAST important is his ability to
    A. coordinate work
    B. plan, organize, and direct the work under his control
    C. cooperate with others
    D. perform the duties of the employees under his jurisdiction

    1.____

2. When subordinates request his advice in solving problems encountered in their work, a certain chief occasionally answers the request by first asking the subordinate what he thinks should be done.
    This action by the chief is, on the whole,
    A. *desirable*, because it stimulates subordinates to give more thought to the solution of problems encountered
    B. *undesirable*, because it discourages subordinates from asking questions
    C. *desirable*, because it discourages subordinates from asking questions
    D. *undesirable*, because it undermines the confidence of subordinates in the ability of their supervisor

    2.____

3. Of the following factors that may be considered by a unit head in dealing with the tardy subordinate, the one which should be given LEAST consideration is the
    A. frequency with which the employee is tardy
    B. effect of the employee's tardiness upon the work of other employees
    C. willingness of the employee to work overtime when necessary
    D. cause of the employee's tardiness

    3.____

4. The MOST important requirement of a good inspectional report is that it should be
    A. properly addressed   B. lengthy
    C. clear and brief   D. spelled correctly

    4.____

5. Building superintendents frequently inquire about departmental inspectional procedures.
    Of the following, it is BEST to
    A. advise them to write to the department for an official reply
    B. refuse as the inspectional procedure is a restricted matter
    C. briefly explain the procedure to them
    D. avoid the inquiry by changing the subject

    5.____

6. Reprimanding a crew member before other workers is a
    A. *good* practice; the reprimand serves as a warning to the other workers
    B. *bad* practice; people usually resent criticism made in public
    C. *good* practice; the other workers will realize that the supervisor is fair
    D. *bad* practice; the other workers will take sides in the dispute

7. Of the following actions, the one which is LEAST likely to promote good work is for the group leader to
    A. praise workers for doing a good job
    B. call attention to the opportunities for promotion for better workers
    C. threaten to recommend discharge of workers who are below standard
    D. put into practice any good suggestion made by crew members

8. A supervisor notices that a member of his crew has skipped a routine step in his job.
    Of the following, the BEST action for the supervisor to take is to
    A. promptly question the worker about the incident
    B. immediately assign another man to complete the job
    C. bring up the incident the next time the worker asks for a favor
    D. say nothing about the incident but watch the worker carefully in the future

9. Assume you have been told to show a new worker how to operate a piece of equipment.
    Your FIRST step should be to
    A. ask the worker if he has any questions about the equipment
    B. permit the worker to operate the equipment himself while you carefully watch to prevent damage
    C. demonstrate the operation of the equipment for the worker
    D. have the worker read an instruction booklet on the maintenance of the equipment

10. Whenever a new man was assigned to his crew, the supervisor would introduce him to all other crew members, take him on a tour of the plant, tell him about bus schedules and places to eat.
    This practice is
    A. *good*; the new man is made to feel welcome
    B. *bad*; supervisors should not interfere in personal matters
    C. *good*; the new man knows that he can bring his personal problems to the supervisor
    D. *bad*; work time should not be spent on personal matters

11. The MOST important factor in successful leadership is the ability to
    A. obtain instant obedience to all orders
    B. establish friendly personal relations with crew members
    C. avoid disciplining crew members
    D. make crew members want to do what should be done

12. Explaining the reasons for departmental procedure to workers tends to
    A. waste time which should be used for productive purposes
    B. increase their interest in their work
    C. make them more critical of departmental procedures
    D. confuse them

13. If you want a job done well do it yourself.
    For a supervisor to follow this advice would be
    A. *good*; a supervisor is responsible for the work of his crew
    B. *bad*; a supervisor should train his men, not do their work
    C. *good*; a supervisor should be skilled in all jobs assigned to his crew
    D. *bad*; a supervisor loses respect when he works with his hands

14. When a supervisor discovers a mistake in one of the jobs for which his crew is responsible, it is MOST important for him to find out
    A. whether anybody else knows about the mistake
    B. who was to blame for the mistake
    C. how to prevent similar mistakes in the future
    D. whether similar mistakes occurred in the past

15. A supervisor who has to explain a new procedure to his crew should realize that questions from the crew USUALLY show that they
    A. are opposed to the new practice
    B. are completely confused by the explanation
    C. need more training in the new procedure
    D. are interested in the explanation

16. A good way for a supervisor to retain the confidence of his or her employees is to
    A. say as little as possible
    B. check work frequently
    C. make no promises unless they will be fulfilled
    D. never hesitate in giving an answer to any question

17. Good supervision is ESSENTIALLY a matter of
    A. patience in supervising workers   B. care in selecting workers
    C. skill in human relations   D. fairness in disciplining workers

18. It is MOST important for an employee who has been assigned a monotonous task to
    A. perform this task before doing other work
    B. ask another employee to help
    C. perform this task only after all other work has been completed
    D. take measures to prevent mistakes in performing the task

4 (#2)

19. One of your employees has violated a minor agency regulation. 19.____
The FIRST thing you should do is
   A. warn the employee that you will have to take disciplinary action if it should happen again
   B. ask the employee to explain his or her actions
   C. inform your supervisor and wait for advice
   D. write a memo describing the incident and place it in the employee's personnel file

20. One of your employees tells you that he feels you give him much more work 20.____
than the other employees, and he is having trouble meeting your deadlines.
You should
   A. ask if he has been under a lot of non-work related stress lately
   B. review his recent assignments to determine if he is correct
   C. explain that this is a busy time, but you are dividing the work equally
   D. tell him that he is the most competent employee and that is why he receives more work

21. A supervisor assigns one of his crew to complete a portion of a job. A short 21.____
time later, the supervisor notices that the portion has not been completed.
Of the following, the BEST way for the supervisor to handle this is to
   A. ask the crew member why he has not completed the assignment
   B. reprimand the crew member for not obeying orders
   C. assign another crew member to complete the assignment
   D. complete the assignment himself

22. Supposes that a member of your crew complains that you are *playing favorites* 22.____
in assigning work.
Of the following, the BEST method of handling the complaint is to
   A. deny it and refuse to discuss the matter with the worker
   B. take the opportunity to tell the worker what is wrong with his work
   C. ask the worker for examples to prove his point and try to clear up any misunderstanding
   D. promise to be more careful in making assignments in the future

23. A member of your crew comes to you with a complaint. After discussing the 23.____
matter with him, it is clear that you have convinced him that his complaint was not justified.
At this point, you should
   A. permit him to drop the matter
   B. make him admit his error
   C. pretend to see some justification in his complaint
   D. warn him against making unjustified complaints

24. Suppose that a supervisor has in his crew an older man who works rather 24.____
slowly. In other respects, this man is a good worker; he is seldom absent, works carefully, never loafs, and is cooperative.

5 (#2)

The BEST way for the supervisor to handle this worker is to
- A. try to get him to work faster and less carefully
- B. give him the most disagreeable job
- C. request that he be given special training
- D. permit him to work at his own speed

25. Suppose that a member of your crew comes to you with a suggestion he thinks will save time in doing a job. You realize immediately that it won't work. Under these circumstances, your BEST action would be to
    - A. thank the worker for the suggestion and forget about it
    - B. explain to the worker why you think it won't work
    - C. tell the worker to put the suggestion in writing
    - D. ask the other members of your crew to criticize the suggestion

25.____

KEY (CORRECT ANSWERS)

1.	D	11.	D
2.	A	12.	B
3.	C	13.	B
4.	C	14.	C
5.	C	15.	D
6.	B	16.	C
7.	C	17.	C
8.	A	18.	D
9.	C	19.	B
10.	A	20.	B

21. A
22. C
23. A
24. D
25. B

SUPERVISION STUDY GUIDE

Social science has developed information about groups and leadership in general and supervisor-employee relationships in particular. Since organizational effectiveness is closely linked to the ability of supervisors to direct the activities of employees, these findings are important to executives everywhere.

IS A SUPERVISOR A LEADER?

First-line supervisors are found in all large business and government organizations. They are the men at the base of an organizational hierarchy. Decisions made by the head of the organization reach them through a network of intermediate positions. They are frequently referred to as part of the management team, but their duties seldom seem to support this description.

A supervisor of clerks, tax collectors, meat inspectors, or securities analysts is not charged with budget preparation. He cannot hire or fire the employees in his own unit on his say-so. He does not administer programs which require great planning, coordinating, or decision making.

Then what is he? He is the man who is directly in charge of a group of employees doing productive work for a business or government agency. If the work requires the use of machines, the men he supervises operate them. If the work requires the writing of reports, the men he supervises write them. He is expected to maintain a productive flow of work without creating problems which higher levels of management must solve. But is he a leader?

To carry out a specific part of an agency's mission, management creates a unit, staffs it with a group of employees and designates a supervisor to take charge of them. Management directs what this unit shall do, from time to time changes directions, and often indicates what the group should not do. Management presumably creates status for the supervisor by giving him more pay, a title, and special privileges.

Management asks a supervisor to get his workers to attain organizational goals, including the desired quantity and quality of production. Supposedly, he has authority to enable him to achieve this objective. Management at least assumes that by establishing the status of the supervisor's position, it has created sufficient authority to enable him to achieve these goals— not his goals, nor necessarily the group's, but management's goals.

In addition, supervision includes writing reports, keeping records of membership in a higher-level administrative group, industrial engineering, safety engineering, editorial duties, housekeeping duties, etc. The supervisor as a member of an organizational network, must be responsible to the changing demands of the management above him. At the same time, he must be responsive to the demands of the work group of which he is a member. He is placed in the difficult position of communicating and implementing new decisions, changed programs and revised production quotas for his work group, although he may have had little part in developing them.

It follows, then, that supervision has a special characteristic: achievement of goals, previously set by management, through the efforts of others. It is in this feature of the supervisor's job that we find the role of a leader in the sense of the following definition: *A leader is that person who most effectively influences group activities toward goal setting and goal achievements.*

This definition is broad. It covers both leaders in groups that come together voluntarily and in those brought together through a work assignment in a factory, store, or government agency. In the natural group, the authority necessary to attain goals is determined by the group membership and is granted by them. In the working group, it is apparent that the establishment of a supervisory position creates a predisposition on the part of employees to accept the authority of the occupant of that position. We cannot, however, assume that mere occupation confers authority sufficient to assure the accomplishment of an organization's goals.

Supervision is different, then, from leadership. The supervisor is expected to fulfill the role of leader but without obtaining a grant of authority from the group he supervises. The supervisor is expected to influence the group in the achieving of goals but is often handicapped by having little influence on the organizational process by which goals are set. The supervisor, because he works in an organizational setting, has the burdens of additional organizational duties and restrictions and requirements arising out of the fact that his position is subordinate to a hierarchy of higher-level supervisors. These differences between leadership and supervision are reflected in our definition: *Supervision is basically a leadership role, in a formal organization, which has as its objective the effective influencing of other employees.*

Even though these differences between supervision and leadership exist, a significant finding of experimenters in this field is that supervisors must be leaders to be successful.

The problem is: How can a supervisor exercise leadership in an organizational setting? We might say that the supervisor is expected to be a natural leader in a situation which does not come about naturally. His situation becomes really difficult in an organization which is more eager to make its supervisors into followers rather than leaders.

LEADERSHIP: NATURAL AND ORGANIZATIONAL

Leadership, in its usual sense of *natural* leadership, and supervision are not the same. In some cases, leadership embraces broader powers and functions than supervision; in other cases, supervision embraces more than leadership. This is true both because of the organization and technical aspects of the supervisor's job and because of the relatively freer setting and inherent authority of the natural leader.

The natural leader usually has much more authority and influence than the supervisor. Group members not only follow his command but prefer it that way. The employee, however, can appeal the supervisor's commands to his union or to the supervisor's superior or to the personnel office. These intercessors represent restrictions on the supervisor's power to lead.

The natural leader can gain greater membership involvement in the group's objectives, and he can change the objectives of the group. The supervisor can attempt to gain employee support only for management's objectives; he cannot set other objectives. In these instances leadership is broader than supervision.

The natural leader must depend upon whatever skills are available when seeking to attain objectives. The supervisor is trained in the administrative skills necessary to achieve management's goals. If he does not possess the requisite skills, however, he can call upon management's technicians.

A natural leader can maintain his leadership, in certain groups, merely by satisfying members' need for group affiliation. The supervisor must maintain his leadership by directing and organizing his group to achieve specific organizational goals set for him and his group by management. He must have a technical competence and a kind of coordinating ability which is not needed by many natural leaders.

A natural leader is responsible only to his group which grants him authority. The supervisor is responsible to management, which employs him, and also to the work group of which he is a member. The supervisor has the exceedingly difficult job of reconciling the demands of two groups frequently in conflict. He is often placed in the untenable position of trying to play two antagonistic roles. In the above instance, supervision is broader than leadership.

ORGANIZATIONAL INFLUENCES ON LEADERSHIP

The supervisor is both a product and a prisoner of the organization wherein we find him. The organization which creates the supervisor's position also obstructs, restricts, and channelizes the exercise of his duties. These influences extend beyond prescribed functional relationships to specific supervisory behavior. For example, even in a face-to-face situation involving one of his subordinates, the supervisor's actions are controlled to a great extent by his organization. His behavior must conform to the organization policy on human relations, rules which dictate personnel procedures, specific prohibitions governing conduct, the attitudes of his own superior, etc. He is not a free agent operating within the limits of his work group. His freedom of action is much more circumscribed than is generally admitted. The organizational influences which limit his leadership actions can be classified as structure, prescriptions, and proscriptions.

The organizational structure places each supervisor's position in context with other designated positions. It determines the relationships between his position and specific positions which impinge on his. The structure of the organization designates a certain position to which he looks for orders and information about his work. It gives a particular status to his position within a pattern of statuses from which he perceives that (1) certain positions are on a par, organizationally, with his, (2) other positions are subordinate, and (3) still others are superior.

The organizational structure determines those positions to which he should look for advice and assistance, and those positions to which he should give advice and assistance.

For instance, the organizational structure has predetermined that the supervisor of a clerical processing unit shall report to a supervisory position in a higher echelon. He shall have certain relationships with the supervisors of the work units which transmit work to and receive work from his unit. He shall discuss changes and clarification of procedures with certain staff units, such as organization and methods, cost accounting, and personnel. He shall consult supervisors of units which provide or receive special work assignments.

The organizational structure, however, establishes patterns other than those of the relationships of positions. These are the patterns of responsibility, authority, and expectations.

The supervisor is responsible for certain activities or results; he is presumably invested with the authority to achieve these. His set of authority and responsibility is interwoven with other sets to the end that all goals and functions of the organization are parceled out in small, manageable lots. This, of course, establishes a series of expectations: a single supervisor can perform his particular set of duties only upon the assumption that preceding or contiguous sets of duties have been, or are being carried out. At the same time, he is aware of the expectations of others that he will fulfill his functional role.

The structure of an organization establishes relationships between specified positions and specific expectations for these positions. The fact that these relationships and expectations are established is one thing; whether or not they are met is another.

PRESCRIPTIONS AND PROSCRIPTIONS

But let us return to the organizational influences which act to restrict the supervisor's exercise of leadership. These are the prescriptions and proscriptions generally in effect in all organizations, and those peculiar to a single organization. In brief these are the *thou shalt's* and the *thou shalt not's*.

Organizations not only prescribe certain duties for individual supervisory positions, they also prescribe specific methods and means of carrying out these duties and maintaining management-employee relations. These include rules, regulations, policy, and tradition. It does no good for the supervisor to say, *This seems to be the best way to handle such-and-such,* if the organization has established a routine for dealing with problems. For good or bad, there are rules that state that firings shall be executed in such a manner, accompanied by a certain notification; that training shall be conducted, and in this manner. Proscriptions are merely negative prescriptions; you may not discriminate against any employee because of politics or race; you shall not suspend any employee without following certain procedures and obtaining certain approvals.

Most of these prohibitions and rules apply to the area of interpersonal relations, precisely the area which is now arousing most interest on the part of administrators and managers. We have become concerned about the contrast between formally prescribed relationships and interpersonal relationships, and this brings us to the often discussed informal organization.

FORMAL AND INFORMAL ORGANIZATIONS

As we well know, the functions and activities of any organization are broken down into individual units of work called positions. Administrators must establish a pattern which will link these positions to each other and relate them to a system of authority and responsibility. Man-to-man are spelled out as plainly as possible for all to understand. Managers, then, build an official structure which we call the formal organization.

In these same organizations, employees react individually and in groups to institutionally determined roles. John, a worker, rides in the same carpool as Joe, a foreman. An unplanned communication develops. Harry, a machinist knows more about high-speed machining than his foreman or anyone else in his shop. An unofficial tool boss comes into being. Mary, who fought with Jane, is promoted over her. Jane now gives Mary's directions. A planned relationship fails to develop. The employees have built a structure which we call the informal organization.

Formal organization is a system of management-prescribed relations between positions in an organization.

Informal organization is a network of unofficial relations between people in an organization.

These definitions might lead us to the absurd conclusion that positions carry out formal activities and that employe4es spend their time in unofficial activities. We must recognize that organizational activities are in all cases carried out by people. The formal structure provides a needed framework within which interpersonal relations occur. What we call informal organization is the complex of normal, natural relations among employees. These personal relationships may be negative or positive. That is, they may impede or aid the achievement of organizational goals. For example, friendship between two supervisors greatly increases the probability of good cooperation and coordination between their sections. On the other hand, *buck passing* nullifies the formal structure by failure to meet a prescribed and expected responsibility.

It is improbable that an ideal organization exists where all activities are carried out in strict conformity to a formally prescribed pattern of functional roles. Informal organization arises because of the incompleteness and ambiguities in the network of formally prescribed relationships, or in response to the needs or inadequacies of supervisors or managers who hold prescribed functional roles in an organization. Many of these relationships are not prescribed by the organizational pattern; many cannot be prescribed; many should not be prescribed.

Management faces the problem of keeping the informal organization in harmony with the mission of the agency. One way to do this is to make sure that all employees have a clear understanding of and are sympathetic with that mission. The issuance of organizational charts, procedural manuals, and functional descriptions of the work to be done by divisions and sections helps communicate management's plans and goals. Issuances alone, of course, cannot do the whole job. They should be accompanied by oral discussion and explanation. Management must ensure that there is mutual understanding and acceptance of charts and procedures. More important is that management acquaint itself with the attitudes, activities, and peculiar brands of logic which govern the informal organization. Only through this type of knowledge can they and supervisors keep informal goals consistent with the agency mission.

SUPERVISION STATUS AND FUNCTIONAL ROLE

A well-established supervisor is respected by the employees who work with him. They defer to his wishes. It is clear that a superior-subordinate relationship has been established. That is, status of the supervisor has been established in relation to other employees of the same work group. This same supervisor gains the respect of employees when he behaves in as certain manner. He will be expected, generally, to follow the customs of the group in such matters as dress, recreation, and manner of speaking. The group has a set of expectations as to his behavior. His position is a functional role which carries with it a collection of rights and obligations.

The position of supervisor usually has a status distinct from the individual who occupies it: it is much like a position description which exists whether or not there is an incumbent. The status of a supervisory position is valued higher than that of an employee position both because of the functional role of leadership which is assigned to it and because of the status symbols of titles, rights, and privileges which go with it.

Social ranking, or status, is not simple because it involves both the position and the man. An individual may be ranked higher than others because of his education, social background, perceived leadership ability, or conformity to group customs and ideals. If such a man is ranked higher by the members of a work group than their supervisor, the supervisor's effectiveness may be seriously undermined.

If the organization does not build and reinforce a supervisor's status, his position can be undermined in a different way. This will happen when managers go around rather than through the supervisor or designate him as a straw boss, acting boss, or otherwise not a real boss.

Let us clarify this last point. A role, and corresponding status, establishes a set of expectations. Employees expect their supervisor to do certain things and to act in certain ways. They are prepared to respond to that expected behavior. When the supervisor's behavior does not conform to their expectations, they are surprised, confused, and ill-at-ease. It becomes necessary for them to resolve their confusion, if they can. They might do this by turning to one of their own members for leadership. If the confusion continues, or their attempted solutions are not satisfactory, they will probably become a poorly motivated, non-cohesive group which cannot function very well.

COMMUNICATION AND THE SUPERVISOR

In a recent survey, railroad workers reported that they rarely look to their supervisor for information about the company. This is startling, at least to us, because we ordinarily think of the supervisor as the link between management and worker. We expect the supervisor to be the prime source of information about the company. Actually, the railroad workers listed the supervisor next to last in the o5rder of their sources of information. Most surprising of all, the supervisors, themselves, stated that rumor and unofficial contacts were their principal sources of information. Here we see one of the reasons why supervisors may not be as effective as management desires.

The supervisor is not only being bypassed by his work group, he is being ignored, and his position weakened, by the very organization which is holding him responsible for the activities of his workers. If he is management's representative to the employee, then management has an obligation to keep him informed of its activities. This is necessary if he is to carry out his functions efficiently and maintain his leadership in the work group. The supervisor is expected to be a source of information; when he is not, his status is not clear, and employees are dissatisfied because he has not lived up to expectations.

By providing information to the supervisor to pass along to employees, we can strengthen his position as leader of the group, and increase satisfaction and cohesion within the group. Because he has more information than the other members, receives information sooner, and passes it along at the proper times, members turn to him as a source and also provide him with information in the hope of receiving some in return. From this, we can see an increase in group cohesiveness because:

- Employees are bound closer to their supervisor because he is *in the know*.
- There is less need to go outside the group for answers
- Employees will more quickly turn to the supervisor for enlightenment

The fact that he has the answers will also enhance the supervisor's standing in the eyes of his men. This increased status will serve to bolster his authority and control of the group and will probably result in improved morale and productivity.

The foregoing, of course, does not mean that all management information should be given out. There are obviously certain policy determinations and discussions which need not or cannot be transmitted to all supervisors. However, the supervisor must be kept as fully informed as possible so that he can answer questions when asked and can allay needless fears and anxieties. Further, the supervisor has the responsibility of encouraging employee questions and submissions of information. He must be able to present information to employees so that it is clearly understood and accepted. His attitude and manner should make it clear that he believes in what he is saying, that the information is necessary or desirable to the group, and that he is prepared to act on the basis of the information.

SUPERVISION AND JOB PERFORMANCE

The productivity of work groups is a product; employees' efforts are multiplied by the supervision they receive. Many investigators have analyzed this relationship and have discovered elements of supervision which differentiate high and low production groups. These researchers have identified certain types of supervisory practices which they classify as *employee-centered* and other types which they classify as *production centered*.

The difference between these two kinds of supervision lies not in specific practices but in the approach or orientation to supervision. The employee-centered supervisor directs most of his efforts toward increasing employee motivation. He is concerned more with realizing the potential energy of persons than with administrative and technological methods of increasing efficiency and productivity. He is the man who finds ways of causing employees to want to work harder with the same tools. These supervisors emphasize the personal relations between their employees and themselves.

Now, obviously, these pictures are overdrawn. No one supervisor has all the virtues of the ideal type of employee-centered supervisor. And, fortunately, no one supervisor has all the bad traits found in many production-centered supervisors. We should remember that the various practices that researchers have fond which distinguish these two kinds of supervision represent the many practices and methods of supervisors of all gradations between these extremes. We should be careful, too, of the implications of the labels attached to the two types. For instance, being production-centered is not necessarily bad, since the principal responsibility of any supervisor is maintaining the production level that is expected of his work group. Being employee-centered may not necessarily be good, if the only result is a happy, chuckling crew of loafers. To return to the researchers' findings, employee-centered supervisors:

- Recommend promotions, transfers, pay increases
- Inform men about what is happening in the company
- Keep men posted on how well they are doing
- Hear complaints and grievances sympathetically
- Speak up for subordinates

Production-centered supervisors, on the other hand, don't do those things. They check on employees more frequently, give more detailed and frequent instructions, don't give reasons for changes, and are more punitive when mistakes are made. Employee-centered supervisors were reported to contribute to high morale and high production, whereas production-centered supervision was associated with lower morale and less production.

More recent findings, however, show that the relationship between supervision and productivity is not this simple. Investigators now report that high production is more frequently associated with supervisory practices which combine employee-centered behavior with concern for production. (This concern is not the same, however, as anxiety about production, which is the hallmark of our production-centered supervisor.) Let us examine these apparently contradictory findings and the premises from which they are derived.

SUPERVISION AND MORALE

Why do supervisory activities cause high or low production? As the name implies, the activities of the employee-centered supervisor tend to relate him more closely and satisfactorily to his workers. The production-centered supervisor's practices tend to separate him from his group and to foster antagonism. An analysis of this difference may answer our question.

Earlier, we pointed out that the supervisor is a type of leader and that leadership is intimately related to the group in which it occurs We discover, now, that an employee-centered supervisor's primary activities are concerned with both his leadership and his group membership. Such a supervisor is a member of a group and occupies a leadership role in that group.

These facts are sometimes obscured when we speak of the supervisor as management's representative, or as the organizational link between management and the employee, or as the end of the chain of command. If we really want to understand what it is we expect of the supervisor, we must remember that he is the designated leader of a group of employees to whom he is bound by interaction and interdependence.

Most of his actions are aimed, consciously or unconsciously, at strengthening membership ties in the group. This includes both making members more conscious that he is a member of their group) and causing members to identify themselves more closely with the group. These ends are accomplished by:

- making the group more attractive to the worker: they find satisfaction of their needs for recognition, friendship, enjoyable work, etc.;
- maintaining open communication: employees can express their views and obtain information about the organization
- giving assistance: members can seek advice on personal problems as well as their work; and
- acting as a buffer between the group and management: he speaks up for his men and explains the reasons for management's decisions.

Such actions both strengthen group cohesiveness and solidarity and affirm the supervisor's leadership position in the group.

DEFINING MORALE

This brings us back to a point mentioned earlier. We had said that employee-centered supervisors contribute to high morale as well as to high production. But how can we explain units which have low morale and high productivity, or vice versa? Usually production and morale are considered separately, partly because they are measured against different criteria and partly because, in some instances, they seem to be independent of each other.

Some of this difficulty may stem from confusion over definitions of morale. Morale has been defined as, or measured by, absences from work, satisfaction with job or company, dissension among members of work groups, productivity, apathy or lack of interest, readiness to help others, and a general aura of happiness as rated by observers. Some of these criteria of morale are not subject to the influence of the supervisor, and some of them are not clearly related to productivity. Definitions like these invite findings of low morale coupled with high production.

Both productivity and morale can be influenced by environmental factors not under the control of group members or supervisors. Such things as plant layout, organizational structure and goals, lighting, ventilation, communications, and management planning may have an adverse or desirable effect.

We might resolve the dilemma by defining morale on the basis of our understanding of the supervisor as leader of a group; morale is the degree of satisfaction of group members with their leadership. In this light, the supervisor's employee-centered activities bear a clear relation to morale. His efforts to increase employee identification with the group and to strengthen his leadership lead to greater satisfaction with that leadership. By increasing group cohesiveness and by demonstrating that his influence and power can aid the group, he is able to enhance his leadership status and afford satisfaction to the group.

SUPERVISION, PRODUCTION, AND MORALE

There are factors within the organization itself which determine whether increased production is possible:

- Are production goals expressed in terms understandable to employees and are they realistic?
- Do supervisors responsible for production respect the agency mission and production goals?
- If employees do not know how to do the job well, does management provide a trainer—often the supervisor—who can teach efficient work methods?

There are other factors within the work group which determine whether increased production will be attained:

- Is leadership present which can bring about the desired level of production?
- Are production goals accepted by employees as reasonable and attainable?
- If group effort is involved, are members able to coordinate their efforts?

Research findings confirm the view that an employee-centered supervisor can achieve higher morale than a production-centered supervisor. Managers may well ask what is the relationship between this and production.

Supervision is production-oriented to the extent that it focuses attention on achieving organizational goals, and plans and devises methods for attaining them; it is employee-centered to the extent that it focuses attention on employee attitudes toward those goals, and plans and works toward maintenance of employee satisfaction.

High productivity and low morale result when a supervisor plans and organizes work efficiently but cannot achieve high membership satisfaction. Low production and high morale result when a supervisor, though keeping members satisfied with his leadership, either has not gained acceptance of organizational goals or does not have the technical competence to achieve them.

The relationship between supervision, morale, and productivity is an interdependent one, with the supervisor playing an integral role due to his ability to influence productivity and morale independently of each other.

A supervisor who can plan his work well has good technical knowledge, and who can install better production methods can raise production without necessarily increasing group satisfaction. On the other hand, a supervisor who can motivate his employees and keep them satisfied with his leadership can gain high production in spite of technical difficulties and environmental obstacles.

CLIMATE AND SUPERVISION

Climate, the intangible environment of an organization made up of attitudes, beliefs, and traditions, plays a large part in morale, productivity, and supervision. Usually when we speak of climate and its relationship to morale and productivity, we talk about the merits of *democratic* versus *authoritarian* climate. Employees seem to produce more and have higher morale in a democratic climate, whereas in an authoritarian climate, the reverse seems to be true or so the researchers tell us. We would do well to determine what these terms mean to supervision.

Perhaps most of our difficulty in understanding and applying these concepts comes from our emotional reactions to the words themselves. For example, authoritarian climate is usually painted as the very blackest kind of dictatorship. This is not surprising, because we are usually expected to believe that it is invariably bad. Conversely, democratic climate is drawn to make the driven snow look impure by comparison.

Now these descriptions are most probably true when we talk about our political processes, or town meetings, or freedom of speech. However, the same labels have been used by social scientists in other contexts and have also been applied to government and business organizations, without it, it seems, any recognition that the meanings and their social values may have changed somewhat

For example, these labels were used in experiments conducted in an informal classroom setting using 11-year-old boys as subjects. The descriptive labels applied to the climate of the setting as well as the type of leadership practiced. When these labels were transferred to a management setting, it seems that many presumed that they principally meant the king of leadership rather than climate. We can see that there is a great difference between the experimental and management settings and that leadership practices for one might be inappropriate for the other.

It is doubtful that formal work organizations can be anything but authoritarian, in that goals are set by management and a hierarchy exists through which decisions and orders from the top are transmitted downward. Organizations are authoritarian by structure and need; direction and control are placed in the hands of a few in order to gain fast and efficient decision making. Now this does not mean to describe a dictatorship. It is merely the recognition of the fact that direction of organizational affairs comes from above. It should be noted that leadership in some natural groups is, in this sense, authoritarian.

Granting that formal organizations have this kind of authoritarian leadership, can there be a democratic climate? Certainly there can be, but we would want to define and delimit this term. A more realistic meaning of democratic climate in organizations is the use of permissive and participatory methods in management-employee relations. That is, a mutual exchange of information and explanation with the granting of individual freedom within certain restricted and defined limits. However, it is not our purpose to debate the merits of authoritarianism versus democracy. We recognize that within the small work group there is a need for freedom from constraint and an increase in participation in order to achieve organizational goals within the framework of the organizational movement.

Another aspect of climate is best expressed by this familiar, and true, saying: actions speak louder than words. Of particular concern to us is this effect of management climate on the behavior of supervisors, particularly in employee-centered activities.

There have been reports of disappointment with efforts to make supervisors ore employee-centered. Managers state that, since research has shown ways of improving human relations, supervisors should begin to practice these methods. Usually a training course in human relations is established; and supervisors are given this training. Managers then sit back and wait for the expected improvements, only to find that there are none.

If we wish to produce changes in the supervisor's behavior, the climate must be made appropriate and rewarding to the changed behavior. This means that top-level attitudes and behavior cannot deny or contradict the change we are attempting to effect. Basic changes in organizational behavior cannot be made with any permanence, unless we provide an environment that is receptive to the changes and rewards those persons who do change.

IMPROVING SUPERVISION

Anyone who has read this far might expect to find *A Dozen Rules for Dealing With Employees* or *29 Steps to Supervisory Success*. We will not provide such a list.

Simple rules suffer from their simplicity. They ignore the complexities of human behavior. Reliance upon rules may cause supervisors to concentrate on superficial aspects of their relations with employees. It may preclude genuine understanding.

The supervisor who relies on a list of rules tends to think of people in mechanistic terms. In a certain situation, he uses *Rule No. 3*. Employees are not treated as thinking and feeling persons, but rather as figures in a formula: Rule 3 applied to employee X = Production.

Employees usually recognize mechanical manipulation and become dissatisfied and resentful. They lose faith in, and respect for, their supervisor, and this may be reflected in lower morale and productivity.

We do not mean that supervisors must become social science experts if they wish to improve. Reports of current research indicate that there are two major parts of their job which can be strengthened through self-improvement: (1) Work planning, including technical skills, and (2) motivation of employees.

The most effective supervisors combine excellence in the administrative and technical aspects of their work with friendly and considerate personal relations with their employees.

CRITICAL PERSONAL RELATIONS

Later in this chapter we shall talk about administrative aspects of supervision, but first let us comment on *friendly and considerate personal relations*. We have discussed this subject throughout the preceding chapters, but we want to review some of the critical supervisory influences on personal relations.

Closeness of Supervision: The closeness of supervision has an important effect on productivity and morale. Mann and Dent found that supervisors of low-producing units supervise very closely, while high-producing supervisors exercise only general supervision. It was found that the low-producing supervisors:

- check on employees more frequently
- give more detailed and frequent instructions
- limit employee's freedom to do job in own way

Workers who felt less closely supervised reported that they were better satisfied with their jobs and the company. We should note that the manner or attitude of the supervisor has an important bearing on whether employees perceive supervision as being close or general.

These findings are another way of saying that supervision does not mean standing over the employee and telling him what to do and when and how to do it. The more effective supervisor tells his employees what is required, giving general instructions.

COMMUNICATION

Supervisors of high-production units consider communication as one of the most important aspects of their job. Effective communication is used by these supervisors to achieve better interpersonal relations and improved employee motivation. Low-production supervisors do not rate communications as highly important.

High-producing supervisors find that an important aid to more effective communication is listening. They are ready to listen to both personal problems or interests and questions about the work. This does not mean that they are *nosey* or meddle in their employees' personal lives, but rather that they show a willingness to listen, and do listen, if their employees wish to discuss problems.

These supervisors inform employees about forthcoming changes in work; they discuss agency policy with employees; and they make sure that each employee knows how well he is doing. What these supervisors do is use two-way communication effectively. Unless the supervisor freely imparts information, he will not receive information in return.

Attitudes and perception are frequently affected by communication or the lack of it. Research surveys reveal that many supervisors are not aware of their employees' attitudes, nor do they know what personal reactions their supervision arouses. Through frank discussion with employees, they have been surprised to discover employee beliefs about which they were ignorant. Discussion sometimes reveals that the supervisor and his employees have totally different impressions about the same event. The supervisor should be constantly on the alert for misconceptions about his words and deeds. He must remember that, although his actions are perfectly clear to himself, they may be, and frequently are, viewed differently by employees.

Failure to communicate information results in misconceptions and false assumptions. What you say and how you say it will strongly affect your employees' attitudes and perceptions. By giving them available information, you can prevent misconceptions; by discussion, you may be able to change attitudes; by questioning, you can discover what the perceptions and assumptions really are. And it need hardly be added that actions should conform very closely to words.

If we were to attempt to reduce the above discussion on communication to rules, we would have a long list which would be based on one cardinal principle: Don't make assumptions!

- Don't assume that your employees know; tell them.
- Don't assume that you know how they feel; find out.
- Don't assume that they understand; clarify.

20 SUPERVISORY HINTS

1. Avoid inconsistency.
2. Always give employees a chance to explain their action before taking disciplinary action. Don't allow too much time for a "cooling off" period before disciplining an employee.
3. Be specific in your criticisms.
4. Delegate responsibility wisely.
5. Do not argue or lose your temper, and avoid being impatient.
6. Promote mutual respect and be fair, impartial, and open-minded.
7. Keep in mind that asking for employees' advice and input can be helpful in decision making.
8. If you make promises, keep them.
9. Always keep the feelings, abilities, dignity and motives of your staff in mind.
10. Remain loyal to your employees' interests.
11. Never criticize employees in front of others, or treat employees like children.
12. Admit mistakes. Don't place blame on your employees, or make excuses.
13. Be reasonable in your expectations, give complete instructions, and establish well-planned goals.
14. Be knowledgeable about office details and procedures, but avoid becoming bogged down in details.
15. Avoid supervising too closely or too loosely. Employees should also view you as an approachable supervisor.
16. Remember that employees' personal problems may affect job performance, but become involved only when appropriate.
17. Work to develop workers, and to instill a feeling of cooperation while working toward mutual goals.
18. Do not overpraise or underpraise, be properly appreciative.
19. Never ask an employee to discipline someone for you.
20. A complaint, even if unjustified, should be taken seriously.

NOTES

BASIC FUNDAMENTALS OF PAVING EQUIPMENT AND OPERATIONS

CONTENTS

		Page
I.	PAVING CONSTRUCTION	1
II.	MAINTENANCE OF BITUMINOUS PAVEMENT	19
III.	MAINTENANCE OF EQUIPMENT	22
IV.	PAVING SAFETY	23
V.	CONCRETE TRANSIT MIXERS	24
VI.	OPERATOR'S CARE AND MAINTENANCE	28
VII.	TRANSIT MIXER SAFETY	28

BASIC FUNDAMENTALS OF PAVING EQUIPMENT AND OPERATIONS

This chapter provides information and guidance for the equipment operator engaged in, or responsible for, bituminous and expedient surfacing operations involving roads and airfields. It includes information on construction materials, mix design, equipment, production, placement, repair and maintenance of bituminous and expedient (emergency make shift construction using the natural resources available) surfaces.

Information on starting, operating, and maintaining concrete transit trucks is given in this chapter. Also included is information on the principles of operating asphalt pavers, asphalt distributors, asphalt traveling plants, asphalt kettles, and self-propelled soil stabilization mixers.

Safety precautions must be rigidly observed in paving operations, particularly in the use of flammables. Safety precautions will be noted at pertinent points, where applicable, throughout the chapter.

I. PAVING CONSTRUCTION

Modern paving is broadly divided into RIGID paving and FLEXIBLE paving. Both types consist of AGGREGATE (sand, gravel, crushed stone, and the like), bound together by a hardening or setting agent called a BINDER. The chief difference between the two types of paving, from the standpoint of ingredients used, lies in the character of the binder.

The binder for most rigid paving is PORTLAND CEMENT, and, for this reason, rigid paving is often referred to as CONCRETE paving. In flexible paving, the binder consists of BITUMINOUS material.

Asphalt paving mixes may be produced from a wide range of aggregate combinations, each having its own characteristics and suited to specific design and construction uses. Aside from the asphalt content, the principal characteristics of the mix are determined, in the main, by the relative amounts of aggregates. The aggregate composition may vary from a coarse-textured mix having a predominance of coarse aggregate to a fine-textured mix having a predominance of fine aggregate.

The selection of a particular bituminous material depends upon the type of pavement, temperature extreme, rainfall, type and volume of traffic, and type and availability of equipment. In general, hard penetration grades of asphalt cement are used in warm climates and softer penetration grades in cold climates. Heavier grades of asphalt cutbacks and tars are generally used in warm regions. Asphalt cements are generally more suitable for high traffic volumes than cutbacks. Asphalts and tars will not necessarily bond to each other; thus, bonding becomes a consideration in bitumen selection.

Looking at figure 1 you can see that many types of products, including asphalt materials, are produced by the refining of petroleum. Such asphalt is produced in a variety of types and grades ranging from hard brittle solids to almost water thin liquids. The semisolid form, known as asphalt cement, is the basic material.

Liquid asphaltic products are generally prepared by cutting back or blending asphalt cements with petroleum distillates or by emulsifying them with water. Types of liquid asphaltic products as shown in figure 2.

Table 1 indicates various uses of asphalt for different types of construction.

In a work area, expedient materials and methods may be used when men, materials, equipment, or time are not available for more permanent surfacing construction. With the choice of materials or methods, the determining factors in selecting the type of expedient will be the time allotted for construction, the required permanency, the type of terrain, and the anticipated type of traffic. As an expedient, any material or method that will provide a temporary road or airfield may be used. Expedient pavements and surfaces may be used provided the criteria for

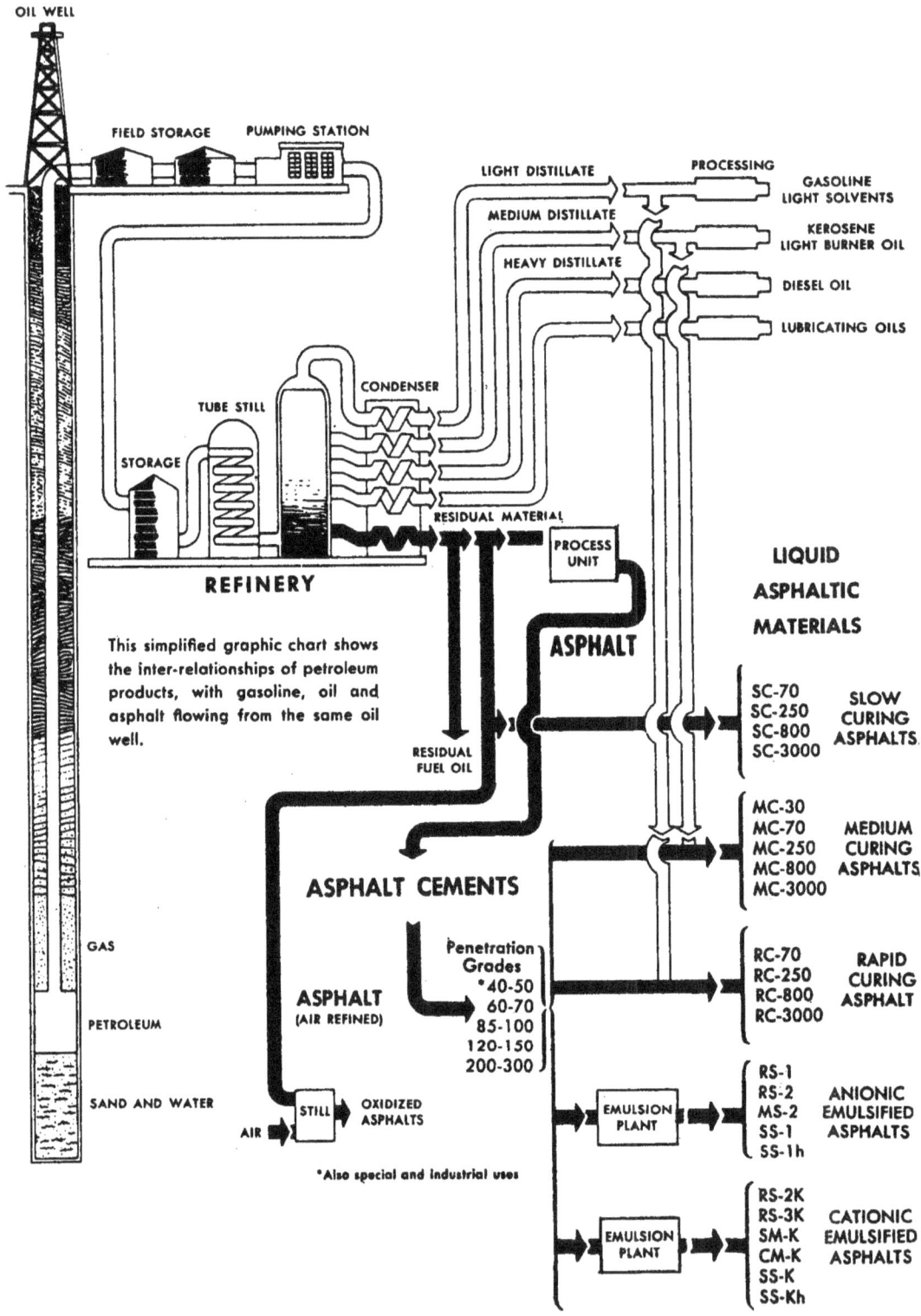

Figure 1.— Petroleum asphalt flow chart.

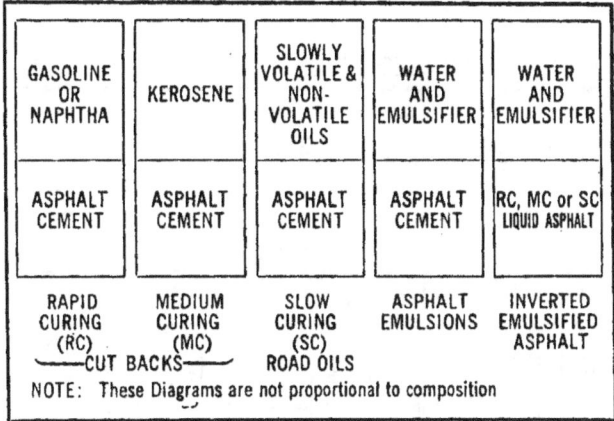

Figure 2.—Liquid asphaltic products.

establishing suitable bases have been met. Sound construction principles and imagination will lead to many improved expedient methods.

ROAD-MIX PAVEMENTS

Road-mix pavements consist of mineral aggregate and mineral filler uniformly mixed in place with a bituminous material and compacted on a prepared base course or subgrade. A single layer, about 1-1/2 inches to 3 inches thick, is generally used. This type of pavement is likely to become defective unless it has a sound, well-drained subgrade and is well mixed, uniformly spread, and properly compacted. Road-mix pavements may be used as a wearing surface on temporary roads and airfields, and as a bituminous base or binder course in construction of more permanent-type roads and airfields. Road mix is an economical method of surfacing small areas when aggregate can be used from the existing base, or when satisfactory aggregate is nearby.

For road-mix pavements, the grade and type of bituminous material depend upon the aggregate and equipment available, as well as weather conditions and time required to complete the project. Good weather is important to the success of a road-mix project. Where possible, road mixing operations should be scheduled when weather conditions are likely to be hot and dry during, and for sometime after, the project. Recommended types of bituminous materials suitable for road mix are asphalt cutbacks, asphalt emulsions, and road tars. A medium-curing cutback is generally used in a moderate climate; and a rapid-curing cutback may be satisfactory for cold climates. Viscosity required is determined by the temperature, aggregate graduation, and method of mixing. The highest viscosity that will completely and uniformly coat the particles of aggregate should be used. In general, open-graded aggregate requires a high viscosity; a gradation containing mineral filler requires a less viscous grade.

Aggregate used in road mix may be scarified from the existing subgrade or hauled in from a nearby source. A wide range of coarse and fine aggregate and mineral filler may be used. The ideal aggregate for road-mix pavement is a well-graded (dense or open) sandy gravel or clean sand. Maximum size of the aggregate, in general, is limited to two-thirds of the compacted thickness of the layer. Loose thickness is approximately 1-1/4 times desired compacted thickness.

Surface moisture is defined as "the film of water around each particle of stone or sand." The amount is determined by heating a weighted sample of aggregate at 212°F in an open pan and stirring with a rod until the surface water disappears (3 to 10 minutes). The difference between the original and final weights is considered to be moisture loss during drying. The loss in weight, expressed as a percent of the final or dry weight, is the moisture content allowed before the aggregate is mixed with asphalt cutbacks or road tars. If the aggregate is too wet, it should be worked with mechanical mixers, graders, or improvised plows to allow the excess moisture to evaporate. For cutbacks and tars, moisture content of coarse-graded aggregate should not exceed 3 percent, and of fine-graded aggregate, 2 percent. For emulsions, moisture content of coarse-graded aggregate should not exceed 5 percent, and of fine-graded aggregate, 3 percent.

Quality of the road-mix pavement depends largely upon the control of the mix. The percentage of bitumen will vary in relation to the absorptive quality of the aggregate, rate of evaporation of the volatile substances, and other factors. Although an exact formula is difficult to follow, proportioning must be controlled within very narrow limits to assure the stability and life of the mix. With dense-graded aggregates especially, too much bitumen should not be used. All particles of the completed mix should be coated and uniform in color. If the mix is too lean, the aggregate in the windrow will stand almost vertically and have a dull

PAVING EQUIPMENT AND OPERATIONS

Table 1. — Recommended Uses of Various Asphalt Grades

TYPE OF CONSTRUCTION	PAVING ASPHALTS					LIQUID ASPHALTS																						
						Rapid Curing (RC)				Medium Curing (MC)					Slow Curing (SC)				Emulsified									
																			Anionic							Cationic		
	40-50	60-70	85-100	120-150	200-300	70	250	800	3000	30	70	250	800	3000	70	250	800	3000	RS-1	RS-2	MS-2	SS-1	SS-1h	RS-2K	RS-3K	SM-K	CM-K	SS-K	SS-Kh
ASPHALT CONCRETE AND PLANT MIX, HOT LAID																													
Highways		x	x	x										x				x											
Airports		x	x																										
Parking Areas		x	x																										
Driveways		x	x																										
Curbs		x	x¹																										
Industrial Floors	x																												
Blocks	x																												
PLANT MIX, COLD LAID																													
Graded Aggregate													x				x					x						x	x
ROAD MIX																													
Open-graded Aggregate							x	x				x	x							x						x			
Dense-graded Aggregate							x	x				x	x			x	x			x	x						x	x	
Clean Sand							x	x				x	x				x				x							x	x
Sandy Soil						x	x	x			x	x	x			x	x				x						x	x	x
PENETRATION MACADAM																													
Large Voids			x					x	x											x					x				
Small Voids		x					x													x					x				
SURFACE TREATMENTS																													
Single, Multiple and Aggregate Seal							x	x				x	x	x			x	x		x	x				x	x		x	
Sand Seal							x	x				x	x				x			x	x	x						x	x
Slurry Seal																						x	x					x	x
Fog Seal																						x²	x²					x²	x²
Prime Coat, open surfaces							x					x				x													
Prime Coat, tight surfaces						x					x	x				x													
Tack Coat						x															x²	x²	x					x²	x²
Dust Laying											x	x			x							x²						x²	
PATCHING MIX																													
Immediate Use								x					x																
Stock Pile								x	x				x	x												x	x		
HYDRAULIC STRUCTURES																													
Membrane Linings, Canals & Reservoirs	x³																												
Hot Laid, Graded Aggregate Mix for Groins, Dam Facings, Canal & Reservoir Linings	x	x																											
CRACK FILLING							x															x⁴	x⁴	x				x⁴	x⁴
MEMBRANE ENVELOPE	x	x																											
EXPANSION JOINTS		Blown asphalts, mineral-filled asphalt cements, and preformed joint compositions																											
UNDERSEALING PCC		Blown asphalts																											
ROOFING		Blown asphalts																											
MISCELLANEOUS		Specially prepared asphalts for pipe coatings, battery boxes, automobile undersealing, electrical wire coating, insulation, tires, paints, asphalt tile, wall board, paper sizing, waterproofing, floor mats, ice cream sacks, adhesives, phonograph records, tree grafting compounds, grouting mixtures, etc.																											

In northern areas where rate of curing is slower, a shift from MC to RC or from SC to MC may be desirable. For very warm climates, a shift to next heavier grade may be warranted.
1 In combination with powdered asphalt.
2 Diluted with water.
3 Also 50-60 penetration blown asphalt and prefabricated panels.
4 Slurry mix.

look while if too rich, it will ooze or slip out of shape. If the mix is correctly proportioned, a handful squeezed into a ball will retain its shape when the hand is opened.

Road-mix pavements should be constructed only on a dry base when the weather is not rainy. Atmospheric temperature should be above 50°F. Mixing should take place at the temperature of the aggregate, but not below 50°F or above the recommended temperature of the liquid asphalt being used. The construction procedure depends upon whether the base is a newly constructed base, a scarified existing base, or an existing pavement.

If a newly constructed base is used, apply the following procedure:

1. Inspect and condition the base.
2. Prime the base and allow the prime to cure.

3. Haul in and windrow the aggregate at the side of the primed base (allow the aggregate to dry or aerate with blade if wet.)
4. Spread the aggregate on the cured prime base 1/2 road bed width.
5. Spray the bitumen on the aggregate in increments of about one-third the total amount required.
6. Mix the bitumen with the aggregate, blade back and forth until a uniform mix is obtained.
7. Repeat as directed in (5) and (6) until thoroughly mixed.
8. Spread the mix to the specified thickness.
9. Compact the surface.
10. Apply a seal coat if necessary.

For a scarified base, the aggregate is scarified if it is not available from other sources. The construction procedure is as follows:

1. Loosen the aggregate from the base.
2. Dry and break up all lumps of material.
3. Blade into parallel windrows of uniform size and one side and/or in the center.
4. Sweep the base, if needed.
5. Prime the base and allow time to cure.
6. Continue as directed in (4) through (10) in the above procedures for a newly constructed base.

If an existing pavement is to be used as a base, the construction procedure is:

1. Sweep the base.
2. Apply a tack coat and allow it to cure.
3. Bring in the aggregate and deposit in windrows at the side of the cured, tacked base.
4. Aerate the aggregate.
5. Spread the aggregate on 1/2 the tacked base.
6. Spray bitumen on the aggregate in increments of about 1/3 the total amount required.
7. Mix the bitumen with the aggregate, by blade.
8. Spread the mix to specified uncompacted thickness.
9. Compact the surface.
10. Apply a seal coat if necessary.

When mixing in place (road mix), here are some helpful hints:

1. Do not buck nature—stop operations when working under adverse weather conditions.
2. Keep the mixture or aggregate in a well packed windrow for better water shedding and control.
3. Provide drainage cuts through the windrow during heavy rains.
4. When a motor grader comes to the end of a section with a full blade, lift it rapidly, to avoid carrying materials into the next section.
5. The distributor spray must be cut sharply at sectional joints; carry-over to the next section will cause undesirable fat joints.
6. Plan the work to avoid inconvenience to traffic.
7. Apply the asphalt at the recommended spraying viscosity to ensure uniform application.
8. A shoe on the outer end of the grader blade or moldboard helps obtain a good edge during spreading operations.
9. Aggregate in shaded areas usually requires extra aeration.

ROAD MIXING METHODS

Three methods of road mixing that the Equipment Operator may use in expedient surfacing operations for roads and airfields are travel plant mixing, blade mixing, and soil asphalt stabilization mixing. These methods are discussed separately below.

Travel Plant Mixing

When a travel plant is used for mixing, the loose aggregate is dumped, mixed, and bladed into uniform windrows, and evened if necessary. The windrow should be sufficient to cover the section of the area to be paved with enough loose material to give the desired compacted depth and width. As the bucket loader tows the mixer and elevates the aggregate to the mixer hopper, the mixer meters the aggregate, sprays it with the correct amount of bitumen, mixes these two uniformally and redeposits the mix into another windrow behind the plant. The rate of travel and the mixing operation should be controlled so that all particles of the aggregate are coated and the mix is uniform. Accuracy in proportioning the mix is extremely important.

The travel plant method usually produces a more uniform mix of higher quality than blade mixing. Heavier types of asphalt cutback and tar may be used. This reduces the time required for curing. The asphalt finisher may be used concurrently with the travel plant. The hopper of the finisher is kept directly under the travel plant output chute. This arrangement reduces

PAVING EQUIPMENT AND OPERATIONS

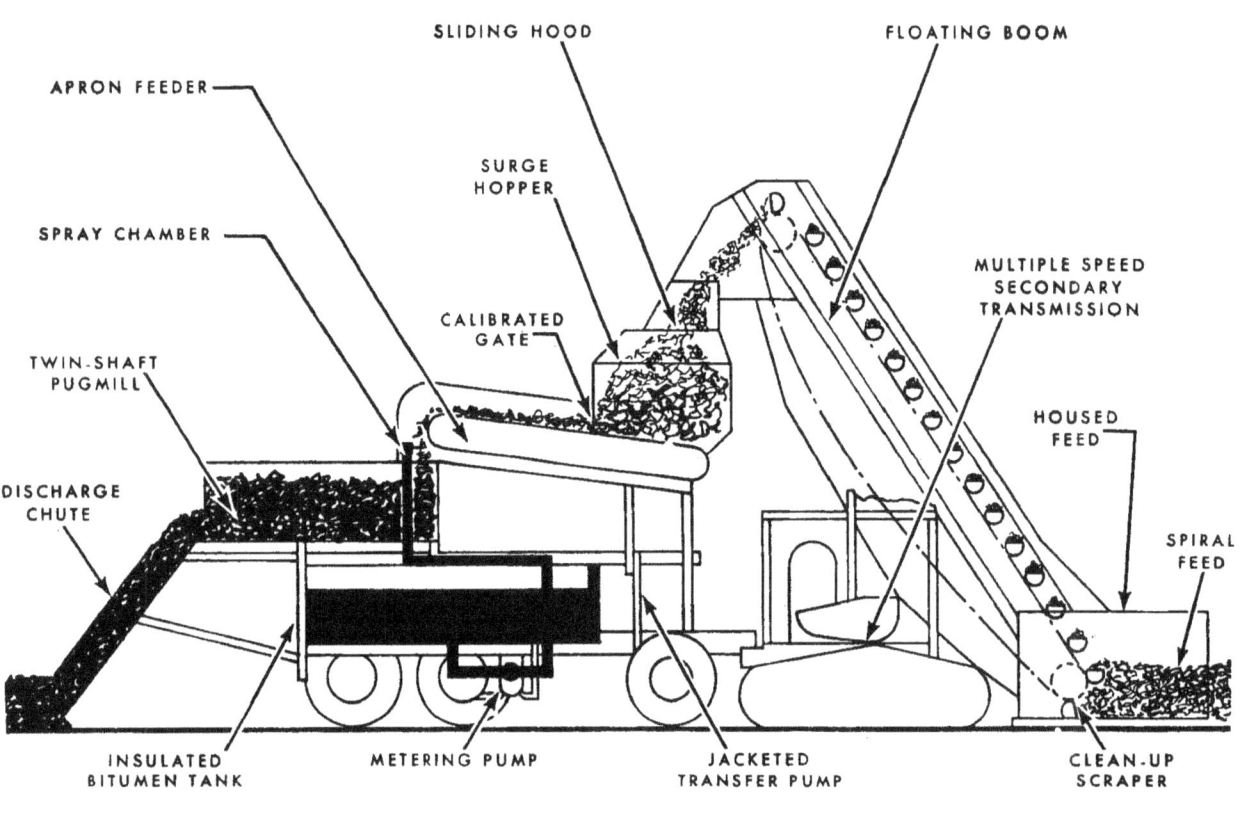

Figure 3. — Schematic layout of a travel plant.

the maximum output of the plant, although it does provide for uniform thickness of the mat being laid.

Windrows must contain no more material than the finisher can place. The major advantage of this setup is that in-place aggregate may be used in an intermediate mix and placed with a finisher without the necessity of loading and transporting aggregate. The finisher must be used with the travel plant for construction of some airfields where surface tolerances are critical. Figure 3 shows a schematic view of a travel plant.

Blade Mixing

In blade mixing, the aggregate is dried and bladed into windrows. The windrows are then flattened and bitumen of the specific temperature is applied with a bituminous distributor in three equal applications. Each application is 1/3 the amount required.

Immediately following each application of the bituminous material, the treated aggregate should be mixed with springtooth or double-disk harrows, motor graders, rotary tillers, or a combination of this equipment, until all the particles of the aggregate are evenly coated. When motor graders are used, the windrow is moved from side to side by successive cuts with the blade.

Several graders can operate, one behind the other, to reduce the total time required for complete mixing. In hilly terrain, blading should be from the bottom to the top as the mix tends to migrate down. After all the aggregate has been mixed, the mix should be bladed into a single windrow at or near the center of the road, and turned not less than four complete turns from one side of the road to the other. Excess bitumen, deficiency of bitumen, or uneven mix should be corrected by the addition of aggregate or bituminous material, followed by remixing. Mixing should continue until it is complete and satisfactory; remember, mix will set up if mixed too long.

Suppose that materials, weather conditions, and equipment are well suited to mixed-in-place paving, but the road or airfield must carry traffic during construction. In such cases, the windrowing of aggregate and the mixing and spreading of bitumen may be done elsewhere, on any area of smooth ground which can be compacted for the purpose, or on any unused road or airfield surface. The road or airfield surface, base, or subbase to be paved is then primed or tack coated as required to complete construction and keep portions of the road or airfield open to traffic. As soon as the prime or tack coat cures the mix is picked up, trucked to the jobsite, dumped, and then bladed into windrows for spreading.

The bituminous mix should not be spread when the surface is damp, or when the mix itself contains an excess of moisture. The mixed material should be spread to the required width in thin, equal layers by a self-propelled motor grader or finisher. (If a finisher is used, additional support equipment is required, and the material must be split into two windrows for an 8- to 12-foot wide pavement.) When spreading the mix from a windrow, care should be taken to prevent cutting into the underlying subgrade or base course. If necessary to prevent such cutting, a layer of mix, approximately 1/2-inch thick, may be left at the bottom of the windrow.

The material being spread should be rolled once, and then leveled with a motor grader to remove irregularities. Remaining material should then be spread and rolled in thin layers, until the entire mix is evenly spread to the depth and width specified. During the spreading and compacting, the surface should be dragged or bladed, as necessary, to fill any ruts and to remove corrugations, waves, or other irregularities. Both pneumatic-tired and steel-wheeled rollers may be used for rolling on all surface treatment jobs; however, the pneumatic-tired roller is the preferred type. While the pneumatic-tired roller will give uniform pressure over the entire area the steel-wheeled roller will hit only the high spots. In any case, two self-propelled rollers should be used with each surface treatment job.

After all layers have been satisfactorily spread, the surface should be rolled with two-axle tandem rollers. Rolling should begin at the outside edge of the surface and proceed to the center, overlapping on successive trips at least one-half the width of the wheel of the roller. Alternate trips of the roller should be different lengths. The speed of the roller at all times should be controlled to avoid displacement of the mix. Light blading (or floating) of the surface with the motor grader during rolling may be required. Rolling should be continued until all roller marks are eliminated, and maximum density obtained. To prevent adhesion of the mix to the roller, the roller wheel should be kept moist with water; use only enough water to avoid picking up the material. The rollers should be in good condition, suitable for rolling asphalt, and should be operated by trained roller operators. At all places not accessible to the roller, the mix should be thoroughly tamped with hand tampers. If the surface course becomes rough, corrugated, uneven in texture, water-soaked, or traffic marked, unsatisfactory portions should be torn up, and reworked, relaid, or replaced. When forms are not used, and while the surface is being compacted and finished, the outside edges should be trimmed neatly in line.

If the road-mix pavement surface course is constructed from an open-graded aggregate, a surface treatment may be required to waterproof the surface. A surface treatment is unnecessary on a dense-graded, well-compacted, road-mix pavement.

Where possible, traffic should be kept off of freshly sprayed asphalt or mixed materials. If it is necessary to route traffic over the new work, speed must be restricted to 25 m.p.h. or less until rolling is completed and the asphalt mixture is firm enough to take high speed traffic.

Soil Asphalt Stabilization Mixing

Soil asphalt stabilization requires a mixture of pulverized soil and bituminous material. By the addition of bituminous material, many soils, which in their natural state would be too unstable for use as a base course, can be made to serve satisfactorily as a base course. The bituminous material serves primarily as a waterproofing agent rather than a binding agent; however, the bitumen does have some binding value.

8

PAVING EQUIPMENT AND OPERATIONS

Figure 4.—Multi-shaft, single-pass soil stabilizer.

If properly constructed, soil asphalt stabilization generally forms an excellent base. However, it is too friable to withstand the abrasive action of traffic, wears rapidly, and often develops uneven surfaces that eventually cause pot holes. Soil asphalt stabilization is recommended only as a base course, on which there is to be placed an approved type of wearing course or surface treatment.

Since most multiple-shaft, single-pass soil stabilization mixing machines such as that shown in figure 16-4 have a high-speed pulverizing rotor, preliminary pulverization is usually unnecessary. The only preparation required is to dig a trench about 18 inches wide and to the depth to be processed (1/4 inch minimum to 8 inches maximum) and across the full width of the roadway to be stabilized. Material removed from this trench should be spread out uniformly over the roadway so that this material will be mixed as the mixing box of the stabilizer unit travels forward.

Processing is done in lanes from 350 to 900 feet depending upon the rate of processing, with a width equal to that of the stabilizing machine. The stabilizing mixer is positioned in the first lane at the point where the cutting rotor is directly above the trench or starting point.

With the bituminous tank truck coupled to the front of the stabilizer, the suction hose connected to the delivery pump, and the mixer moving forward, the high speed cutting rotor cuts and pulverizes the road material to be stabilized. The blending rotor picks up the loose material and trims the subgrade. Turning in the opposite direction of the cutting rotor, the blending rotor provides a shuttle motion that ensures a thorough mixing of the material. The material from the blending rotor is then carried up and over the rotor and tossed into the twin pugmill. While the material is still in mid-air, it passes through an atomized spray of asphalt liquid. The strategic placement of the spray bars, together with controlled pressures, provides the most efficient dispersion of liquid for assuring accurate, uniform coating of all material particles.

All asphalt liquids used in material processing are accurately metered. After passing through the asphalt liquid spray, the thoroughly coated materials are agitated in a transverse, twin pugmill with overlapping blades. The opposed action of the blades provides intensified agitation and squeezing. This important operation renders a thorough job of final mixing and prepares the uniformly mixed mass of materials for subsequent spreading.

The adjustable tailgate provides flexibility for regulating the amount of materials held in the pugmill for thorough mixing and conforming to the processing depth. It strikes off materials to a uniform loose density the full width of the processing chamber. This material is then ready for immediate compaction where aeration is not required.

A small asphalt liquid tank on the machine permits continuous operation while the asphalt tank truck is being switched. The gallons of liquid asphalt required for a soil asphalt stabilization project will be determined by the project supervisor.

BITUMINOUS MATERIALS

Pavements constructed of bituminous materials and aggregates are referred to as "flexible pavements," because of their ability to permit slight deflections without detrimental effect. Flexibility is due to consolidation of the base course or effect of a load. Flexible pavements provide a resilient, waterproof, load-distributing medium which protects the base course from the detrimental effect of water and the abrasive action of traffic. Properly designed, high quality bituminous concrete is affected very little by temperature strains and fatigue stresses. Bituminous concrete pavements are subject to nominal maintenance due to wear, weathering, and deterioration from aging. Also, as load intensities increase, additional layers of bituminous pavement can be added to existing pavement to provide further reinforcement.

Bituminous pavements can be placed easily and quickly. For these reasons, bituminous materials have become of tremendous importance to both the military and civil engineer in the construction of roads and airfields. They can be used not only in pavements but also as soil stabilizers, thereby improving the strength and waterproofness of subgrades, subbases, and base courses.

Tack Coat

A tack coat is an application of asphalt to an existing paved surface to provide bond between the existing surface and the asphalt material to be placed on it. Two essential requirements of a tack coat are: (1) it must be very thin, and (2) it must uniformly cover the entire surface to be treated. A very thin tack coat does no harm to the pavement and it will properly bond the course.

Some of the bituminous materials used for tack coats are rapid-curing cutbacks, road tar cutbacks, rapid-setting emulsions (may be used in warm weather), and medium asphalt cements. Because rapid-curing cutbacks are highly flammable, safety precautions must be very carefully followed.

A tack coat should be applied only when the surface to be tacked is dry and the temperature has not been below 35°F for 12 hours immediately prior to application.

Before applying the tack coat to a surface that is sufficiently bonded, see that all loose material, dirt, clay, or other objectionable materials are removed from the surface to be treated. This operation may be accomplished with a power broom or blower, supplemented with hand brooms if necessary.

Immediately following the preparation of the surface, the bituminous material should be uniformly applied by means of a bituminous distributor (discussed later in this chapter) at the spraying temperature specified. The amount of bitumen application varies with the condition of the existing pavement being tack-coated, but in general 0.10 to 0.25 gal per sq yd is satisfactory. Following the application of bituminous material, the surface should be allowed to dry until it is in a proper condition of tackiness to receive the surface course, otherwise the volatile substances may act as a lubricant and prevent bonding with the wearing surface. Clean, dry sand should be spread on all areas that show an excess of bitumen to effectively blot up and cure the excess.

An existing surface that is to be covered by a bituminous wearing surface should be barricaded to prevent traffic from carrying dust or mud onto the surface, either before or after the tack coat is applied. Should it become necessary for traffic to use the surface, one lane may be tack coated and paved, using the other lane as a traffic bypass. The bypass lane should be primed and sanded before opening to traffic. It should be swept and reprimed after the adjacent lane is completed. This preserves the base and acts as a dust palliative (sheltering).

Prime Coat

Priming consists of the initial treatment on a granular base prior to surfacing with a bituminous material or pavement. The purpose of a prime coat is to penetrate the base (about 1/4" minimum penetration is desired), fill most of the voids, promote adhesion between the base and the bituminous applications placed on top of it, and waterproof the base.

The priming material may be either a low viscosity tar, a low viscosity asphalt, or a diluted asphalt emulsion. The quantities of priming materials to be applied will be determined by the condition of the soil base and climate. The use of rapid-curing asphalt cutbacks, in general 0.2 to 0.5 gal per square yard, in cold climates has proved to be satisfactory. However, the prime coat can be eliminated if the climate is very cold, as this is likely to slow the curing process.

The sequence of operations for the application of a prime coat is the same as described earlier for application of a tack coat. If the base absorbs all of the prime material within 1 to 3 hours, or if penetration is too shallow, the base is underprimed. Underpriming may be corrected by applying a second coating of the prime material.

An overprimed base may fail to cure and contribute to failure of the pavement. A free film of prime material remaining on the base after a 48-hour curing period indicates that the base is overprimed. This condition may be corrected by spreading a light, uniform layer of clean, dry sand over the prime coat to absorb the excess material. Application of the sand is usually followed by light rolling and brooming. Excess prime held in minor depressions should be corrected by an application of clean, dry sand. Any loose sand should be lightly broomed from the primed surface before the wearing surface is laid.

The primed base should be adequately cured before the wearing surface is laid. In general, a minimum of 48 hours should be allowed for complete curing. Ordinarily, proper surface condition is indicated by a slight change in the shiny black appearance to a slightly brown color.

When a soil base is to be covered by a bituminous wearing surface, the area should be barricaded to prevent traffic from carrying dust or mud onto the surface both before and after priming. If it is necessary to open the primed base course to traffic before it has completely cured, a fine sand may be used; and when ready to place the wearing surface, lightly broom the sand from the primed base course.

Single and Multiple Surface
Treatments

A single surface treatment usually consists of a sprayed application of a bitumen and aggregate cover one stone thick. Surface treatment may be referred to as a seal coat, inverted penetration, armor coat, or carpet coat. A single surface treatment is usually less than 1/2 inch thick. Surface treatments serve as an abrasive and weather-resisting medium which waterproofs the base. Generally, they are not as durable as bituminous concrete and may require frequent maintenance. Surface treatments are particularly suitable for surfacing aged or worn bituminous pavements that are cracked, dry, reveled, or beginning to show signs of wear. When bituminous pavements are designed and constructed properly, they should possess a surface texture that does not require surface treatment to fill the voids.

Surface treatments are used largely on roads, shoulders, and parking areas. Although not recommended for airstrips, they may be used as an expedient measure.

Surface treatments will not withstand the action of metal wheels on vehicles, tracked vehicles, or non-skid chains on vehicle wheels. Surface treatment should not be attempted except when the temperature is above 50°F. Three requirements for a surface treatment are:

1. The quantity of the bitumen must be sufficient to hold the stone without submerging it.
2. Sufficient aggregate must be used to cover the bitumen.
3. The base course on which the surface treatment is laid must be sufficiently strong to support the anticipated load.

A single surface treatment consists of an application of bitumen covered with mineral aggregate, rolled to provide a smooth, even-textured surface. Figure 5 shows the sequence of operations for the application of a single surface treatment.

Uniformly graded sand or crushed stone, gravel, or slag may be used for surface treatments. The purpose of the surface treatment determines the size of the aggregate to be selected. For example, coarse sand may be used for sealing a smooth existing surface. For a badly broken surface, the maximum size of the aggregate should be about 1/2 inch, and the mimimum size about 3/16 inch.

Rapid-cure cutbacks, medium-cure cutbacks, road tars, rapid-setting emulsions, and asphalt cements may be used for surface treatment. Rapid-cure cutbacks are most widely used because they evaporate rapidly and the road can be opened to traffic almost immediately after application of the surface treatment.

Surface treatments are usually applied to a thoroughly compacted primed base that has been swept clean. The existing surface or base course

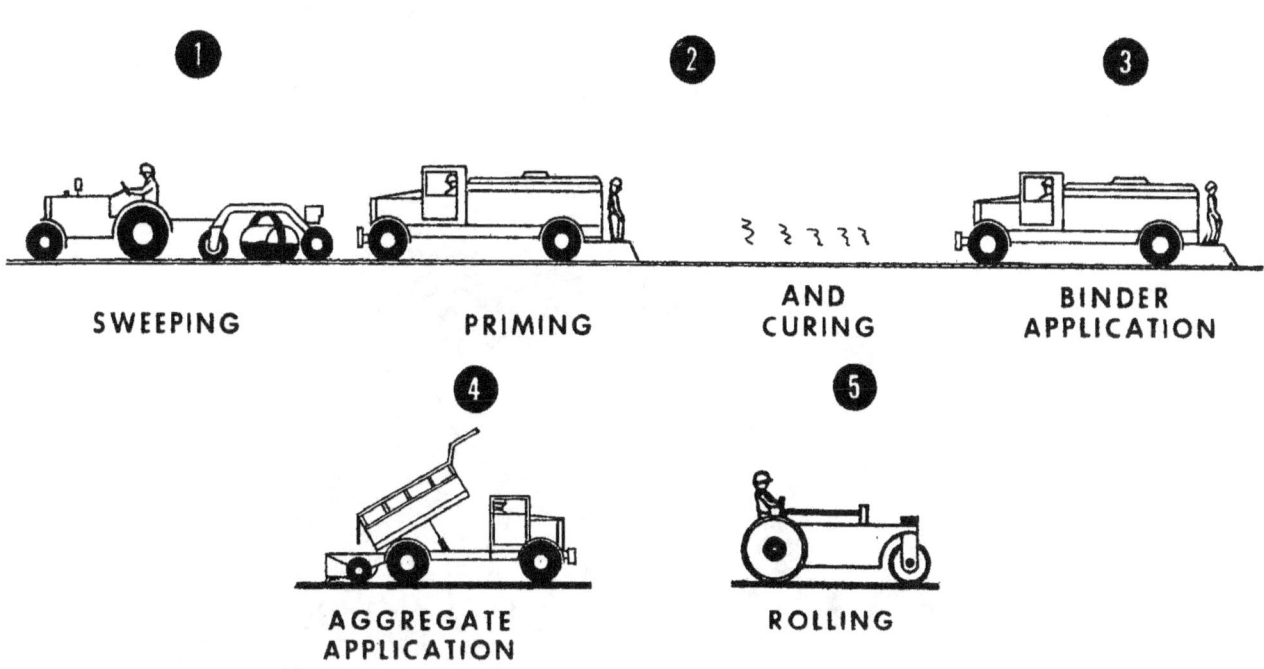

Figure 5.—Sequence of operations for the application of a single surface treatment.

must be dry, or contain moisture not in excess of that which will permit satisfactory bonding of surface treatment to the base. To assure uniform distribution, the bitumen should be applied with a bituminous distributor. The quantity of the bitumen required is based on the average particle size of the coverstone (aggregate). The bitumen must be sufficient to hold the aggregate in place without leaving a sticky surface. The aggregate must not be completely submerged in the bitumen. The viscosity used is dependent upon the size of the coverstone; the larger the coverstone, the higher (or thicker) the viscosity of the bitumen. One-quarter-inch aggregate should be submerged approximately 30 percent; 3/8-inch aggregate, 32 percent; 1/2-inch aggregate, 35 percent; and 3/4-inch aggregate, 43 percent. Approximately 1 gallon of bitumen is usually used for 100 pounds of aggregate.

The aggregate is spread immediately after application of the bitumen, while the bitumen is still fluid. An adjustable mechanical aggregate spreader may be used as shown in figure 6, or the aggregate may be spread from trucks or by hand. Trucks should be operated backwards so that the truck wheels will move over the bitumen that has been covered with aggregate. For handspreading, aggregate should be dumped in piles adjacent to the areas to be treated.

During aggregate spreading, the surface is rolled with a 5- to 8-ton roller. A heavier roller is likely to crush the aggregate rather than embed the aggregate particles in the bitumen. Faulty rolling can be eliminated or minimized if the following practices are adhered to:

1. Rolling should be parallel to the centerline of the roadway to reduce the number of times the roller must change direction.
2. To assure complete coverage, succeeding passes should overlap one-half of the wheel width of the roller.
3. Rolling should be completed before the bitumen hardens. This will ensure that the aggregate becomes well embedded in the bitumen.
4. To maintain surface crown and to prevent feathering at the edges, succeeding passes should be made from the low side to the high side of the surface.
5. Rolling should be done at a slow speed.
6. Rolls should be wet to prevent bitumen from sticking to wheels.

PAVING EQUIPMENT AND OPERATIONS

Figure 6. — Hopper-type spreader applying aggregate to a surface treatment.

7. The power roll should pass over the unrolled surface before the steering roll.

After rolling and curing, the surface is ready for traffic. If the surface is used on an airfield, excess aggregate must be swept from the surface to avoid damage to aircraft. This practice is also recommended for roads, although it is not essential.

When a tougher, more resistant surface is desired than that obtained with a single surface treatment, multiple surface treatment may be used. Multiple surface treatment is two or more successive layers of a single surface treatment. Smaller particles of aggregate and correspondingly less bitumen are used for each successive layer. Although multiple surface treatments are usually more than 1 inch thick, they are still considered surface treatments because each layer is usually less than 1 inch and the total surface treatment does not add appreciably to the load-carrying capacity of the base.

The first layer of a multiple surface treatment is laid in accordance with instructions given earlier for a single surface treatment.

Loose aggregate remaining on the first layer must be swept from the surface so that the layers may be bonded together. Remember that the size of the aggregate and the bitumen will decrease for each successive layer. For the second layer, the bitumen will usually be reduced one-third or one-half of the amount used in the first application. The aggregate used in the second application should be approximately one-half the diameter of that used in the first application. The final application is drag-broomed, if necessary, to provide an even layer of aggregate. At the time the surface is being drag-broomed, it should also be rolled with a 5- to 8-ton

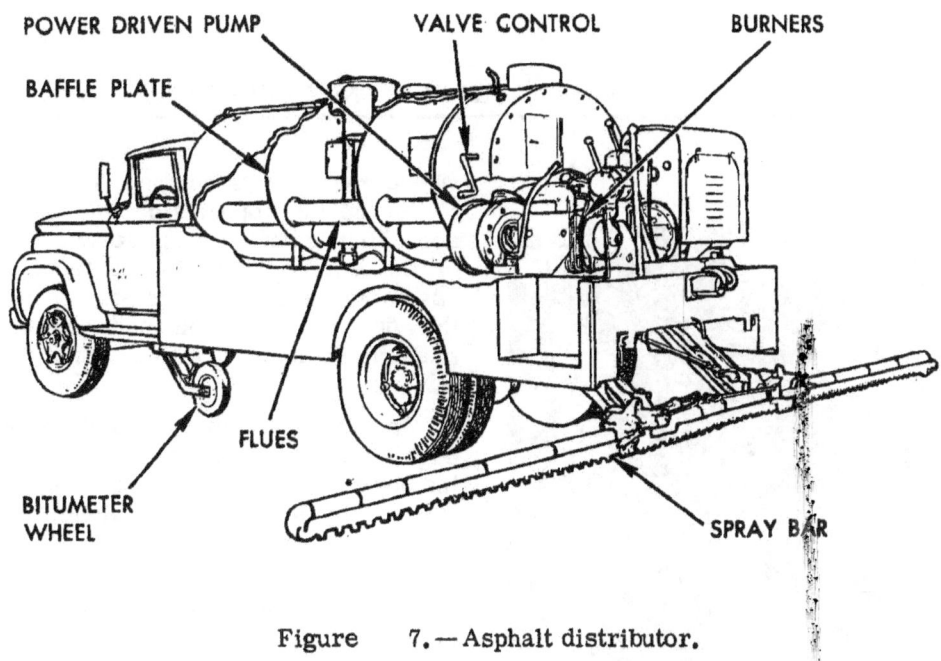

Figure 7.—Asphalt distributor.

roller so that the aggregate will become embedded in the bitumen. After the surface is rolled and cured, it is ready for traffic. If the multiple surface treatment has been laid on an airfield, loose aggregate must be swept from the surface so that it will not damage the aircraft. Final sweeping is also recommended for roads.

To prevent a soil wearing surface (dirt road) from becoming excessively dusty, a bituminous dust palliative (covering) is applied to hold down the dust. The bituminous material used as a dust palliative must be thin enough to soak easily into the surface. It must also retain fluidity indefinitely so that dust particles raised by the traffic will become coated with the bituminous material. A medium-cure or slow-cure cutback is the best material for this purpose.

ASPHALT DISTRIBUTOR

An asphalt distributor, illustrated in figure 7, is frequently used to spray bituminous material on a prepared surface. The insulated bitumen tank is equipped with heating flues for application of heat from an oil burner. A gasoline engine, mounted to the rear of the truck, provides power for an asphalt pump, fuel pump, and air blower. The asphalt pump has an output range from 30 to 350 gallons per minute. The application rate of bitumen is controlled by the width of the spray bar, pump output, and forward speed of the truck after the bitumeter indicator has been set. The spray bar width can vary from 6 to 24 feet in width. The output of bitumen will range from 1/10 to 3 gallons per square yard. Where necessary, bituminous material may be applied through an adjustable length spray bar or a hand spray gun. The spray bar may be of the circulating or noncirculating type, depending upon the model of the distributor. Flow of bituminous material is controlled by a system of hand-operated valves. A tachometer registers the pump discharge in gallons per minute and/or speed of the engine, and a bitumeter shows the forward speed of the truck in feet per minute. (See fig. 8.)

When applying asphalt for a prime or tack coat, an over application of asphalt should be avoided. For this reason, each distributor load should be started out over building paper (sometimes called tar paper). This will also prevent transverse overlap of material.

To maintain uniform pressure and temperature on all spray nozzles, the fan of the spray from each nozzle must be uniform and set at the proper angle with the spray bar (according to the manufacturer's instructions) so that the spray fans do not interfere with each other. The spray bar must be maintained at the proper height

PAVING EQUIPMENT AND OPERATIONS

Figure 8.—Bitumeter and tachometer dials.

above the road surface to provide complete and uniform overlap of the spray fans. The overlap can vary from 6 to 15 inches depending on the desired coverage and type of distributor used. The road speed must be uniform as determined by the type of surface treatment being applied.

ASPHALT FINISHER

While various makes and models of asphalt finishers are used in asphalt paving operations, the finisher most used for training and field operations is the Barber-Greene model SA-35 shown in figure 9.

When the surface has been cleaned, primed, and allowed to cure, it is ready for paving. In spreading mix, whether a hot or cold bituminous mixture, an asphalt finisher is used to lay the mixture into a smooth mat of required thickness and width. While the asphalt finisher shown in figure 16-9 is capable of handling up to 200 tons of mix per hour, its effective capacity is 100 tons per hour. The mat width may be varied from 8 to 14 feet, the depth from 1/2 to 6 inches, and the laydown speed from 12 to 64 feet per minute. The finisher consists essentially of a crawler-mounted tractor unit and a screed unit that is attached to the tractor. An 8-ton charging hopper is mounted on the front of the finisher where the mix is dumped from a truck. A bar feeder on the hopper floor moves the mix to the spreading screws, which spread the mix in front of the screed unit. At the front of the screed assembly, a tamper bar strikes off the mat to the desired elevation and compacts it to as much as 85 percent of final density.

As shown in figure 10, the forward, beveled edge of the tamper does the compacting, while the lower edge does the striking off. Behind the tamper the screed slides along, giving the mat the final smooth finish.

A burner unit, figure 11, permits heating of the screed to prepare it for proper operating temperature. In general, the reason for heating the screed is to keep the asphalt material from sticking to it, and causing what is known as a drag to tear. Thickness of the mat is controlled by two thickness control screws as shown in figure 12. The screed may be adjusted at center to produce a crown. Normal width of the screed is 10 feet, but the width may be increased to 14 feet by use of screed extensions, or reduced to 8 feet by use of cutoff shoes. The finisher is usually powered by a gasoline engine, with a diesel engine being optional.

The manually operated dual controls of the model SA-35 finisher allow the operator to sit on the same side of the machine as the guideline or the edge of the existing mat (see fig. 13). This feature greatly eases longitudinal joint alignment control. Dual controls are most advantageous for paving in narrow places, such as parking areas and around airfield facilities. Operators may be stationed on both sides in such restricted places, greatly reducing the chance of collision and resulting damage to both the machine and objects nearby. Dual controls also allow operators to be trained in minimum time.

Assuming that the operations ahead of the paver have been properly performed, that the equipment is in good condition and properly adjusted, and that the paver is not placing the mix at an excessive rate of speed, there should be no need for hand work. Hand raking should not be done unless absolutely necessary. The most uniform surface texture can be obtained by keeping the hand work back of the paver to a minimum, except when it is required around obstacles.

Figure 9.—Asphalt finisher.

On many jobs there are places where spreading with a paver is either impractical or impossible. In these cases, hand spreading is required. Placing and spreading by hand should be done very carefully and the material distributed uniformly so that segregation of the coarse aggregate and the bituminous binder will be avoided. If the asphalt mix is broadcast with shovels, almost complete segregation of the coarse and fine portions of the mix will result. The material should be deposited from the shovels into small piles which, in turn, are spread with LUTES or RAKES. In the spreading process, all material should be thoroughly loosened and evenly distributed. Any part of the mix that has formed into lumps and does not break down easily should be discarded. After the material has been placed, it is then rolled. In areas difficult to reach with a roller, hand tampers are used.

COMPACTION EQUIPMENT

The following discussion on compaction equipment is limited to that used in bituminous operations. Remember that the initial use of any compaction method should be on a trial-and-error basis.

Rollers used for compaction and final rolling of hot asphalt mix are the 10-ton three-wheel, two- and three-axle tandem, and multiple-wheel pneumatic rollers. Navy two-axle tandems usually weigh from 5 to 8 tons, and three-axle tandems

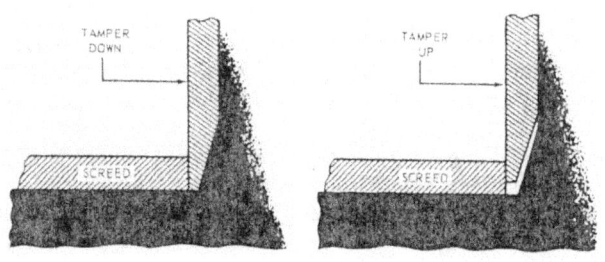

Figure 10.—Cross section of asphalt finisher tamper and screed.

PAVING EQUIPMENT AND OPERATIONS

Figure 11.—Screed heater.

from 9 to 14 tons. Pneumatic tired rollers usually weigh 9 tons, fully ballasted.

Most compaction required in asphalt construction is achieved by the tamper on the finisher. Additional compaction and final surface texture are achieved by applying the rollers in the proper sequence. The hot mix should be at its optimum temperature for rolling when the rollers start to operate on the mat being laid. This optimum temperature will range between 225° to 250°F.

Breakdown rolling is done by the 10-ton three-wheel roller, secondary rolling by the two-axle tandem roller, and finish rolling by the penumatic-tired roller. With this combination of rollers, specified density should be obtained.

If the required density is not obtained during construction, subsequent traffic will further consolidate the asphalt surface and cause ruts.

Rolling of the longitudinal joint should be done immediately behind the finisher. The initial, or breakdown, pass with the roller should be made as soon as it is possible to roll the mixture without cracking the mat or having the mix pick up on the roller wheels. The second rolling should follow the breakdown rolling as closely as possible. The finish rolling should be done while the material is still workable enough for removal of roller marks. Generally speaking, longitudinal joint rolling should start directly behind the spreader; breakdown less than 200 feet behind the spreader; second rolling 200 feet or more behind the breakdown rolling; and

Figure 12.—Thickness control.

finish rolling as soon as possible behind the second rolling.

During rolling, the roller wheels should be kept moist, using only enough water to avoid picking up material. Rollers should move at a slow but uniform speed, with the drive rolls nearest the finisher. With the drive rolls moving toward the finisher, the material will have less tendency to be displaced, as shown in figure 14.

The line of rolling should not be suddenly changed or the direction of rolling suddenly

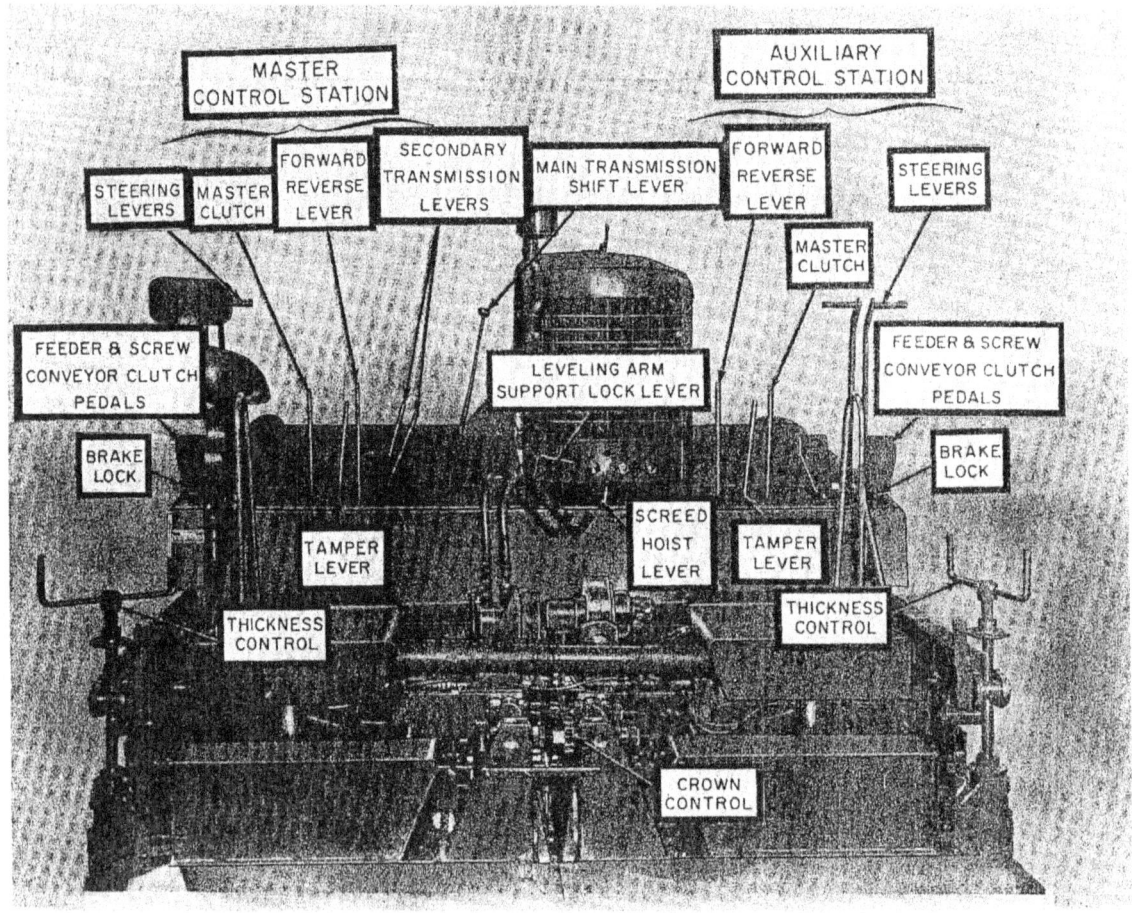

Figure 13.—Operating controls, Barber Greene model SA-35 finisher.

reversed, thereby displacing the mix. Any pronounced change in direction of the roller should be made on stable material. If the rolling causes displacement of the material, the affected areas should be loosened at once with rakes and restored to the original grade with loose material before being rerolled. Heavy equipment or rollers should not be permitted to stand on the finished surface until it has properly cooled or set. Rollers allowed to stand on a hot mat will sink in, thus causing depressions in the new mat.

When paving with a single finisher, the first lane placed should be rolled in the following order:

(1) Transverse joints.
(2) Outside edge.
(3) Breakdown rolling, beginning on the low side and working toward the high side.
(4) Second rolling, same procedure as (3).
(5) Finish rolling.

When paving with two finishers working in echelon, or abutting a previously placed lane, the mix should be rolled in the following order:

(1) Transverse joints.
(2) Longitudinal joints.
(3) Outside edge.
(4) Breakdown rolling.
(5) Second rolling.
(6) Finish rolling.

When paving in echelon, 6 to 8 inches of the edge which the second paver is following should

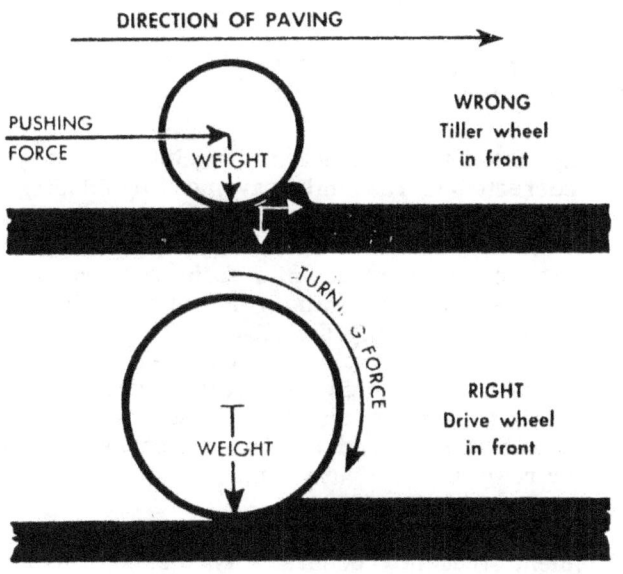

Figure 14.—Rolling—direction is important.

be left unrolled. Then the second strip can be laid the same depth as the unrolled part of the first strip, and the roller can then compact the joint while the material is hot.

II. MAINTENANCE OF BITUMINOUS PAVEMENT

Maintenance and repair of roads and airfields are particularly important because of the constant and heavy mobility in modern warfare. Damage caused by the weight of heavy loads, by the abrasive action of military traffic, and by combat conditions must be repaired as quickly as possible. Repairs must often be made under difficulties, such as shortages of manpower, materials, and equipment; a lack of time; and the possibility of continuing or imminent attack.

Priority of maintenance and repair depends upon tactical requirements, traffic volume, and hazards that will result from complete failure of the paved area. A single pothole in a heavily used road, which is otherwise in excellent condition, should take priority over a pothole in an infrequently used road.

CAUSES OF SURFACE FAILURE

The principal causes of surface failure are subgrade or base failure, disintegration of the surface, instability, or combat failure.

As you may know, an asphaltic concrete pavement is directly dependent upon its base for its load-carrying capacity. WHENEVER THE SUBGRADE OR BASE COURSE FAILS, THAT PART OF THE WEARING SURFACE IMMEDIATELY ABOVE THE WEAKENED AREA WILL ALSO FAIL. Factors which may cause a base to fail include inadequate drainage, frost action, poor compaction, improper materials used for the subgrade or base, and overloading by transporting of exceptionally heavy equipment and materials.

The disintegration, or decomposition, of a wearing surface may be the result of hardening of the bituminous film. This hardening process, usually referred to as oxidation, starts at the time the bitumen is applied and continues during the life of the wearing surface. Continuous exposure to the weather slowly hardens the bitumen, which loses its resiliency and becomes brittle. Hardening may be caused by poorly designed mix, incorrect proportioning of the aggregate and bitumen, or inadequate mixing.

Water may be responsible for surface failure by causing the asphalt film to separate from the surface of the aggregate. If the aggregate absorbs too much water, the aggregate and bitumen may separate.

An unstable wearing surface is likely to deform under the impact of traffic. Causes of instability are as follows:

1. Too much bitumen.
2. Smooth aggregate.
3. Bitumen that is too soft.
4. Low density resulting from insufficient compaction.
5. Unsuitable mix design or gradation of the aggregates, and unsatisfactory placement.
6. Uncured prime.
7. Overpriming or excessive tack coat.
8. Dirt between the surface and base course.

Continuous use of bituminous paved airfields by jet aircraft is likely to burn or scorch the surface, causing a pavement failure.

Other causes of surface failure are the use of unsuitable or insufficient bitumen, inadequate mixing, or a combination of these factors. The bitumen may also strip from dirty aggregate or be cut away by a petroleum distillate.

TYPES OF SURFACE FAILURE

Potholes are the most frequent type of failure found in bituminous wearing surfaces. Potholes may be caused by defective drainage, front action in the base, settlement of the base, or heavy traffic. A small pothole may be repaired with a hot or cold premix patch or a penetration patch. If a large area has many potholes, the entire area must be entirely reworked or replaced, depending upon the type of bituminous material used in the original pavement.

When the bond breaks down between the aggregate and bitumen a condition called raveling occurs. Raveling is disintegration of the surface, with damage starting at the top. This condition is frequently caused by a bitumen that becomes brittle and can no longer bind the aggregate together. A scorched bitumen or any of the factors that cause disintegration may produce reveling. Reveling is repaired by applying a skin patch or a seal coat (described later), as well as a fog seal or slurry seal.

Surface cracking first appears as minute hairline cracks visible only under careful scrutiny. The cracks run lengthwise of the road and appear to be numerous toward the edges of the traveled area. Surface water may seep through the cracks to the base and cause serious base failure and the formation of potholes. Cracks are cleaned with compressed air. Cracks wider than 1/8 inch are filled with lean sand-asphalt mix. The sand-asphalt mix is broomed into the cracks until they are full, then tamped with a spading tool. The filled cracks are sealed with asphalt and covered with sand. When surface cracks and checks are so extensive that water seeps through the cracks into the base course and endangers the pavement, a sand seal is applied. The pavement should be cleaned thoroughly and not more than 1/4 gallon per square yard of bituminous material applied. An even coating of clean, dry sand should be applied directly on the bitumen and rolled until the sand is well set. The area should not be opened to traffic until the bituminous seal has set and will not pick up under traffic.

Rutting and shoving of the wearing surface may be caused by instability. Defects caused by too much cutback in the bitumen may be corrected in road-mix pavement by blading the material from one side of the strip to the other until the volatile substances evaporate. For excess bitumen in the mix, sufficient new aggregate is added and mixing is continued until the bitumen is evenly distributed. The mix is then reshaped and rerolled, and a seal coat may be applied. In hot-mix pavements, excess bitumen requires removal and replacement of the affected area. Weakness of the base must be corrected by reworking the pavement.

Corrugation of a bituminous surface treatment frequently occurs when the bond has been broken between the surface and the underlying course. To repair this defect, the surface should be removed, the base reconditioned and primed, and a new surface treatment applied. Corrugation of a bituminous wearing surface may also be caused by any of the conditions discussed in the preceding paragraph and corrected in the same manner.

Bituminous materials that have been burned or overheated in processing of the mix become brittle and lifeless. The full depth of the pavement course constructed from such materials must be removed and replaced.

Bituminous surfaces frequently bleed, or exude bitumen, in hot weather. Bleeding causes a slippery condition that is hazardous to traffic and may possibly cause the surface to become rutted and grooved. This condition should be remedied as quickly as possible. Bleeding can be caused by too much bitumen being applied during prime coating or tack coating or by inadequate curing; in such cases the wearing surface must be replaced or reworked. As an expedient method for light bleeding, a light, uniform coat of fine aggregate or coarse sand should be applied. Fine sand is unsatisfactory. The pavement should be rolled, if possible, or the traffic permitted to compact the aggregate or sand. A light drag should be used to keep the aggregate or sand spread uniformly, and additional applications made as required. For heavy bleeding, a large aggregate is used.

When settlement is caused by failure of pipes, culverts, or supporting walls, repairs to these structures must be made before surfacing. Minor settlements and depressions frequently are repaired by surface treatments. The edge of a depression should be marked with chalk or paint,

The surface of the pavement within the marking should be cleaned thoroughly and a tack coat applied of not more than 0.1 gallon per square yard. Materials should be used similar in character and texture to those in the adjacent pavement. The patching material should be placed, raked, and rolled. Larger settled areas are repaired with one or more applications of bituminous material on top of the existing surface, or by removing the surface course and bringing the base up to proper grade. Under suitable weather conditions, many types of bituminous surfaces may be bladed to one side of the affected area and then relaid after the base is readjusted.

TYPES OF PATCHES

The types of patches used for repair of bituminous wearing surfaces are: premixed patch, penetration patch, skin patch, and seal coat (surface treatment). If damage is extensive, the entire paving system should be reworked or replaced.

Both hot and cold mixes are used for premixed bituminous patches. Small quantities of hot mix or cold mix often may be obtained locally or the mix may be prepared on the job. Hot mixes prepared at a central plant are generally used for extensive repair. Hot mix can be used with less delay from inclement weather than cold mix, and hot-mix patches can be opened to traffic in a shorter time. New cold-mix patches displace easily under traffic before the volatile substances have evaporated. Hot-mix patches have a longer life than cold-mix patches and less tendency to ravel at the edges. Hot-mix patching material is prepared in accordance with instructions set down at the central plant. In most cold-mixes, dry aggregate is required for a satisfactory mix. The amount of bitumen to be used is just as important in patching mixes as it is in mixes for construction of new pavements.

A penetration patch is made with macadam aggregate (which should be broken stone or slag, with a maximum size of 2 to 3 inches, depending on the depth of the hole) and a suitable bitumen. Layers of suitable base material should be placed, compacted, lightly tacked, and a coarse layer of aggregate tamped into the hole which has been prepared in accordance with the procedures shown in figure 15. The bitumen used may be asphalt cement or a rapid-curing emulsion. Rate of application is usually 1 gallon per square yard for the top inch, and 1/2 gallon per square yard for each additional inch of depth. Ensure that the final surface patched is slightly high to allow for compaction by traffic. Excess bituminous material should be avoided in a penetration patch. If time and personnel availability permit, a firm compaction of subbase material can be accomplished by repeatedly filling the pothole with materials on hand until the traffic has fully compacted the subbase. When traffic has sufficiently compacted the subbase, repair can proceed as illustrated in figure 15.

A skin patch is a single surface treatment used to correct cracking and raveling in small areas of the wearing surface. Skin patches seal the defective areas and recondition the wearing surface. In applying a skin patch, the damaged area is swept clean and a coat of asphalt cutback applied. The bituminous coat is then covered with fine aggregate and lightly rolled or tamped to seal the aggregate. The aggregate generally used is about 1/4-inch stone or clean, coarse sand. In general, approximately 1 gallon of bitumen is used for 100 pounds of aggregate, regardless of the size of the aggregate.

A seal coat is a single surface treatment used to seal large cracked or raveled areas. Basically, a seal coat is a sprayed application of bitumen covered with a thin layer of aggregate. The amount of bitumen depends upon the type of aggregate; usually about 1 gallon of bitumen is needed for every 100 pounds of aggregate. Double surface treatments may be used if necessary.

ASPHALT KETTLE

The asphalt kettle shown in figure 16 is equipped for hand-spraying bituminous materials for dressing stretches or road or runway shoulders, filling surface cracks, and spray coating areas for sheet asphalt repairs, surface treatment, or seal coating.

The trailer-mounted tank consists of an outer shell with a 165-gallon capacity storage and melting tank mounted inside. A removable fuel burner, mounted inside the kettle outer shell, provides heat to the melting tank through a baffle. A flue stack, located on the forward end of the melting tank over the top of the baffle and burner assembly, provides an escape for exhaust gases. A thermometer, inserted through

PAVING EQUIPMENT AND OPERATIONS

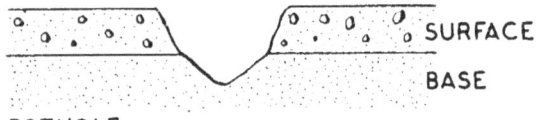
POTHOLE

CLEAN AND TRIM TO RECTANGULAR LINES AND VERTICAL FACES

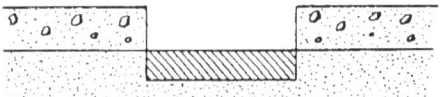
REPLACE BASE MATERIAL AND COMPACT THOROUGHLY BY TAMPING

PRIME BOTTOM AND PAINT SIDES OF HOLE WITH LIGHT-GRADE BITUMINOUS MATERIAL. LET DRY UNTIL BITUMEN BECOMES TACKY

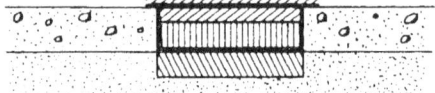
BUILD UP WITH 3" OR SMALLER LIFTS OF COMPACTED BITUMINOUS PRE-MIXED MATERIAL

Figure 15. — Steps in patching a pothole or burned area.

an insulated pipe into the interior of the melting tank, indicates the temperature reading of the heating bituminous material. If the bituminous material is overheated, a fire or explosion can result.

A two-cylinder gasoline engine provides power for the bitumen pumping system. By shifting the clutch shifter lever, the engine is engaged

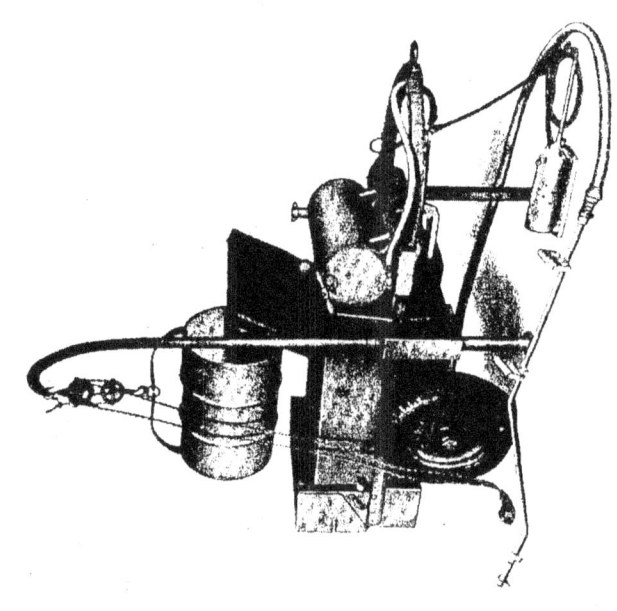

Figure 16. — Asphalt kettle.

to the pump assembly which provides the pressure for all pumping operations. A flexible, metal spray hose, which connects the pump to the hand-held spray bar assembly, is used to convey bitumen to the surface being repaired.

III. MAINTENANCE OF EQUIPMENT

As an Equipment Operator, it is your responsibility to coordinate the proper operation, care, use, adjusting, cleaning, preservation, and lubrication of paving and support equipment. This includes daily inspections and adjustments required for good operation. Malfunctions in equipment, which go beyond those operating adjustments performed by the EO, should be referred to the field mechanic for corrective action. This does not release you from working with the field mechanic unless directed otherwise.

You, the EO, serve a very important function in preventive maintenance. You are required to perform specific daily and scheduled maintenance services on your equipment. Proper performance of these services does much to prolong the life of the equipment, to avoid major repairs, and to assure that your equipment will perform its mission consistently and dependably. Acceptable maintenance standards applicable to any particular piece of equipment you operate have been established by the manufacturer of that equipment and should be followed. Instructions and directives put out by your unit must also be followed. They may include periodic inspections, testing, and observation of your operational techniques. You are responsible for certain forms, records, and reports in the performance of your maintenance services and daily operations. Get to know the applicable maintenance procedures and carry out the directives accordingly.

IV. PAVING SAFETY

This section deals with safety precautions applicable to paving operations. We are particularly interested in such topics as the heating of asphalt materials, traffic control, plant safety, equipment operation, cleaning bituminous handtools, and safe practices applicable to the personal safety of the operator and other persons who may be working as crewmembers.

Construction with bituminous materials involves several hazards. One of the most serious dangers is associated with the heating required to convert the solid or semi-solid materials to a degree of fluidity which will permit their application and/or mixing. As a safety measure, make sure fire extinguishing equipment (foam-type) is present at all times.

When readying the distributor and/or asphalt kettle, be sure they are in a level position before heating and are located a safe distance from buildings and other flammable materials. Keep covers closed during the heating period to prevent escape of flammable vapors, and avoid exposure to fumes from hot bituminous material—stay on the windward side.

When heating bituminous materials for spraying purposes, check the temperature suggested in table 2 for the type and grade being used. Remember that most of the flash points are exceeded before the materials reach spraying or working temperature; therefore, additional caution must be exercised to prevent the exposure of rising fumes to an open flame. A dense yellow cloud or vapor rising from the distributor or kettle is an indication that the material is being overheated to the extent that a small spark is sufficient to ignite the vapors.

Always extinguish burners before spraying bituminous material. When spraying, stand at least 25 feet clear of the spray bar on the bituminous distributor; spray bars have been known to blow open or rip with sudden pressure of heated materials. Remember that bituminous material must be heated to a high temperature, and any of this material coming in contact with the skin will leave a serious burn.

When handling asphalt being processed, wear proper protective apparel. Wear loose, heavy

Table 2.—Suggested Temperatures for Uses of Asphalt

Type and Grade of Asphalt	Pugmill Mixing Temperature of Aggregates*	Distributor Spraying Temperature
Asphalt Cements		
(For Open-Graded Mixes, Types I & II)**		
40-50	225-310°F	
60-70	225-305°F	
85-100	225-300°F	
120-150	225-300°F	
200-300	225-300°F	
(For Dense-Graded Mixes, Types III-VIII)**		
40-50	275-350°F	
60-70	265-330°F	
85-100	255-325°F	
120-150	245-325°F	
200-300	225-300°F	
(For Distributor Spray Applications)		
40-50***		300-410°F
60-70***		295-405°F
85-100		290-400°F
120-150		285-395°F
200-300		275-385°F
Liquid Asphalts		
RC, MC, and SC Grades		
30	60-105°F	
70	95-140°F	
250	135-175°F	
800	165-205°F	
3000	200-240°F	
Asphalt Emulsions		
RS-1	****	75-130°F
RS-2	****	110-160°F
MS-2	50-140°F	100-160°F
SS-1	50-140°F	75-130°F
SS-1h	50-140°F	75-130°F
RS-2K	****	75-130°F
RS-3K	****	110-160°F
CM-K	50-140°F	100-160°F
SM-K	50-140°F	100-160°F
SS-K	50-140°F	75-130°F
SS-Kh	50-140°F	75-130°F

*The temperature of the aggregates and asphalt immediately before mixing should be approximately that of the completed batch.
**Mix Type III is intermediate between dense- and open-graded mixes. As the gradation of the mix changes from dense-graded to open-graded the mixing temperature should be lowered accordingly.
***Not normally used for spray applications in pavement construction.
****Not used for mixing.

PAVING EQUIPMENT AND OPERATIONS

clothing—in good condition. Clothing should be closed at the neck, sleeves rolled down over the top of gloves, and trousers (without cuffs) extending well down over the top of shoes (safety type). Goggles should be worn to prevent eye burn from bubbling or splashing asphalt. In addition, wear a safety hat.

Frequently, bituminous operations will be planned for roads that must carry traffic while work is in progress. Slow signs or other warning devices should be conspicuously placed at both 100 yards and 20 yards from each entrance of the project. Flagmen, dressed in safety vests or some other attire, should aid in traffic control.

It will be necessary for most airfields to remain operational (if possible) during bituminous operations. The construction schedule, equipment routing, and maximum height of equipment should be discussed with the airfield safety officer. Liaison with air traffic control must be established if trucks and other equipment are to cross runways that are in use.

Guards, safety appliances, and similar devices are placed on moving parts in both asphalt and concrete plants for the protection of personnel. They must not be removed or made ineffective except for the purpose of making immediate repairs, lubrication, or adjustments, and then, only after the power has been shut off. All guards and devices must be replaced immediately after completion of repairs and adjustments by maintenance personnel.

There should be a platform near the truck loading or unloading area from which the mix or materials may be observed. There should also be a horn or buzzer for the plant operator to signal a truckdriver to move his vehicle. In addition, a "panic button," or switch, should be located a short distance from the plant. This panic button, or switch, can be used to stop all plant operations in event of an emergency. The area around mixing plants should be kept clean and clear of any waste material.

Machinery and mechanized equipment must be operated only by qualified and authorized personnel. It must not be operated in a manner that will endanger personnel or property, and the safe operating speeds or loads be exceeded. Equipment requiring an operator must not be permitted to run unattended. Mounting or dismounting equipment while in motion, or riding on equipment by unauthorized personnel, is prohibited. All equipment using fuel must be shut down, with ignition off, prior to and during refueling operations.

When operating paving equipment, frequent inspections of running mechanisms and attachments are the operator's responsibility. He is also responsible for inspecting such items as the power train, power plant, transmission, tracks, controls, skip guards, cables, sheaves, loading or unloading warning devices, and receiving hoppers.

In applying paving materials, crewmembers often become so occupied with their particular job that they are unaware of equipment operating near them. For this reason, at least one crewmember should be designated as safety inspector to ensure that reasonable precautions are observed within the assigned working areas. In addition, the safety inspector periodically holds short (approximately 5 to 15 minutes) safety meetings, called Stand-up Safety meetings, during which he briefs his crew on hazards and precautions relating to current work.

All handtools used for paving purposes must be kept in good repair and used only for the purpose for which designed. When using handtools such as rakes, shovels, lutes, and hand tampers on asphalt paving jobs, these tools should be heated before use and cleaned immediately after use. It is common practice to clean these handtools by burning off the bitumen collected during paving operations. Crewmembers should exercise caution and be forewarned that flames are not always visible. One man should stand by with a fire extinguisher capable of controlling a petroleum fire.

All personnel should be instructed to report promptly all personal injuries and property damage regardless of how minor. Reports should be prepared in accordance with instructions set forth in base of command publications.

V. CONCRETE TRANSIT MIXERS

The concrete transit mixer is a production tool designed to deliver and mix concrete. You, as an EO, are responsible for the safe and timely delivery of your load. You are also responsible

Figure 17.— Concrete transit mixer.

for manufacturing concrete and safeguarding the quality of the concrete en route to and at the jobsite until the concrete has been discharged.

OPERATING CONCRETE TRANSIT MIXERS

The information given below is on the Challenge series 01 concrete transit mixer (fig. 17), and applies ONLY to that machine. This information will give you an idea of how one of the several types of transit mixers is operated.

Before operating the transit mixer, you should first become familiar with its controls (fig. 18). The purpose of the various controls is explained below; the numbers in parentheses correspond to those used in figure 18 to indicate the location and purpose of the controls.

The CLUTCH LEVER (1) is known as the "Uni-Lever" in that the actions of the clutch, throttle, and drum rotation are incorporated in the one lever. The "Uni-Lever" located at the rear of the mixer has three functions. In addition to serving as clutch and throttle, the lever also controls the direction of drum rotation. The shifting of drum rotation may be accomplished ONLY at the rear station (2).

The HAND THROTTLE (3) is mounted on the auxiliary frame runner at the left front control station. The hand throttle is used (1)

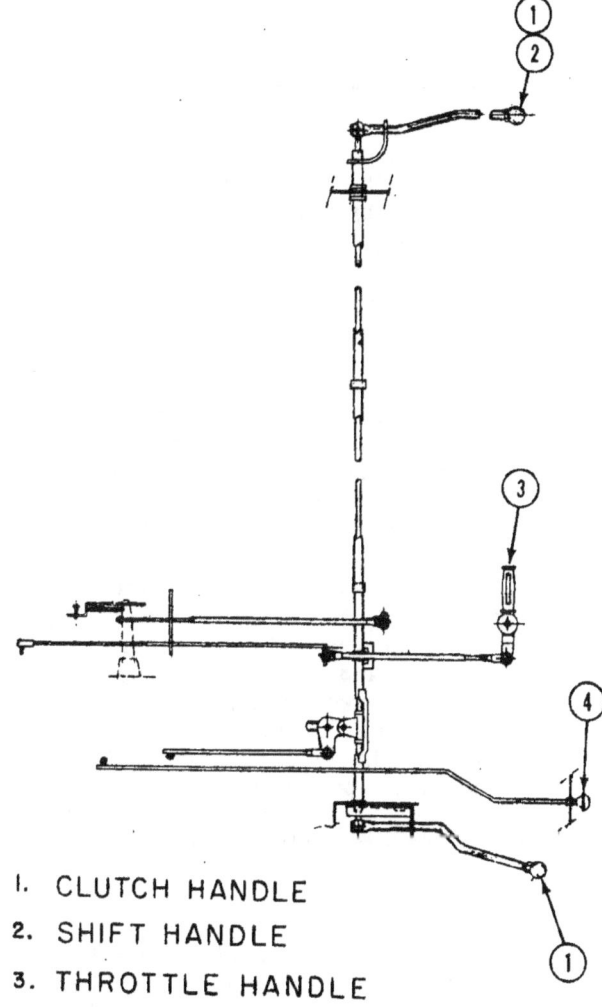

1. CLUTCH HANDLE
2. SHIFT HANDLE
3. THROTTLE HANDLE
4. CHARGING RANGE HANDLE

Figure 18.— Transit mixer controls.

to regulate engine speed while charging the mixer, (2) to set the engine speed for transit, and (3) for any other applications which may require a constant engine speed.

The CHARGING RANGE CONTROL LEVER (4) is located on the UPPER left corner of the instrument panel at the front control station. This lever is mechanically connected to the two-speed transmission; this gives the operator an additional speed range for charging. To select the desired speed range, disengage the clutch, select the appropriate speed range, and re-engage the clutch.

PAVING EQUIPMENT AND OPERATIONS

Before you can fulfill your responsibility as a transit truck mixer operator, some basic knowledge of the nature of concrete and of its proper mixing procedures must be known.

The basic ingredients of concrete are aggregates (such as gravel and crushed stone), sand, cement, and water. Small quantities of admixtures may also be added to achieve certain characteristics such as air entrainment or better workability. The aggregates normally comprise approximately 65 to 80 percent of the total volume of ingredients, while the cement and water together comprise about 20 to 35 percent.

Various kinds of concrete are produced to meet specific needs in construction work. Concrete of the desired quality is obtained by varying the sizes, types, and quantities of aggregates, as well as the type and amount of cement, the amount of water, and the types and amounts of admixtures. The kinds and quantities of each material are spelled out in a "mix design" for specific jobs and are standardized for many jobs that are similar in nature.

Types of Mixer Operation

The transit truck mixer is used with any type of ready mix concrete mixing and hauling procedure, including central mixing, shrink mixing, transit mixing and jobsite mixing. In hauling central mixed concrete the truck mixer serves as an agitator keeping the concrete well mixed en route to the job by turning the drum at agitating speed. In shrink mix operations the materials are combined and the mixing process is begun at the plant. Then the concrete is loaded into the mixer, and the mixing is completed in the truck mixer. In transit mixing the materials are loaded into the truck mixer at the plant, and all of the mixing is accomplished by the truck mixer en route to the job. Some project plans specify that the concrete must be mixed at the jobsite. On this type of operation, all the materials except the water are loaded into the truck mixer drum at the plant. The mixer, equipped with one of the optional large water tanks and water measuring devices, adds the mixing water at the jobsite and performs the entire mixing operation there.

Ideal Mixing Conditions

Ideal conditions for mixing concrete include simultaneous loading of cement, sand, water and aggregate (to obtain initial intermingling of materials), followed by 70 to 100 turns of the mixer drum at normal mixing speeds of approximately 7 to 11 rpm. Of these three critical steps: proper charging, adequate drum speed, and the correct number of drum revolutions during the mixing cycle, the charging operation (described later in this chapter) is most important.

At variations from simultaneous loading will make mixing more difficult and will require additional drum revolutions at mixing speed.

Avoid Overmixing

Overmixing damages the quality of the concrete, tends to grind the aggregates into smaller pieces, increases the temperature of the mixture, lowers the slump, decreases air entrainment, and decreases the strength of the concrete. Overmixing also puts NEEDLES WEAR on the drum and blades.

In selecting the best mixing speed for each trip, the operator of a transit mixer should estimate the travel time (in minutes) to the job and divide this into the minimum desired number of revolutions at mixing speed — 70. The result will be the best drum speed. For instance, if the haul is 10 minutes, 70 divided by 10 equals 7. With this drum speed, the load will arrive on the job with exactly 70 turns at mixing speed — no overmixing and no unnecessary equipment wear. If the load cannot be discharged immediately, the driver should turn it at 2 rpm (minimum agitating speed) until he can discharge it. Since he arrived on the job with no more than the minimum number of mixing turns completed, he is able to wait longer (if necessary) without accumulating more than the maximum permissible number of total turns (250).

To simplify the selection of proper mixing speeds and to allow a margin for error that will cover variations in driving conditions, the operator may choose to use mixing speeds between 5 and 10 rpm, rather than 4 to 12 rpm. Working within the 5 to 10 rpm range, dividing 70 by estimated travel time will produce the desired drum speed for any trip from 7 to 14 minutes in length. For trips shorter than 7 minutes, the driver will continue to turn his drum at 10 rpm for the full 7 minutes, even though a portion of that time is at the jobsite. For trips longer than 14 minutes in length, the driver will maintain a drum speed of 5 rpm for 14 minutes (producing a total of 70 turns at mixing speed), then change to 2 rpm (agitating speed) for the balance of the trip, and for waiting time on the job, if any.

Batching and Charging Procedures

In order to produce quality concrete, you should strive to obtain uniform ribbon loading of all materials throughout the entire charging operation. Ribbon loading is best because it allows intermingling of the materials as they enter the drum, providing a head start on the mixing operations.

For transit mixing and jobsite mixing, the mixer should be charged with the truck engine running at near full throttle and the mixer control lever in the charge position. This will produce a drum speed of about 16 rpm. For central mix and shrink mix operations a little less throttle, which will produce a charge speed of 12 to 14 rpm, is generally adequate. As soon as the load is charged, the hand throttle or remote throttle should be closed and the drum speed reduced to the desired mixing speed.

Discharging

The unloading operation can be controlled from the control station at the rear or from the cab, whichever seems to best suit the job conditions. In either case, the throttle should be set partially open and the discharge speed controlled with the mixer control lever. Returning the control lever to its neutral position will automatically stop the drum. If the interruption is of any significant length, the control lever should be moved to agitate speed. The load can also be discharged with the truck in motion if required, such as in curb and gutter placement. With the mixer engine throttle positioned for slow speed, the "Uni-Lever" can be moved to whatever position will produce the needed discharge rate to fill the forms.

When discharging concrete from a mixer equipped with a sealing door, the door should be opened wide to prevent segregation or straining of materials. When discharging is intermittent as in wheelbarrows, buggies, buckets, etc., the rate should be controlled by manipulation of the mixer control lever—not the engine throttle.

Mixer Cleaning

At the jobsite: Immediately after discharging all concrete to the required project, you should wash off the excess concrete in the mixer drum and blades, the discharge opening, and the discharge chutes before it has a chance to harden. Spraying 15 to 25 gallons of water into the drum while it is revolving will clean the inside of the drum as well as remove all grout which may have collected in the water nozzle during discharge. This may be carried back to the plant and subtracted from the next load. A washdown hose is provided to clean areas accessible from the outside. A clean mixer produces a more satisfactory mixing and discharging of concrete.

> CAUTION: Wash the mixer with water only for the first 30 days of operation. Any stains occurring within the first 30 days can be washed off with a mild detergent. Thoroughly rinse with clear water. Avoid washing in the sun. The use of acids or abrasives may cause severe loss of gloss.

At the plant: A minimum of 150 to 250 gallons of water, depending on the size of the mixer, should be used to thoroughly clean the drum immediately at the end of each day's run. With the flush water in the drum, rotate the drum in the mixing direction for a few minutes, then discharge the flush water at maximum drum rpm. Complete cleaning the outside of the mixer, particularly around the discharge end.

By using a mixture of half paraffin oil and half diesel oil, the truck and concrete mixer can be sprayed in a few minutes; this prevents or retards the concrete from adhering to the structural members. After the entire unit has been thoroughly sprayed, it can be washed down with an ordinary garden hose at the prescribed line pressure.

If the above procedure is followed daily, it will result in increased efficiency, as well as reduce maintenance costs, of the equipment.

Hydraulic Chute Hoist

The manual hydraulic chute hoist is simple to operate and requires very little maintenance.

PAVING EQUIPMENT AND OPERATIONS

This hoist consists of an oil reservoir and a hydraulic pump with a flow control valve and a hydraulic cylinder secured to the chute. By hand pumping and manipulation of the flow control valve, the operator may raise, hold, or lower the chute to any desired position.

Hints for trouble free operation:

1. Check oil level in reservoir.
2. Keep breather on top of reservoir clean. If this breather becomes clogged, a vacuum will result.
3. Use clean oil when adding oil.

The friction lock chute brake is designed to control the swing of the chute through a 180° range. The operator may lock it at any position simply by tightening down on the handle, or it may be desirable to apply just enough drag so that a slight tug will move the chute. This arrangement may save damage to the chute in case it is forced against a solid object.

SECURING

When securing a concrete transit mixer, position the concrete discharge chute so that it is parallel to the mixer drum. Wash down the unit as described in previous paragraphs, place mixer controls in neutral, and secure mixer engine. Drive the transit truck to the designated securing area and position in a safe manner.

VI. OPERATOR'S CARE AND MAINTENANCE

Every operator is required to perform certain daily maintenance services on the concrete transit mixer he operates. This maintenance includes the required inspection service, lubrication, and adjustments required to maintain the concrete transit mixer in a safe and operable condition, prevent malfunctions, and avoid or delay major repairs.

In order to maintain efficient operation of the mixer, it is important that you clean the mixer thoroughly once a day, in addition to washing it down after discharging each load. Lubricate the mixer and the mixer engine daily, in accordance with the manufacturer's instructions. Service the engine air filter regularly, check the truck frame and mixer mounting bolts, and maintain correct drum chain adjustment.

Oils which are used in the hydraulic system perform the dual function of lubrication and transmission of power. Select and use only the type recommended by the manufacturer.

Special worm gear or compound steam cylinder oil is used in the worm gear drive. Do not use automotive or hypoid type "all purpose" oil. Do not add any compound. Check oil level daily, change oil after 2 weeks of operation and every 3 months thereafter. The oil capacity is given on the instruction plate attached to the mixer housing.

The frequency of oil change and oil filter element replacement for the mixer engine depends upon the operating conditions encountered. Under normal operating conditions, the oil and filter element should be changed after every 100 hours of operation.

Since engines used in mixers may vary, it is advisable that you comply with the recommended oil viscosity, general care, and maintenance procedures outlined in the manufacturer's operating manual.

The lubricant used on the mixer roller chain must be thin enough to enter a chain joint and must be applied frequently enough that a film of lubrication is constantly maintained inside the joints. A coating of hard grease will collect and hold abrasive particles, resulting in undue wear on both chains and sprockets. To prevent corrosion, reduce wear rate of chains, and lengthen sprocket life, use of SAE 30 engine oil is recommended by the manufacturer for mixer chain lubrication. Apply oil to the chain joints daily with an oil can or brush.

VII. TRANSIT MIXER SAFETY

The increased use of transit mix trucks on construction projects imposes traffic problems which must be considered. Caution must be used during backing of the transit truck. Backing should be controlled by a signalman, positioned so that the operator can clearly observe the directions given.

Use extreme caution when traveling over uneven terrain on a construction site. The stability of the mixer is greatly reduced with the extra weight of the concrete in the mixer unit. In such cases, a slow speed is recommended.

Some additional safety precautions that must be observed are as follows:

1. Reduce speed before making a turn or applying the truck brakes.

2. Secure discharge chute properly, using the friction brake lock provided.

3. Check to make certain that other personnel are in the clear before starting the mixer charging or discharging.

4. Before making any adjustments, make certain that the mixer engine is not running; this is particularly important when the clutch or drum chain is to be adjusted.

5. Secure mixer engine before refueling.

HIGHWAY MAINTENANCE GUIDELINES

CONTENTS

Section	
4.000	Maintenance and Repair of Highways Structures
4.100	Definition of Terms
4.120	Loads on Structures
4.130	Deck Elements
4.140	Superstructures
4.150	Bearings
4.160	Substructures
4.170	Miscellaneous
4.200	Bridge Inspection Program
4.210	General
4.220	Frequency of Inspection
4.230	Requirements for Inspections
4.240	Inspection Equipment
4.300	Routine and Preventive Maintenance
4.320	Types of Work
4.330	Work Procedures
4.400	Channel Maintenance
4.500	Foundations and Substructure Maintenance
4.520	Piles
4.530	Footings
4.540	Abutments and Piers
4.550	Backwalls
4.560	Bridge Seats
4.570	Wingwalls
4.600	Superstructure Maintenance and Repair
4.620	Steel Superstructure
4.630	Concrete Superstructure
4.640	Bridge Bearings
4.700	Deck Elements and Wearing Course
4.720	Bridge Decks
4.730	Wearing Surfaces, Concrete
4.740	Wearing Surfaces, Asphalt
4.750	Curbs and Sidewalks
4.760	Railing
4.770	Joints
4.800	Painting
4.820	Surface Preparation
4.830	Paint Application

HIGHWAY MAINTENANCE GUIDELINES

4.000 MAINTENANCE AND REPAIR OF HIGHWAY STRUCTURES

Note: As a general reference, the Standard Construction Specifications sections 551 through 589, especially section 580 through 589, Bridge Repair may be consulted. Appropriate materials references and other useful information can be found in these sections.

4.100 DEFINITION OF TERMS

4.110 Purpose: Before undertaking a comprehensive discussion of the Maintenance and Repair of Highway Structures it is important to first develop a series of uniform definitions. These definitions will provide a common vocabulary for the understanding of the subject, the development of maintenance methods, and the exchange of ideas.

An additional benefit to be derived from the establishment of a common set of definitions is an understanding of the various component parts that comprise highway structures and the purpose these individual parts play in providing load carrying capacity. This understanding of the importance of the individual structural members in carrying the bridge loadings will have considerable bearing on the nature and urgency of the maintenance and repair procedures that are developed.

It will therefore be the purpose of Section 4.100 to develop a common frame of reference to be used in the discussion of the maintenance and repair of highway structures. In the following definitions it must be realized that this manual will be used by individuals with a wide variety of backgrounds. It is not unlikely that this manual will be utilized by individuals ranging from registered professional engineers with considerable structural training through individuals in the bridge maintenance crews with little or no formal structural training. Therefore, in the following material an attempt will be made to treat the subject with as little reference to theoretical aspects as possible. Theory will be interjected only when it lends itself to the clarity of the subject being discussed.

4.120 Loads on Structures

4.121 Dead Load: The dead load on a stucture is the weight of the structure itself and the weight of any permanent fixtures which are carried by the structure. It is a fixed load which remains in position during the life of the structure unless removed. It could be increased. Some examples are:

- A. Wearing Courses
- B. Structural Decks
- C. Structural Steel Members
- D. Curbs and Sidewalks
- E. Pipes or Conduits

4.122 Live Load: The live load on a structure includes all other loads or forces, excluding dead load, acting on the structure.

The live load stresses can result from one or a combination of the following:

- A. Traffic: These loadings, for the purpose of highway structures are divided into the following two general classifications:

    1. H-Loadings which consist of a two axle truck. The H-Loadings are designated H, followed by a number indicating the gross weight in tons of the standard truck. For example, H-10 would designate a 10-ton truck.

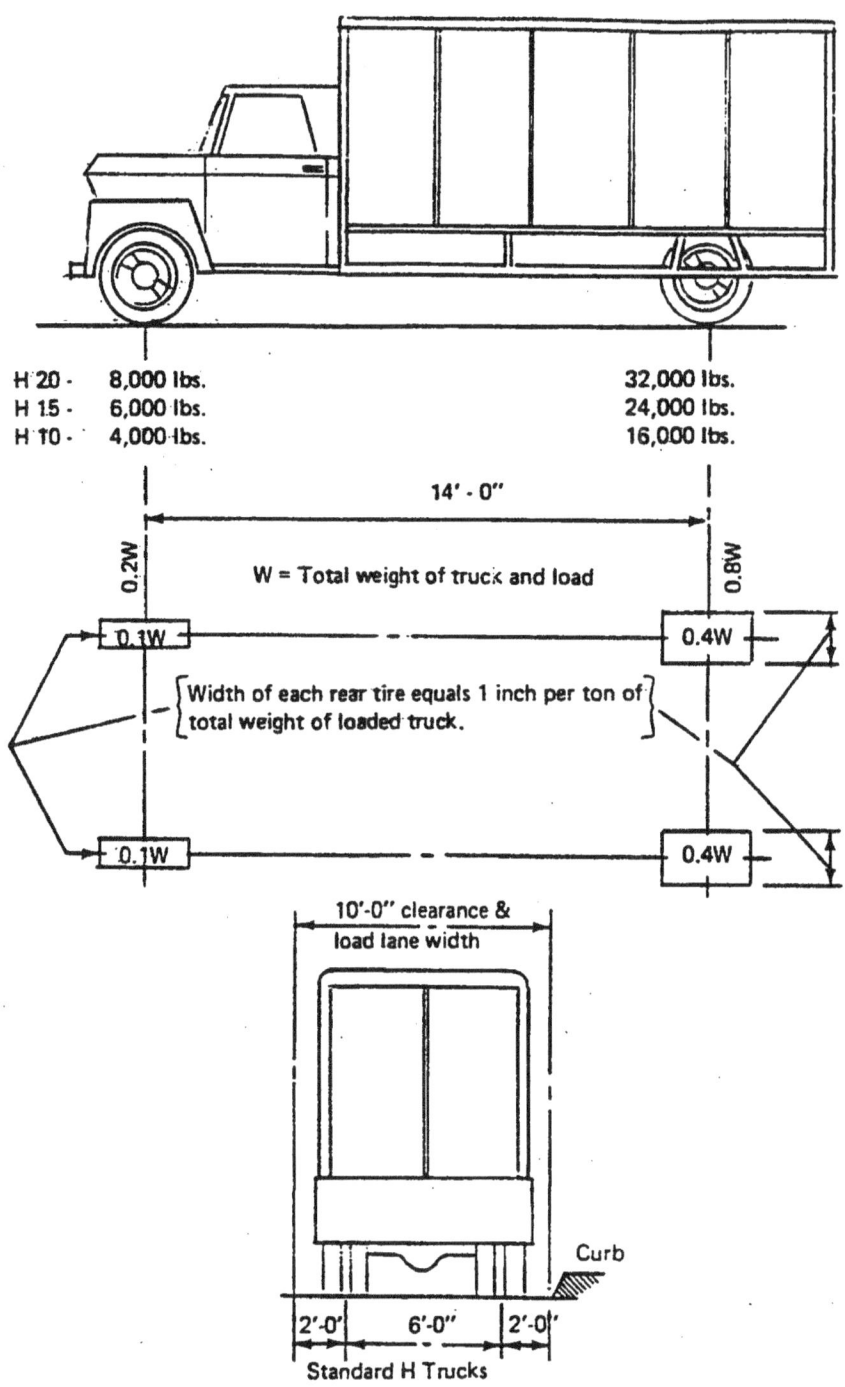

2. H-S Loadings consist of a tractor truck with semi-trailer. The H-S Loadings are designated by the letter H, followed by a number indicating the gross weight in tons of the tractor truck and the letter S followed by the gross weight in tons of the single axle of the semi-trailer.

A variable axle spacing is also utilized in order that the spacing of the axles may approximate more closely the tractor trailers now in use. For example, an H20-S16 loading would be a twenty-ton tractor truck with a sixteen-ton semi-trailer.

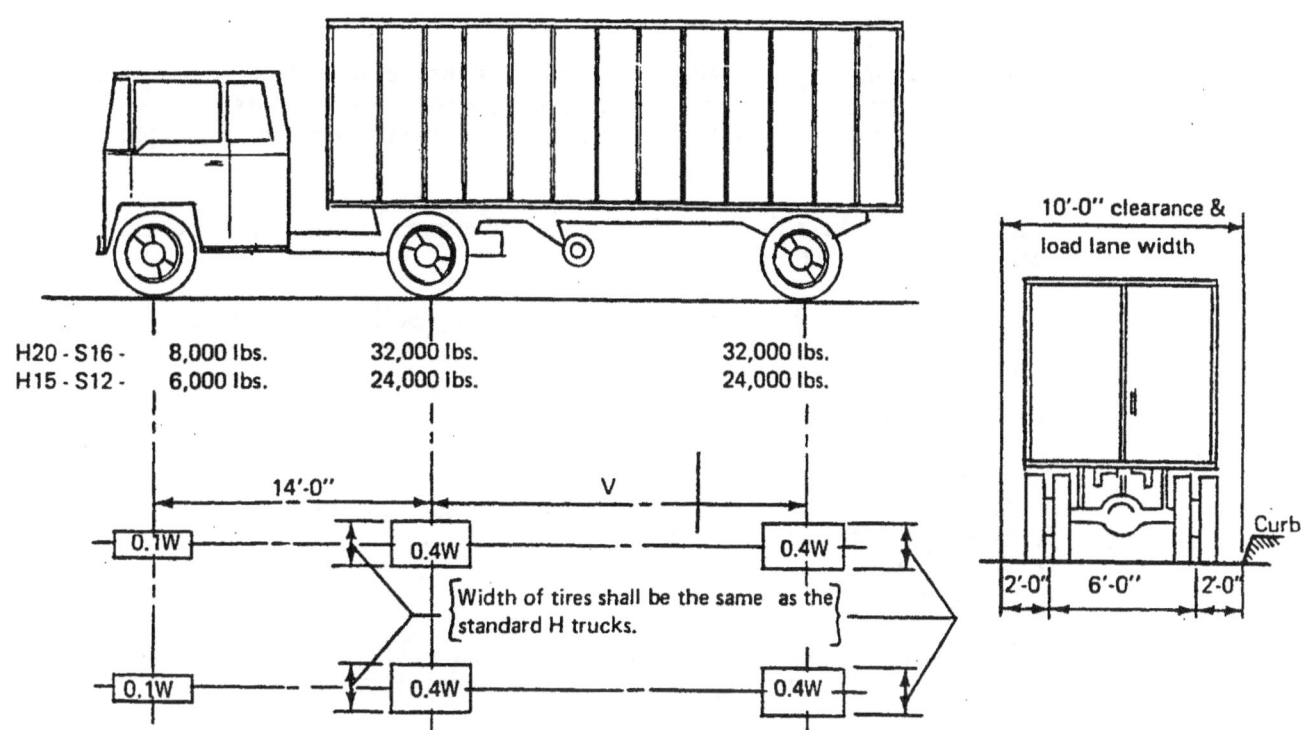

W = Combined weight on the first two axles which is the same as for the corresponding H truck.
V = Variable spacing - 14 feet to 30 feet inclusive. Spacing to be used is that which produces maximum stresses.

Standard H-S Truck

- B. **Impact**: This is an allowance, equal to a calculated percentage of the live load which is added to the live load of a structure to provide for the dynamic and vibratory effects of traffic loadings.

- C. **Wind**: The wind loading is an allowance for the effect of wind blowing against the structure. This loading is computed on the basis of a given number of pounds per square foot, dependent on wind velocity, acting against the exposed vertical surface of the bridge.

- D. **Longitudinal Forces**: This is an allowance for the effect of the forces created by traffic moving across the bridge. These forces act longitudinally, i.e., parallel to the center line of bridge, and are generally considered to be equivalent to five percent of the live load value.

- E. **Thermal Forces**: This is a stress created in the structure due to the variation in temperature.

Although there are load factors other than those mentioned above, the foregoing loadings can be considered the primary factors influencing the design of a typical highway structure.

The final decision as to the loads and/or combinations of loads applied to a particular structure is, of course, the responsibility of the designing engineer and should only be made after a careful and complete structural analysis.

4.130 Deck Elements

4.131 Wearing Course: The wearing course provides the riding surface for traffic and is placed on top of the structural slab. There are also wearing courses poured integral with the structural slab. When this technique is used it is generally referred to as a monolithic deck.

Wearing courses can be either asphalt concrete or cement concrete and are not considered to provide load carrying capacity.

4.132 Structural Deck: The structural deck or slab provides the load carrying capacity of the deck system.

Typical structural deck systems are:

- A. Reinforced concrete
- B. Steel plates (Orthotropic decks) with thin wearing course overlay.
- C. Steel grid (open or concrete filled)
- D. Wood planking.
- E. Prestressed concrete beams

4.133 Sidewalks: Sidewalks are provided on structures where pedestrian traffic counts warrant their use. Otherwise, safety walks are generally recommended.

Typical sidewalks are:

- A. Reinforced concrete
- B. Steel plate
- C. Wood planking

4.134 Curbs: Curbs are provided in conjunction with sidewalks and safety walks. Curbs can be constructed of reinforced concrete, pre-cut granite, heavy timber, or steel plate.

4.135 Railings: Railings are placed along the extreme edges of the deck system and provide protection for traffic and pedestrians. There are a wide variety of railing materials and configurations.

Some of the more common are:

- A. Metal multiple rail systems
- B. Box Beam
- C. W-Beam
- D. Reinforcec concrete.

4.140 Superstructures

4.141 Trusses: The truss is one form of structural system which, because of its characteristics, provides high load carrying capacities and can be used to span greater lengths than rolled beams and girders. The truss functions basically in the same manner as a rolled beam or girder in resisting loads. The top and bottom chords acting as the flanges of the beam and the diagonal members acting as the web.

Typical types of truss systems that are used for highway structures are illustrated as follows: (These truss types may be used as "Thru Type" or "Deck Type".

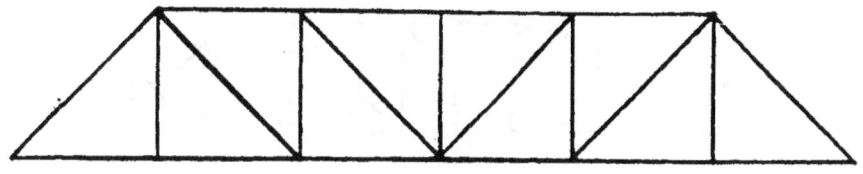
PRATT TRUSS

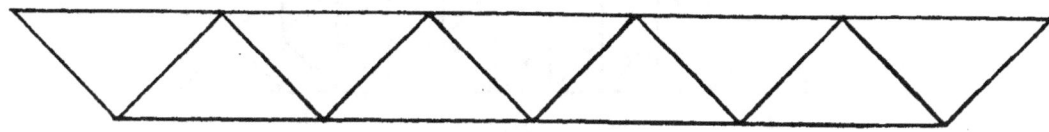
WARREN TRUSS
(DECK TYPE)

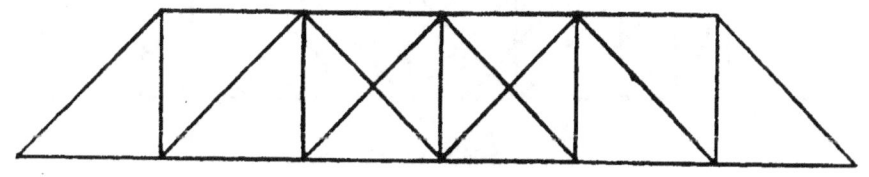
HOWE TRUSS

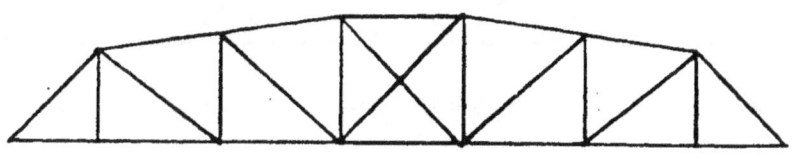
PARKER TRUSS

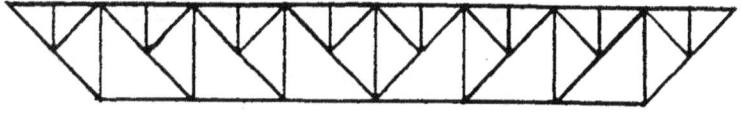
BALTIMORE TRUSS
(DECK TYPE)

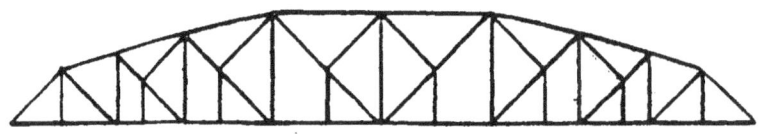

PETTIT TRUSS

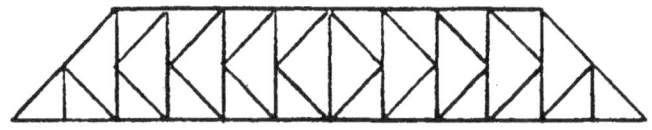

K - TRUSS

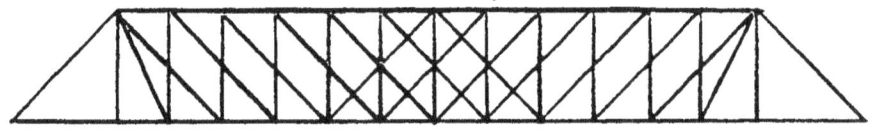

WHIPPLE TRUSS

DOUBLE TRIANGULAR TRUSS

LATTICE TRUSS

GENERAL BRIDGE TYPES

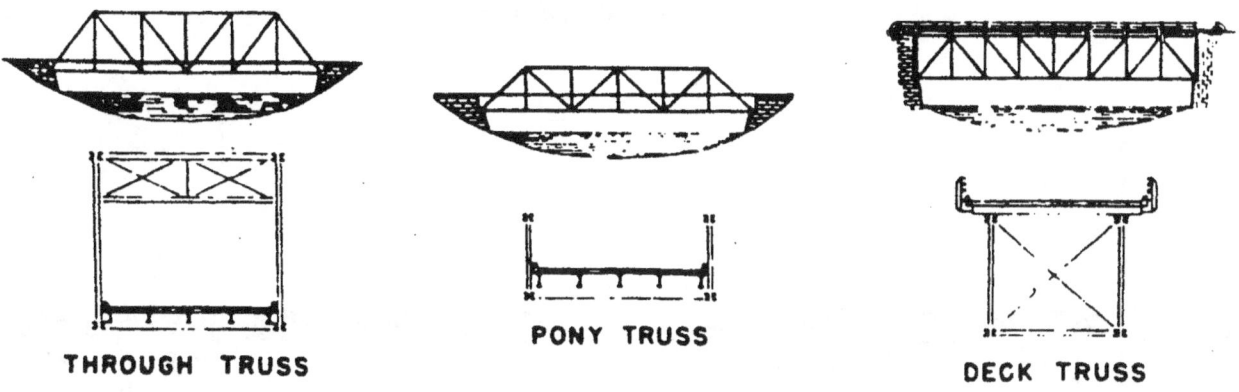

THROUGH TRUSS   PONY TRUSS   DECK TRUSS

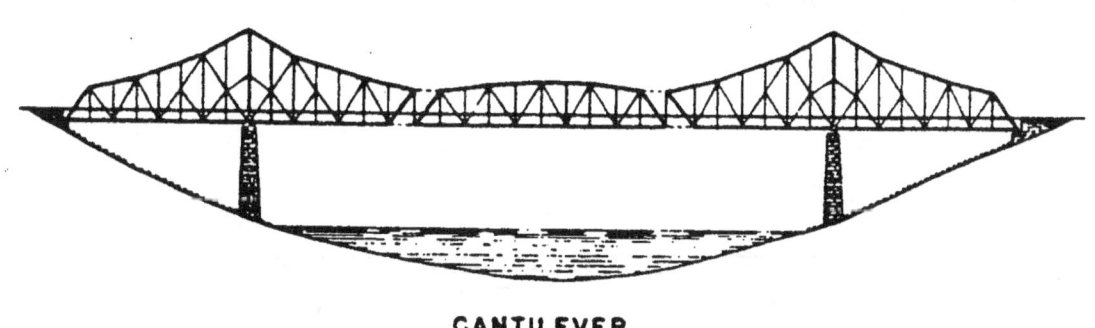

CANTILEVER

THROUGH GIRDER   DECK GIRDER   I BEAM

SUSPENSION

CONTINUOUS GIRDER

SPANDREL-FILLED ARCH

OPEN SPANDREL ARCH

RIGID FRAME - CONCRETE

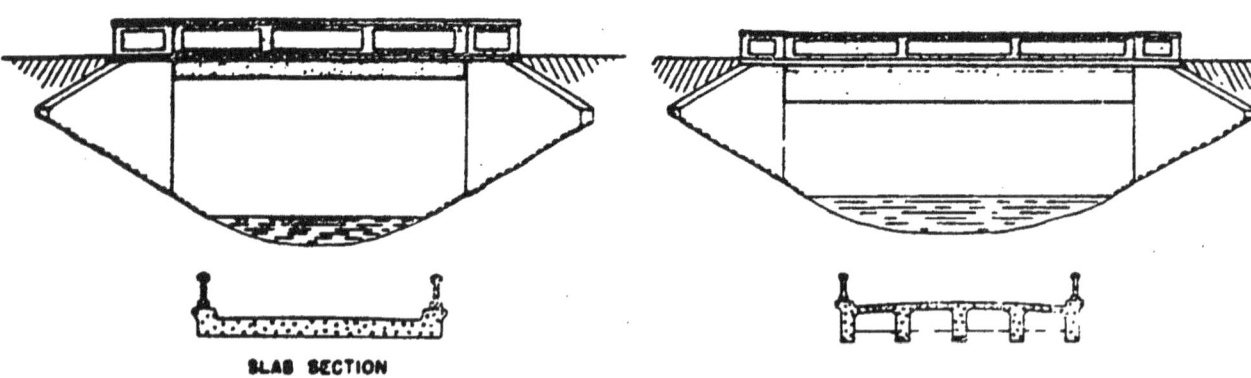
CONCRETE SLAB (PLAIN)

SLAB SECTION

CONCRETE DECK GIRDER

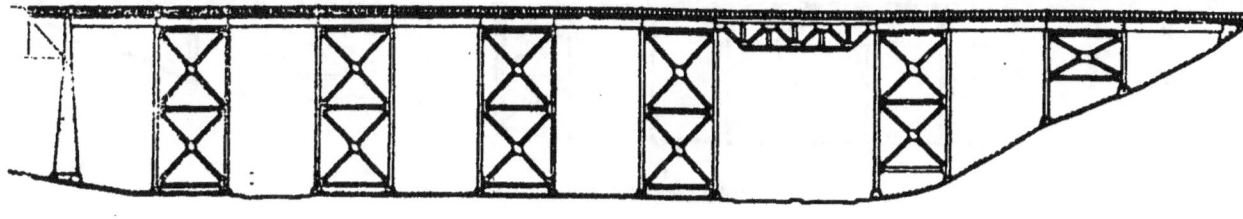

STEEL VIADUCT

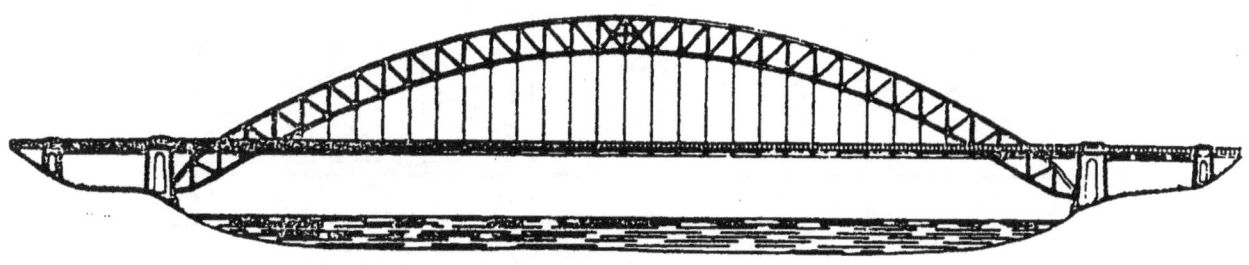

THROUGH-ARCH TRUSS

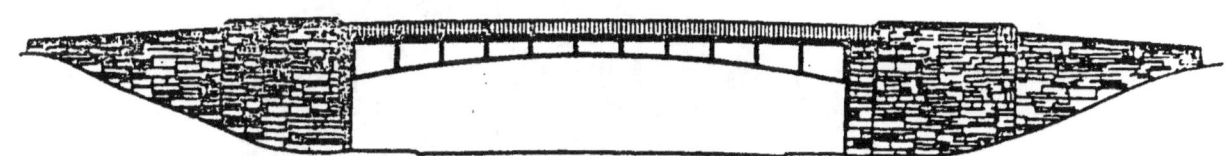

RIGID FRAME - STEEL

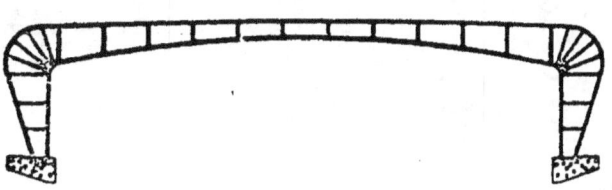

RIGID FRAME
(STEEL GIRDER ELEMENT)

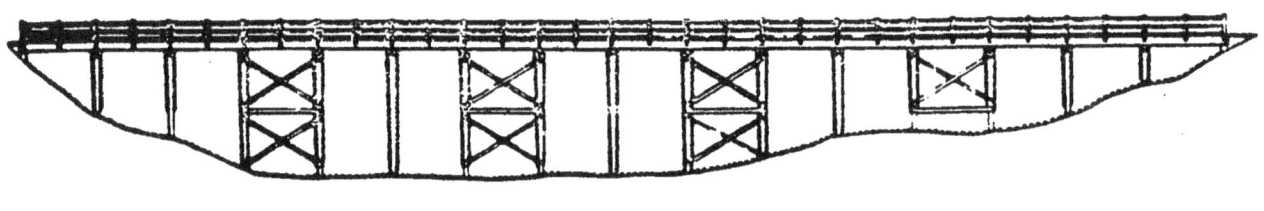

TIMBER TRESTLE

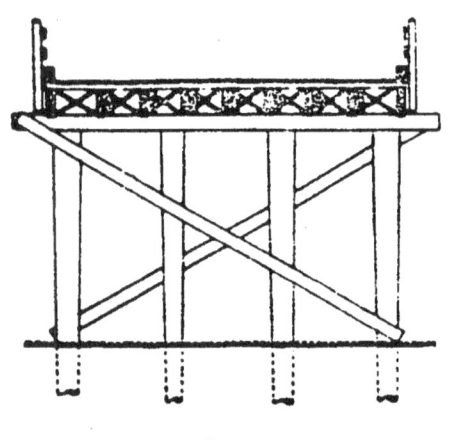

PILE BENT

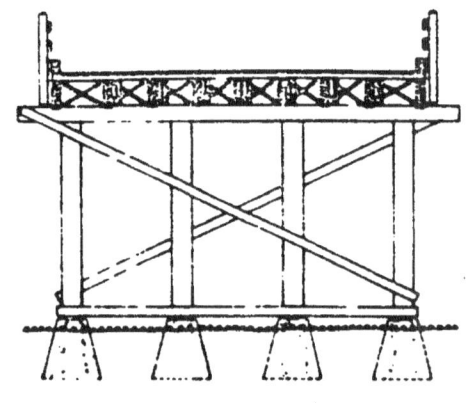

FRAME BENT

COVERED BRIDGE

The component parts of a typical truss system are illustrated and defined below with a brief statement regarding their purpose and importance as regards the load carrying capacity of the structural system.

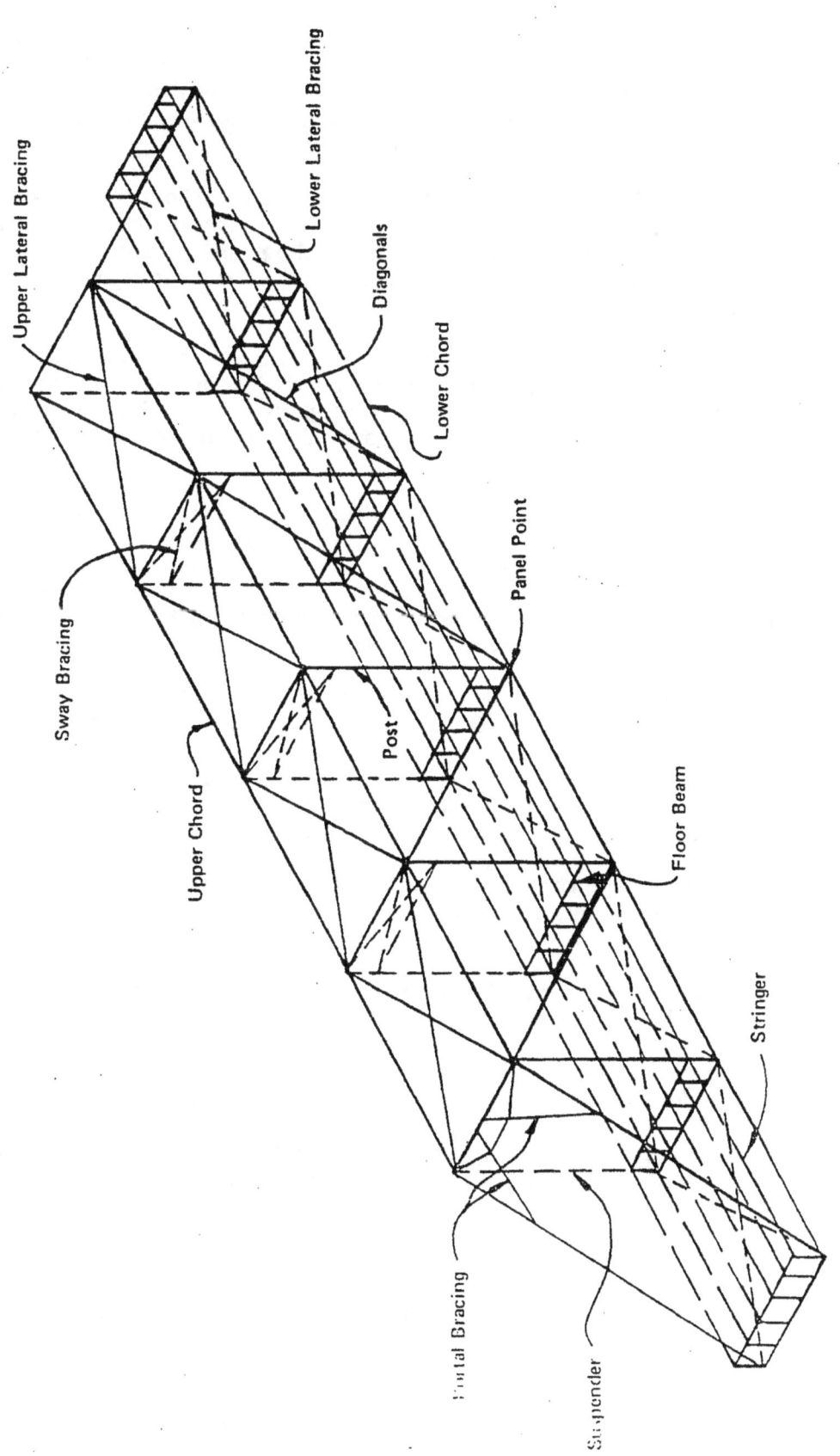

A. **Upper Chord:** The upper chord of a truss is the uppermost structural member in the system. This member will always be in compression for simple span structures and should be considered a primary structural member. Failure of this member is an extremely critical situation and will render the truss unsound as a load carrying system.

B. **Lower Chord:** The lower chord of a truss is the lower-most structural member in the system. This member will always be in tension for simple span structures and should be considered a primary structural member. Failure of this member is an extremely critical situation and will render the truss unsound as a load carrying system.

C. **Diagonals:** The diagonal members span between top and bottom panel points and will either resist tension or compression depending on their location in the truss configuration. The diagonals are also primary structural members and their failure is extremely critical and will render the truss unsound as a load carrying system.

D. **Vertical Posts:** Vertical posts will resist either tension or compression stresses depending on whether the deck system is located at the level of the bottom chord or top chord respectively. Vertical posts are also primary structural members and their failure is critical and will render the truss unsound as a load carrying system.

Failure of any of these members (A thru D) presents an extremely critical situation and will render the truss unsound as a load carrying system.

Items F through L below can be considered secondary structural members and although their failure should receive immediate attention an individual member, failure will not render the structure unsound.

F. **Portal Bracing:** The portal bracing is found overhead at the ends of a thru truss and provides lateral stability and shear transfer between trusses.

G. **Sway Bracing:** Sway bracings are secondary structural members spanning between the trusses and provide lateral stability and shear transfer between trusses.

H. **Upper Lateral Bracing:** The upper lateral bracing lies in the plane of the top chord and provides lateral stability between the two trusses and resistance to wind stress.

I. **Lower Lateral Bracing:** The lower lateral bracing lies in the plane of the lower chord and provides lateral stability and resistance to wind stresses.

J. **Floor Beam:** The floor beam spans between trusses at the panel points and provides main support for the floor stringers and deck system.

K. **Floor Stringers:** The floor stringers span between floor beams and provide the primary support for the deck system. The deck loading is transmitted to the stringers and through the stringers to the floor beams and to the truss.

L. **Gusset Plates:** These plates are used for connecting the structural members of a truss and provide a means of transmitting stress between members.

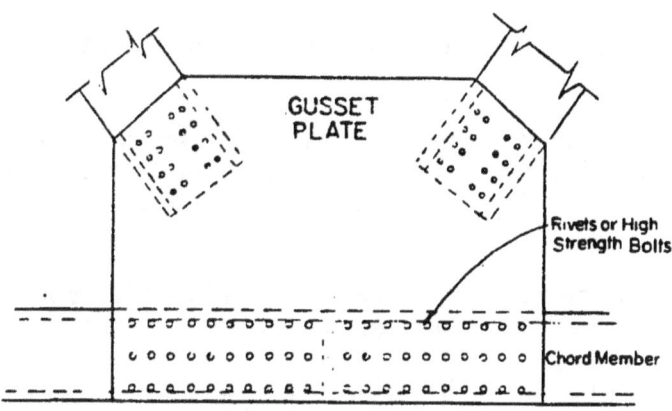

TYPICAL GUSSET PLATE CONNECTION

4.142 Plate (built up) girders: This type of structural member is used for intermediate span lengths not requiring the depth provided by a truss and yet requiring greater depth than available from a rolled beam. The basic elements of a plate girder are a web to which flanges are riveted or welded at the top and bottom edges. The most common forms of cross section are shown below:

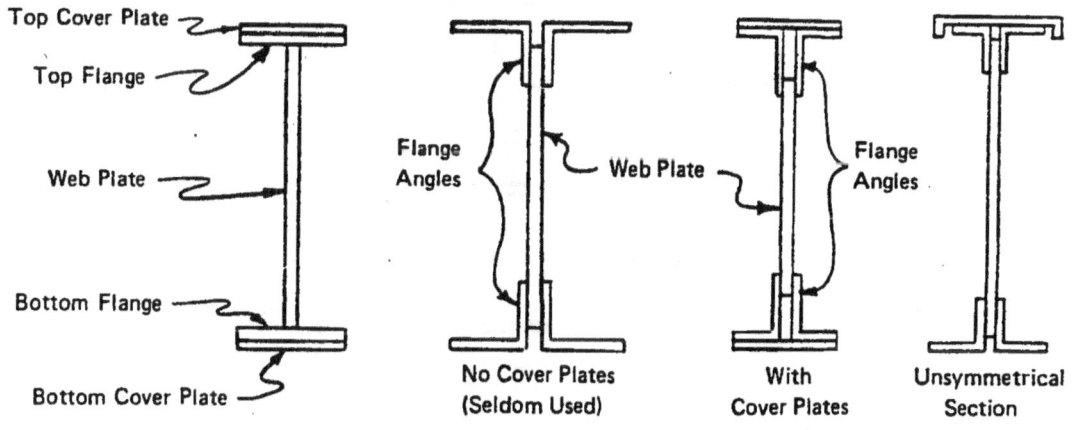

The component parts of a typical plate girder are illustrated below:

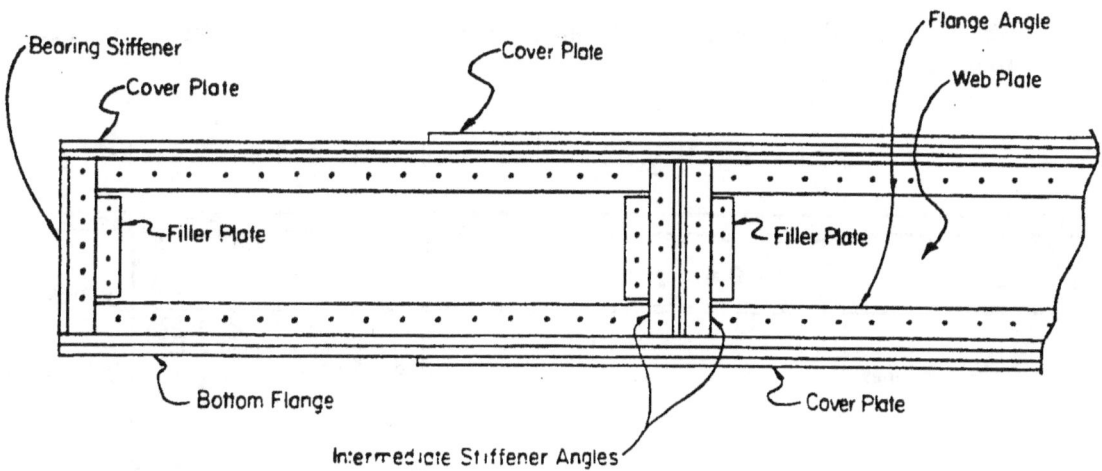

The top half of the plate girder will be in compression and the bottom half will be in tension for simple span structures.

Bearing Stiffeners: These are either plates or angles placed vertically at the ends of the girder and attached to the web. Their primary function is to transmit the shearing stresses in the web plate to the end bearing, and by so doing prevent web crippling.

Intermediate Stiffeners: Intermediate stiffeners with or without fillers are used at points of concentrated loads or for deep girders and prevent web crippling.

Cover Plates: Cover plates are welded or riveted to the top and/or bottom flanges of the girder to increase the load carrying capacity.

Flange Angles: Flange angles are used for riveted plate girders and provide a means of connecting the web and flange plates.

4.143 **Rolled Beams**: The rolled beam is used for short spans. The beam comes from the rolling mill as an integral unit composed of two flanges and a web. The more common types of rolled beam shapes are:

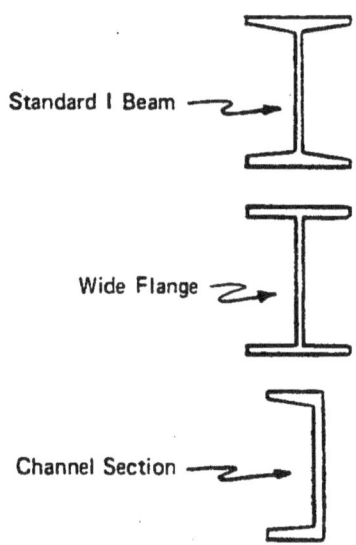

The following illustrates a typical longitudinal and transverse section for a rolled beam span:

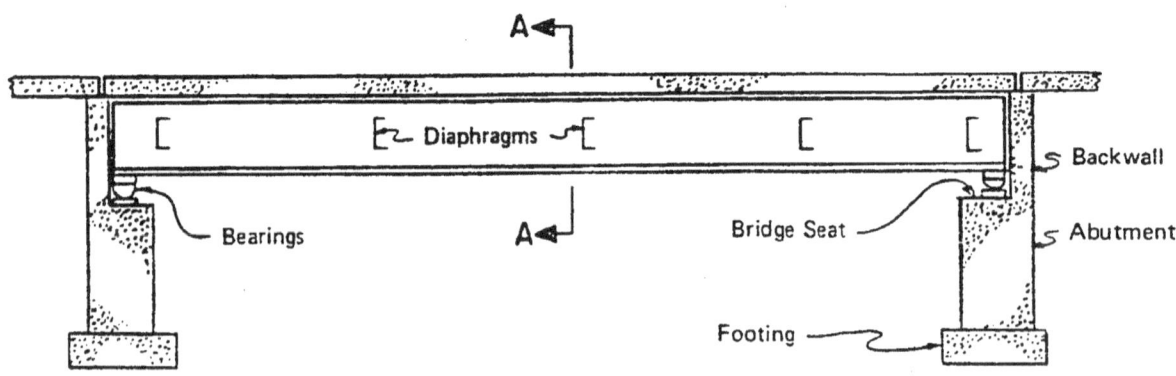

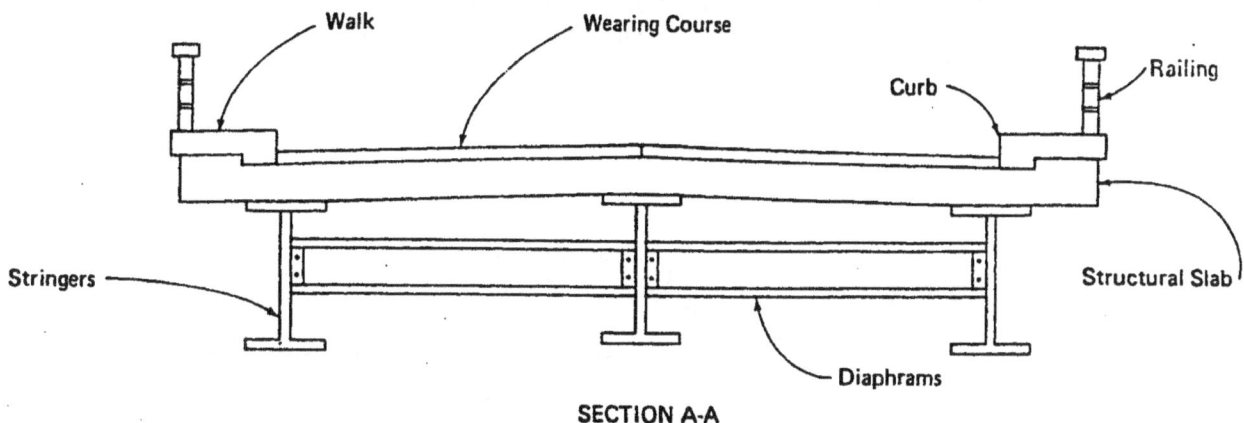

SECTION A-A

4.144 Continuous Spans: When a truss, plate girder, or rolled beam is continuous over multiple supports it is designated as a continuous span. The primary benefits from this type of construction are the reduction in depth of truss, plate girder or beam and the reduction in the number of deck joints.

Examples of continuous structures follow:

CONTINUOUS TRUSS

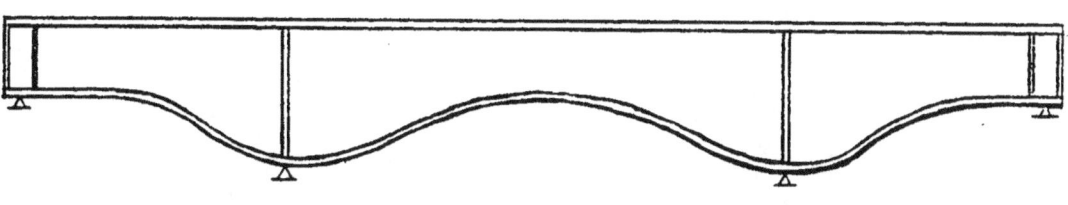

CONTINUOUS GIRDER

CONTINUOUS ROLLED BEAM

4.145 Cantilever Suspended Span: This type of design provides some of the benefits of continuous spans. The main difference being that a hinge is introduced in the beam to facilitate design and construction.

A typical suspended span design is illustrated below:

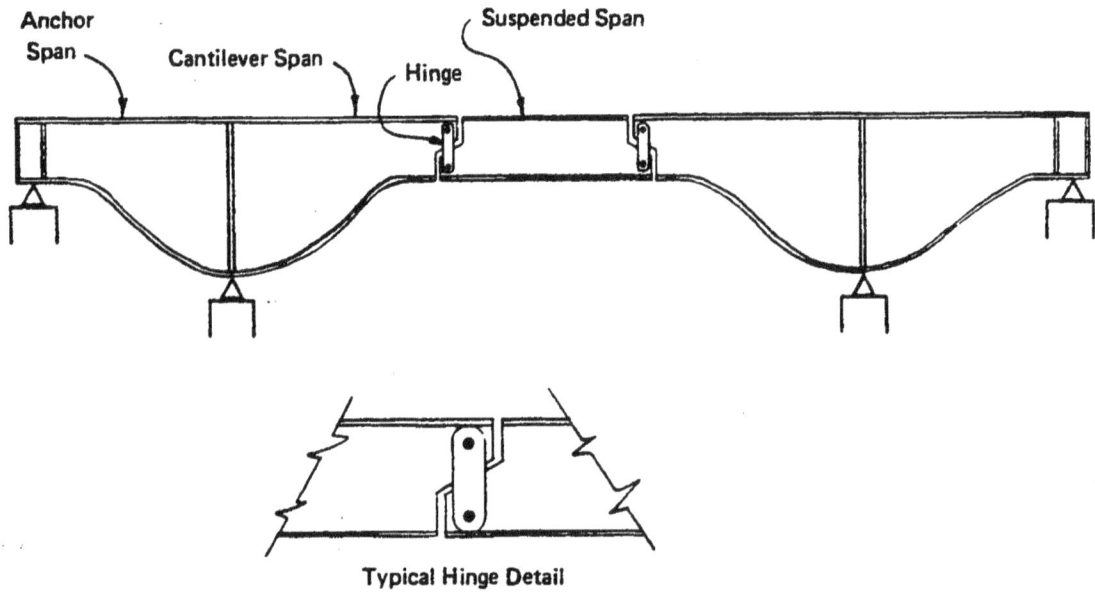

Typical Hinge Detail

CANTILEVER SUSPENDED SPAN

4.146 Composite Beams: Composite Structural Members - as the name implies - are composed of two or more construction materials.

A composite beam has shear connectors welded to the top flange and when the slab is poured on the beam the slab and beam work as a unit to resist loads. Three generally used types of shear connectors are:

STUD　　　　　　　　　　　　　　CHANNEL

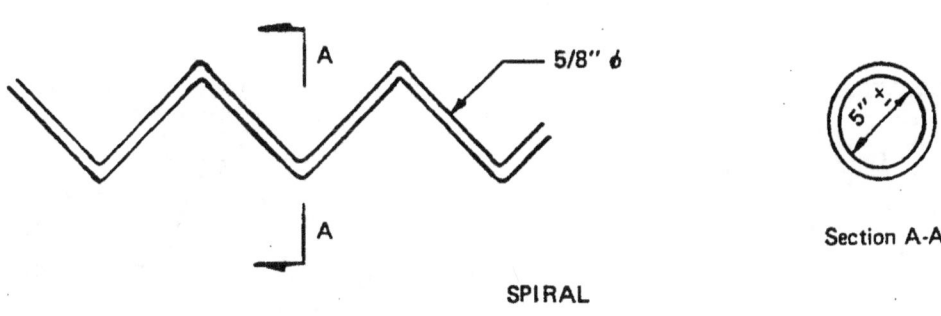

SPIRAL

Section A-A

A typical composite section is illustrated below:

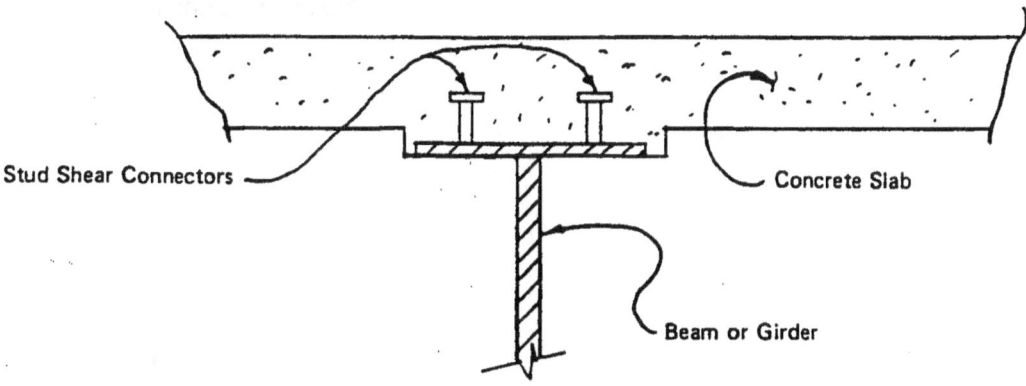

4.150 Bearings: Bearings transmit the full load of the superstructure to the substructure. They also provide for longitudinal movement due to expansion and contraction and rotational movement due to deflection. The bridge bearings are vitally important for the load carrying capacity of the structure and if not kept in good working order can induce stresses in the structure that will shorten the useable life of the bridge.

Some typical bridge bearings are shown on the following pages:

18

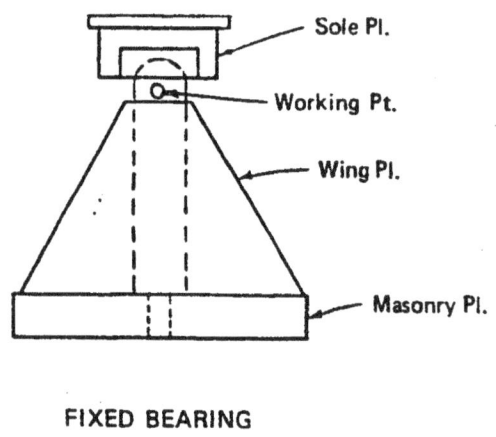

FIXED BEARING

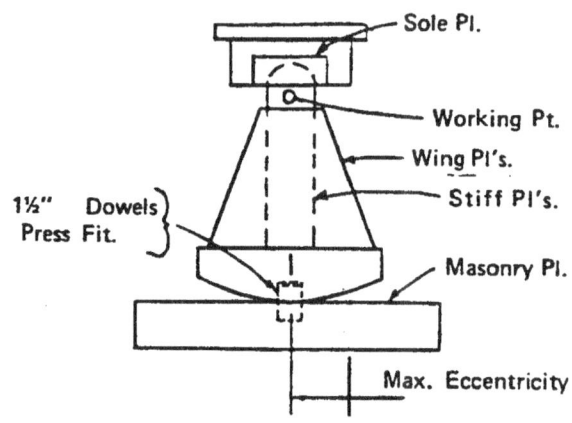

EXPANSION BEARING

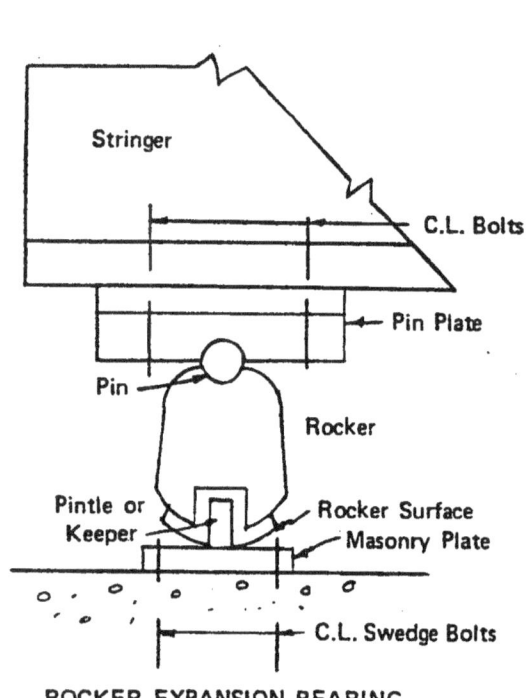

ROCKER EXPANSION BEARING
(Large Spans)

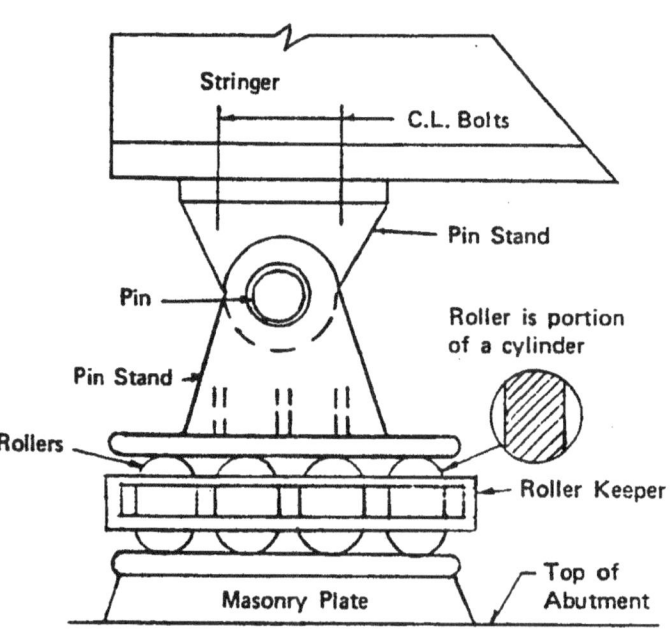

ROLLER EXPANSION BEARING

132

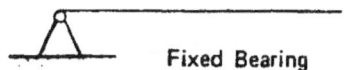 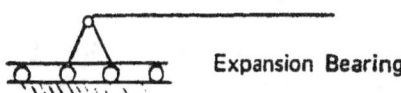

BEARING NOMENCLATURE

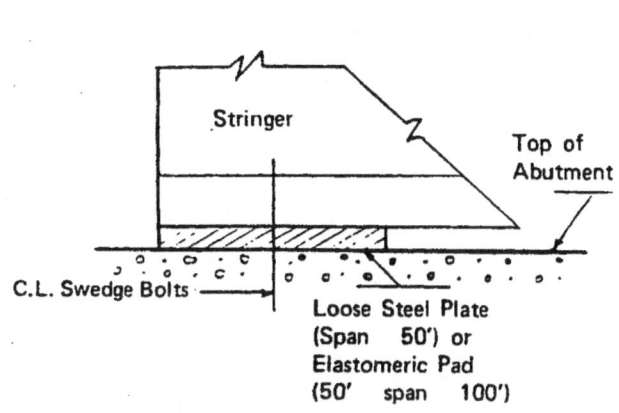

SIMPLE EXPANSION BEARING

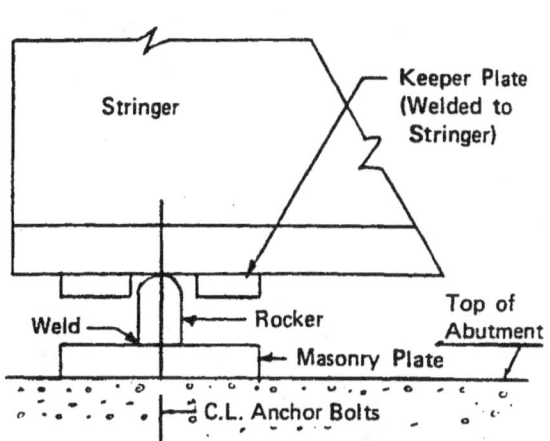

OR

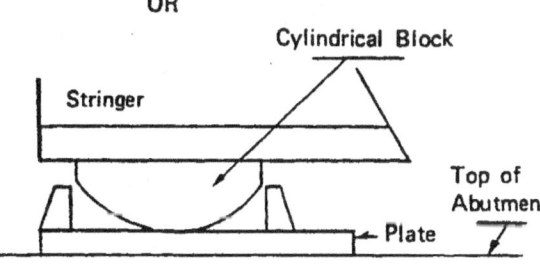

SIMPLE FIXED BEARING

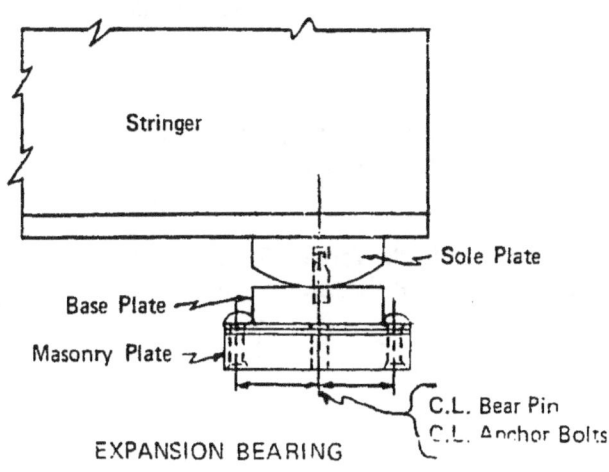

SLIDING EXPANSION BEARING

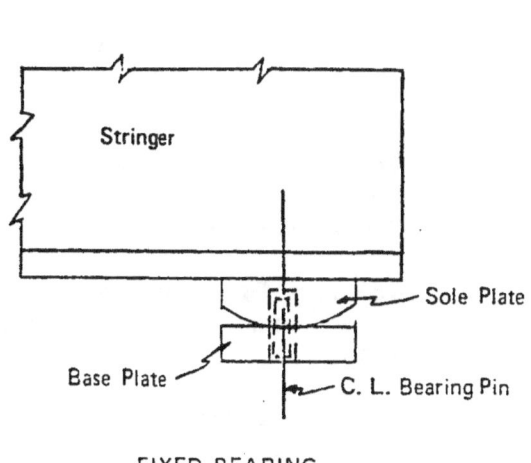

EXPANSION BEARING   **FIXED BEARING**

4.160 Substructures

4.161 Abutments: The bridge abutment is constructed at each end of the structure and transmits the load of the superstructure to the foundation material. Abutments are generally of two types:

- A. Stub Abutments which are generally less than 6 feet in height.
- B. High Wall Abutments which are greater than 6 feet in height.

A typical bridge abutment and related terminoligy is provided below:

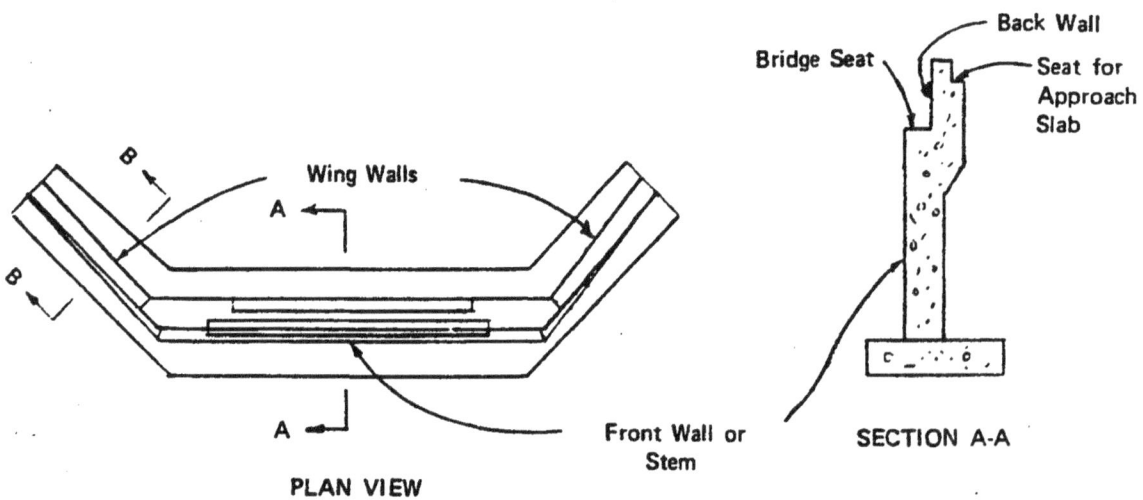

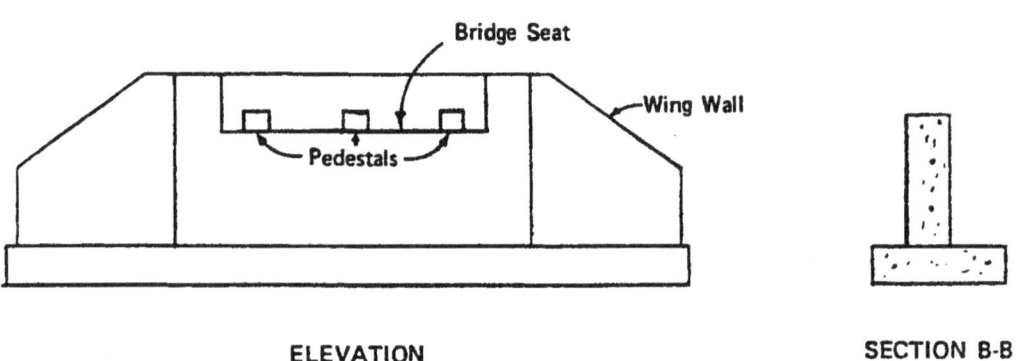

4.162 Piers: Bridge Piers similar to Abutments transmit the load of the superstructure to the foundation material and provide intermediate supports between abutments.

4.163 Piles: Piles are used to transmit the bridge loadings to the foundation material when soil conditions are not suitable for receiving the load in bearing. Typical pile types are:

- A. Steel H Piles
- B. Wood
- C. Concrete cast in place piles
- D. Concrete filled pipe piles.

4.170 Miscellaneous

4.171 Clearances: Clearances refer to the minimum distances that are provided by the bridge as regards the passage of traffic. Typical clearance measurements are shown below:

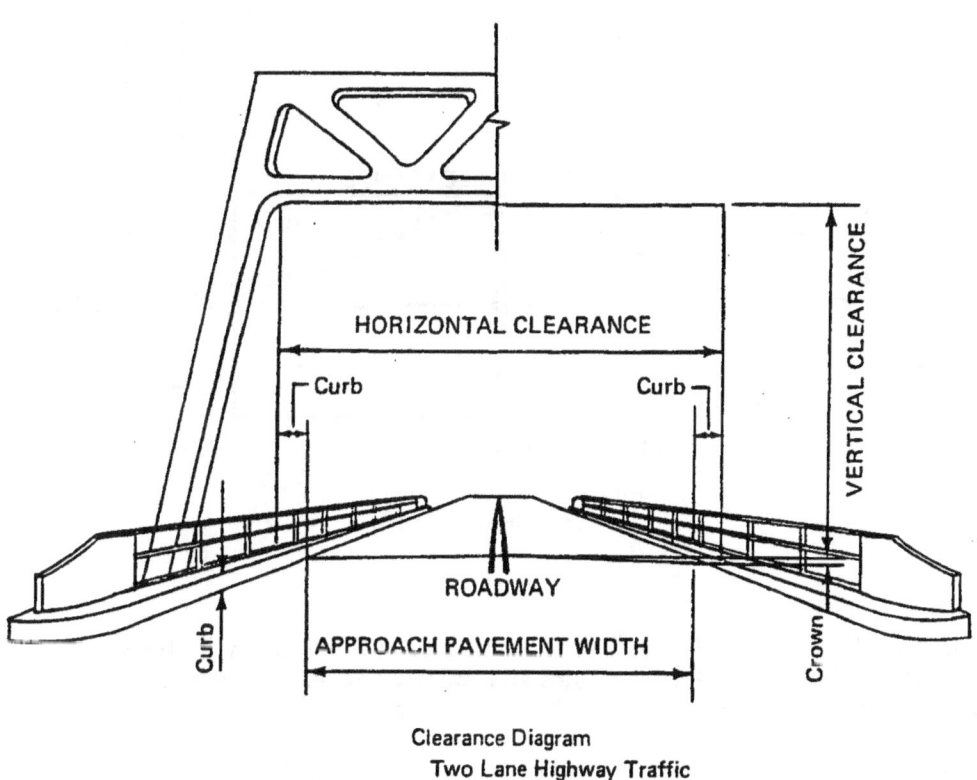

Clearance Diagram
Two Lane Highway Traffic

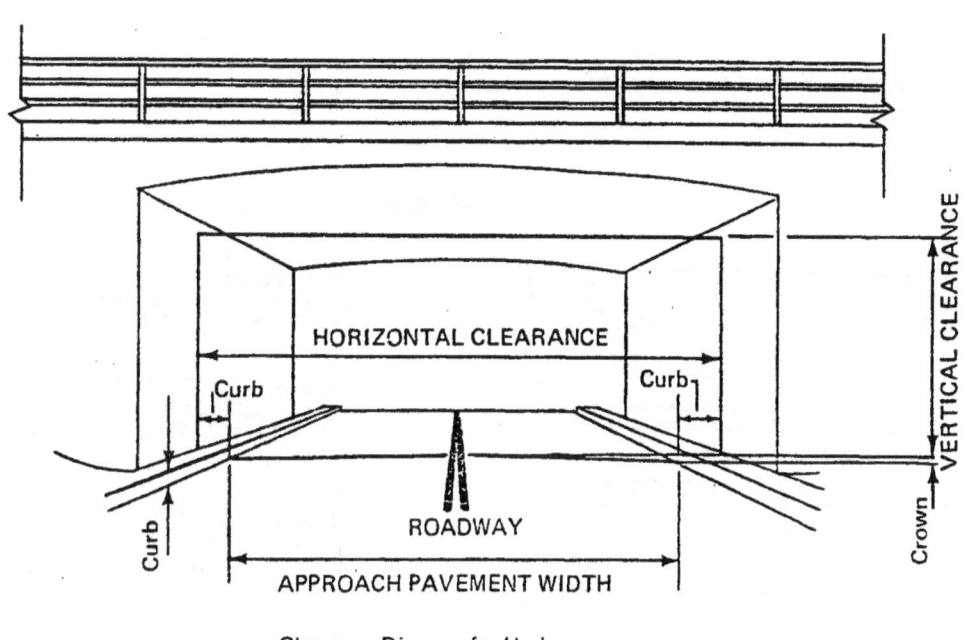

Clearance Diagram for Underpasses
Two Lane Highway Traffic

22

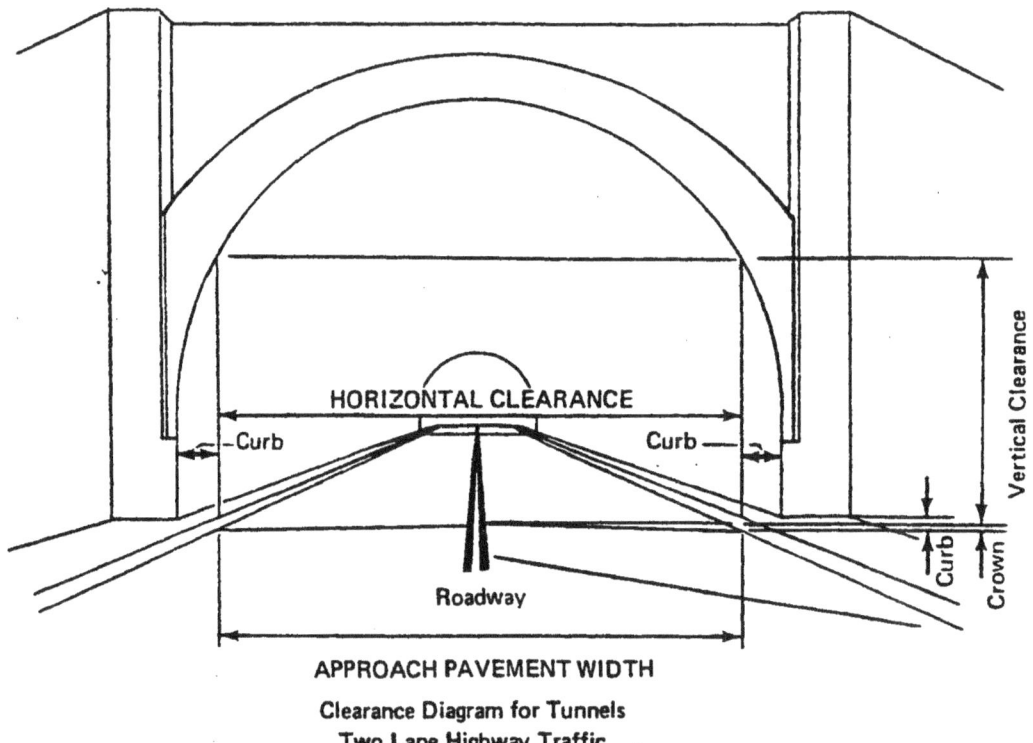

Clearance Diagram for Tunnels
Two Lane Highway Traffic

4.172 Camber: This is an initial deflection built into a beam girder or truss to eliminate unsightly geometrical effects, dips and water traps on the bridge surface and allow for vertical curves or cross slopes in the road section.

4.173 Reinforcement for Concrete: Concrete cannot resist tension stresses and therefore is reinforced with steel.

Two types illustrated on the next page, are generally used for concrete reinforcement.

   A. Deformed Bars - for main reinforcement.

DEFORMED BARS

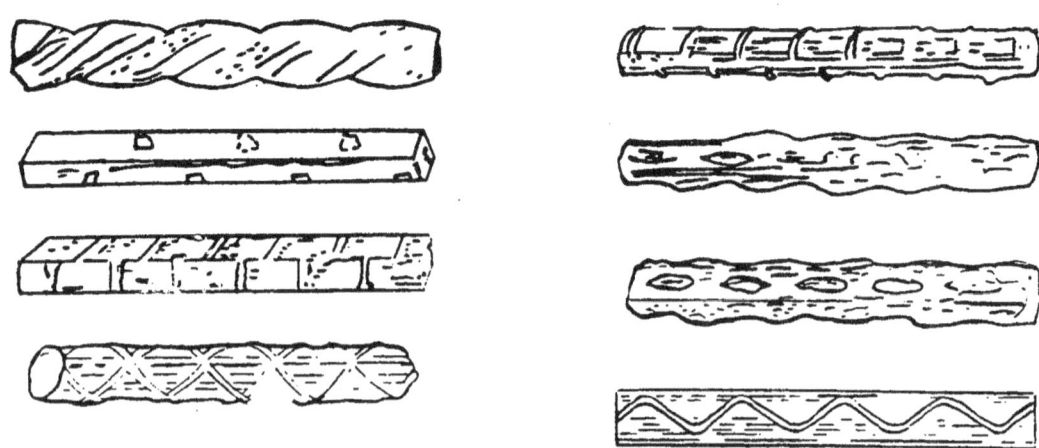

136

B. Wire mesh for low stress areas, for example, temperature stresses.

WIRE MESH

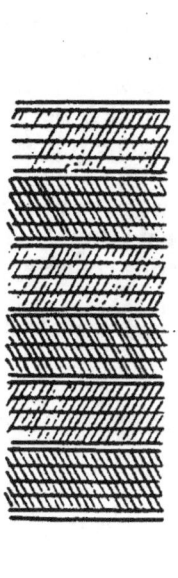
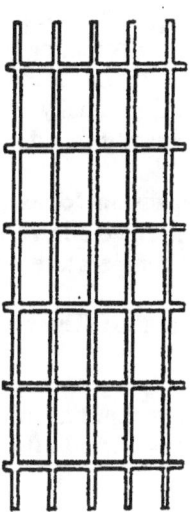
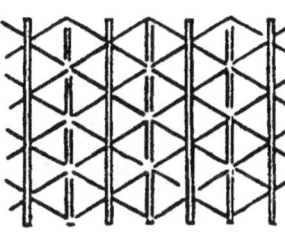

4.174 Welds: Welding is a method of joining two metals together by melting metal at the joints and fusing it with an additional metal from a welding rod. When cool, weld metal and base metal form a continuous and almost homogeneous joint. Two typical welds are shown below:

SINGLE V-BUTT WELD

FILLET WELD

4.175 High Strength Bolts: These bolts are called high strength because of their high strength in tension. Within the last 15 years, the A325 high-strength bolt has become the prime field fastener of structural steel. The specifications call for a heavy hexagon structural bolt, a heavy semifinished hexagon nut and either one or two washers. Bevel washers may be required.

4.176 Fatigue: This term applies to the phenomenon whereby a structural member, subjected to alternating tension and compression stresses due to moving loads on the bridge, has its load carrying capacity decreased. A crack, very often minute, will develop and gradually enlarge on the member, thereby further decreasing its load carrying capacity to a dangerous point at which a sudden failure is possible.

4.177 Expansion Joints: These are joints placed in the bridge wearing course and in the deck itself to allow for longitudinal movement by the structural members due to changes in temperature. They prevent cracking in the wearing course and deck.

4.178 Scuppers: These are located along the curb line and provide drainage from the deck.

4.179 Down Spouts: When it is not desirable to allow water from the scuppers to fall free, it is carried off by the use of pipes.

4.200 BRIDGE INSPECTION PROGRAM

4.210 General: Two published documents are available in the Department and they are to be followed except where specifically noted. They are:

I. Manual for Maintenance Inspection of Bridges published by American Association of State Highway and Transportation Officials (prepared by the Highway subcommittee on Bridges and Structures).

II. NYSDOT Bridge Inspection Manual published by NYSDOT Structures Design and Construction Division as part of the Bridge Inventory and Inspection System.

4.211 Objective: Only through inspection, investigation and careful appraisal of each component member comprising a structure can the true condition of a bridge become known. A systematic inspection is necessary for the following reasons:

1. To insure the discovery of any critical weakness due to deterioration, corrosion, material defects, and damage caused by man or nature.

2. To appraise the degree of deterioration, corrosion, material defects, and damage so that appropriate action can be taken to safeguard the traveling public and to prevent additional deterioration of the structure.

3. To provide a basis for the programming of repair work and for the estimating of time and materials to complete the repairs.

4. To provide a periodic inspection record showing the bridge condition at the time of each inspection, thus enabling detection of progressive changes.

5. To establish service records from which the relative value of different types of details, both design and construction, can be determined.

4.212 Inventory and Inspection System: The Department has a formal computerized data system for its Structures Inventory and Inspection as described in Reference I. For convenience in administering the system, NYSDOT has classified the activities into three main categories. These are:

1. Inventory
2. Inspection
3. Load Rating

The computer data file includes all three parts but provides for separate input for each. These three parts are administered separately.

4.213 Administration of System: The overall management of the Structures Inventory and Inspection System is by Structures Design and Construction Division. This includes applications management of the data system and the development and upkeep of standards for the entire system. They publish documentation for all parts of the system and provide editing and files management for the data.

4.214 System Data Collection: Primary responsibility for system data collection is Structures Design and Construction Division. This includes data for locality, municipality and privately owned as well as State owned structures. They also supervise all significant consulting services for system data.

Within this context, Highway Maintenance Division provides the coordination and field survey for the inspection portion of those structures which are direct state inspection responsibility.

4.220 Frequency of Inspection: Inspections for state bridges are scheduled on a calendar year basis. Reference I requires that regular inspections be performed at an interval not to exceed two years. As implementation of this requirement every bridge shall be scheduled for inspection such that inspection is not omitted from more than one calendar year's inspections before a subsequent inspection. All those bridges having a general recommendation (See Reference II) of 3 or less shall be inspected at some time during each calendar year. In order to avoid inordinately long internals between inspections, an attempt should be made to schedule successive inspections (for either one or two year cycle category) at approximately the same time of year. Otherwise it is possible to have nearly an additional year elapse between inspections. This is not desirable.

4.230 Requirements for Inspections: Details of the requirements are set forth in References I and II. Reference I states the overall requirements including qualifications of personnel and general methods of inspection. It also defines requirements for load rating which are not applicable to regular inspections.

Reference II gives the specific rules and standards for actually doing the inspections. This includes the coding system and an explanation of the input forms to be used.

4.240 Inspection Equipment.

4.241 General Inspection Equipment: Certain equipment is required for a complete inspection of a structure. The following equipment should be made available to each inspection team during an annual bridge inspection:

    1 - long level rod
    1 - mason's hammer
    1 - chipping hammer
    1 - pair binoculars (7 x 35 or 7 x 50)
    1 - 35 mm. camera with flash (automatic)
    1 - 100' cloth tape
    1 - 50' metal tape
    1 - 12' metal pocket tape
    1 - 6' ruler
    1 - wire brush
    1 - scraper
    1 - plumb bob
    1 - line level
    1 - small pick
    1 - small square shovel
    crayons for marking

In addition to the above list, the inspector shall have other tools or instruments he requires to appraise the condition of the structure.

Each member of the inspection team shall be equipped with the following personnel safety equipment:

    1 - hard hat (to be worn)
    1 - safety belt (to be worn)
    1 - life line - 50' long

4.242 Special Equipment: All special equipment, within the Department, should be made available to the inspection team, as required, so that access to all structural elements may be attained. A partial list would include the following:

    A - Vehicles equipped with hydralic lifts
    B - Boats or Barges
    C - Ladders
    D - Minor rigging or scaffolding

The special equipment not only insures a proper close inspection but also is required for the safety of personnel conducting the inspection.

NOTES

4.300 ROUTINE & PREVENTIVE MAINTENANCE

4.310 Description: This type of maintenance may be the most important of all. By performing certain routine tasks on a regularly scheduled basis, much of the corrective type of maintenance and repair can be avoided. The work does not require the hiring of higly skilled craftsmen or the purchase of high priced equipment.

Although routine and preventive maintenance are practically the same it is felt that the following definitions should apply:

1. Routine Maintenance - Involves labor and equipment only
2. Preventive Maintenance - Involves labor, equipment and materials

4.320 Types of Work

4.321 Routine:

A. Cleaning - In general remove from the following bridge elements accumulated salt, salt laden sand, and all other dirt and debris.
   1. Deck elements, gutters, sidewalks, joints, etc.
   2. Scuppers, troughs, downspouts
   3. Pier caps, abutments, and pedestals
   4. Structural elements especially bottom cord members of trusses and members under open joints.
B. Maintain Slope Paving
   1. Clean
   2. Repair minor settlements if any

4.322 Preventive

A. Apply linseed oil and mineral spirits to non-air entrained concrete
   1. two coats initially
   2. additional coat every other year
B. Touch-up Painting
C. Clean and fill cracks and joints
D. Clean and lubricate bearings, hangers, etc.
E. Install pressure relief joints in the concrete pavement just beyond the limits of the reinforced concrete approach slabs.
F. Report major deterioration to the Bridge Maintenance Engineer.

4.330 Work Procedures

4.331 Routine Work Procedures: All the various routine cleaning tasks are basically similar. High pressure water, high pressure air and long handled scraping and breaking tools will help to speed the completion of these tasks.

Sewer cleaning snakes will also be useful in loosening materials caked in troughs and downspouts.

Routine maintenance of slope paving must be limited to cleaning; and repair of minor failures such as edge settlement in a small area, cracking or opening of joints in a small area. If the extent of the work is such that it cannot be completed by the crew in one half day, it should be avoided. In this case, the Foreman of Routine Maintenance Crew should inform the Bridge Maintenance Engineer of the condition requiring extensive repair.

Preventive Work Procedures:

A. Boiled Linseed Oil and Mineral Spirits: The two components should be mixed on a 50%-50% basis. The mixture can best be applied to most elements of a bridge by using a garden type pneumatic sprayer which is slung from the shoulder.

   Uncoated concrete at least 30 days old should be given two coats of the mixture in the first year of application. The second coat must not be applied until the first has completely dried. Thereafter, the concrete should be given one coat of the mixture every other year.

   Boiled linseed oil and mineral spirits can be usefully applied to all the exposed concrete of a structure except pavement with an unbroomed finish.

B. Touch-up Painting: This covers the painting of areas of rust of scaled paint. Loose, scaling paint should be removed from the locations and areas involved. The areas should then be thoroughly wire-brushed and primed followed by two coats of paint.

C. Clean and Fill Cracks and Joints: This operation is the same as filling highway cracks and joints by hand pouring (see Section 1.360). It is most important to blow all cracks and joints clean with compressed air immediately before filling.

D. Clean and Lubricate Bearings, Hangers, etc.: All of these structural elements of a bridge must be kept free of rust, scale, dirt and debris to ensure proper operation during periods of expansion and contraction. Once cleaned, all surfaces requiring it should be lubricated with the proper lubricant.

E. Install pressure relief joints in the highway pavement adjacent to the reinforced concrete approach slab. This is accomplished by cutting out a strip, of appropriate width, from the highway slab. This should be done using a concrete saw to provide a clean, straight edge. The concrete should be removed with a pavement breaker and jack hammer or other appropriate equipment. The strip should then be filled with asphalt, preferably of the grade and character of the type used in the top course in paving.

CHANNEL MAINTENANCE

Slope: The physical condition of structures carrying highways over streams is largely dependent on the flow conditions in the channel, its grade and horizontal alignment. Scour, undermining, and subsequent structural damage may result from poor channel conditions. Routine inspection and maintenance should be aimed at preventing occurrence of these detrimental situations. Corrective measures must be taken wherever the conditions exist. Necessary action should be taken to restore satisfactory channel flow conditions.

Any work done by maintenance forces should not extend beyond our right of way or permanent easement line unless prior approval from the property owner is obtained.

Removal of Debris and Siltation: Accumulation of debris and siltation results from floods, particularly where alignment is irregular and the stream bed consists of erodible material.

Objective: To restore and stabilize the original alignment and cross section of the channel and remove all obstructions caught by piers, trees and underwater vegetation.

4.422 Standard: Channels should be cleaned at least once a year, preferably in the spring and after floods. Debris racks should be cleaned after a flood.

4.423 Material: No additional material is required for this operation.

4.424 Method: All depressions in the stream bed should be filled with heavy stone or gravel. Fill material may be obtained from nearby portions of the same channel, if suitable; or may be purchased from a supplier. Siltation, which occurs mainly at the inlet approach, should be removed since it reduces the hydraulic capacity of the structure. Stone and gravel accumulated in these areas may be used to fill scoured areas. Extensive and deep scour occurring at sharp turns in the stream channel will require the use of rip rap or a concrete slab to prevent recurrence of this condition and subsequent instability of abutments and piers due to undermining.

4.430 Arresting Scour at Outlets: A natural stilling basin is formed at the outlets of structures with concrete bottom slabs where flow has a high velocity.

4.431 Objective: Fill scour basin with gravel and cover with rip rap which shall be resistant to erosion and prevent undermining of the floor slab and wingwall footing.

4.432 Standard: Corrective work is deemed necessary before scour progresses 2 feet below the level of the top of the wingwall footing or bottom slab of culvert.

4.433 Materials: Rip rap should consist of stones weighing in excess of 300 lbs. and having a minimum thickness of 18".

4.434 Method: The scour basin shall be filled with suitable material, preferably gravel. Rip rap stones shall be set individually and level with the floor slab over entire fill area. A recommended measure to prevent undermining at the downstream end of the rip rap apron is the construction of a low horizontal sill (approximately 6") across the channel. This tends to produce a roller which tends to pull material against the apron preventing undermining.

4.440 Replacement of Slope Protection: Washout of slope protection generally occurs during floods and usually affects the area adjacent to the structure. Turbulence attributed to constriction of flow at inlets and divergence at outlets has sufficient energy to dislodge slope protection. Outside slopes at sharp turns in the channel are most vulnerable to washout. Spring floods, which often contain ice flow, are more apt to harm slope protection than floods at other times of the year.

4.441 Objective: Reset existing slope protection as it is undermined by rapid flow conditions or dislodged by ice flow or debris. Replace all damaged or washed out slope protection.

4.442 Standard: Inspection of slope protection should be done in the spring of the year and also following serious floods. Repair work should start when the protective device is in danger of not being able to perform its intended function or when minor damage left uncorrected would result in progressive failure.

4.443 Material: Rip rap or stone used as replacement shall conform in quality to the existing material.

4.444 Method: In case of extensive washout, the entire slope should be filled with suitable material and regraded prior to placing new slope protection. Rip rap stone should be set individually. Heavy stone slope protection may be dumped and graded.

4.450 Arresting Scour at Bridge Piers: This potentially destructive condition occurs where the axis of the pier and flow line differ in direction. Undermining of the pier and subsequent settlement may result in serious structural damage to the bridge. A poorly designed streamlining of the pier nose may also creat turbulence leading to scour. Obstructions by debris tend to disturb the flow, creating additional turbulence and aggravating scour conditions at piers.

4.451 Objective: Inspections in depth should be made on all structures susceptible to this condition. Corrective measures should be taken to eliminate scour as needed.

4.452 Standard: Channels should be cleaned a minimum of twice a year in the vicinity of bridges susceptible to this condition. In addition, this same operation should be performed following every flood. Repairs should be made, using heavy stone fill or rip rap before scour progresses to a depth dangerous to the stability of a structure (½ of the thickness of pier footing).

4.453 Method: Permanent corrective measures involve pier reconstruction and are very costly. They should be considered only in the most serious cases. The only measures that should be taken by maintenance are as follows:

1. Periodic dumping of heavy stone fill in the scour hole.
2. Driving of sheet piling to a depth where rock or sound soil conditions exist.
3. Construction of debris control devices since debris accumulation is conducive to scour.

In most cases, the above corrective measures will suffice. However, good judgment is required to resolve each situation. A recommended solution should be made by the Bridge Maintenance Engineer, but the final decision should be made in conjunction with the Resident Engineer and the Regional Highway Maintenance Engineer.

4.500 FOUNDATION & SUBSTRUCTURE MAINTENANCE

4.510 Scour Under Footings

4.511 Description: This occurs generally when there is severe channel misalignment at a structure. The misalignment may have been pre-existing or it may have resulted from circumstances connected with the particular flood flow that caused the scour. During heavy flows in the stream, the misalignment causes a very large volume of water moving at high velocity to act upon the stream bed, carrying away large quantities of material and thus lowering the elevation of the bottom of the stream. When this happens adjacent to a footing, material may possibly be carried away from beneath the footing. In the worst case, sufficient material may be removed by scour so as to cause severe loss of support and hence settlement of the pier or abutment.

4.512 Objective: To repair all incidences of scour under footings by replacing the lost material or underpining.

4.513 Repair Method:

A. Construct a temporary channel to direct the stream flow away from the scoured area and/or construct a temporary cofferdam of sandbags or sheet piling as required to divert stream flow from the scoured area. In severe cases, it may be necessary to resort to dumped rip rap to control the flow before a cofferdam can be built. Make cofferdams large enough to accommodate support cribs if necessary.

B. If measurable settlement has occurred or is progressing, it will now be essential to provide temporary support for the structural members carried on the scoured footing. This can be done by making the cofferdammed area large enough to accommodate timber or steel cribbing on which the members may be temporarily supported. Other methods may also be required depending on the circumstances; such as driving pile bents and carrying the members on heavy transverse beams supported on the pile bents. If possible, pile driving should be avoided since it could cause even greater settlement.

C. It generally will not be feasible to level the settled pier or abutment by jacking. Therefore, the next step will be to underpin the scoured footing with concrete. This must be done in all areas where the foundation soil has been scoured from beneath the footing. All loose material must be removed and the earth bottom and sides dug level and plumb. In some cases it may be necessary to do the underpinning in alternate blocks. This would be necessary where squaring and trimming of the scoured area would dangerously reduce support for the footing.

D. Construct a form which provides at least a 6" projection beyond the footing sides, and extends at least one foot above the footing bottom. In filling this form, vibrate the concrete thoroughly and make every effort to ensure that no voids occur between the bottom of the footing and the new concrete.

E. After the concrete has cured sufficiently, remove the forms and cofferdam and then proceed to realign the stream as described elsewhere in this manual. It may also be advisable to place heavy rip rap to protect the footings from future scour.

F. A final step will be required if there has been appreciable settlement of the pile or abutment. This is to jack the superstructure to its original design elevation after which shims of steel or lifts of concrete can be installed under the settled bearings to correctly position the bridge.

4.520 Piles

4.521 Description: In most cases the piles supporting a structure will not be visible once construction of the footing is completed. There are two cases, however, where the piles will be visible:

A. Where the piles extend upward above the ground or water and are cross-braced and capped to form a pier or abutment.
B. Where the earth is eroded or settled away from underneath the footing leaving the piles exposed to view for a certain, usually short, length.

4.522 Objective: Repair the incidences of pile deterioration in order to restore the load carrying capacity.

4.523 Types of Deterioration:

CASE A. In this case the most severe deterioration problem will occur in the area just above and just below the ground line or the high water line. Also, the pile bents should be checked for damaged piles, bracing, or connections due to ice, snags or vehicle damage.

CASE B. In this case the exposed areas of the piles and the areas just below the ground line (if in the dry) should be checked for deterioration.

4.524 Repair Methods:

CASE A:
1. Where there is extreme deterioration (50-75% loss of section over large and numerous areas) it will probably be best to encase the pile in concrete from approximately 2 ft. above to 2 ft. below the severely deteriorated area. This can be done by jacketing the pile with corrugated galvanized pipe and filling with concrete. The concrete should be adequately reinforced both spirally and vertically.

2. In locations of less severe deterioration (up to 50% loss of section in smaller and fewer areas) repairs can be made by plating the steel piles and other members involved.

3. The decision as to whether to plate or encase will also depend on the amount of underwater work involved. Encasement is generally more suitable for underwater work.

4. In the case of extreme deterioration in the dry or above ground it may be possible to temporarily transfer the load from the member and splice in a length of new section equal to the original.

5. In all cases the new steel plus any of the existing steel that is subject to splash, spray or other corroding action should be given a heavy protective coating of the best available material.

CASE B:
1. If, upon inspection, no serious deterioration is present in the exposed piles, then the void under the footing should be filled using select fill. The fill material should be worked back under the footing and around the pile, and it should be compacted as thoroughly as possible during placement.

    If the void which exposed the piles was caused by erosion the work above must be followed by some measures to prevent recurrence of the erosion. This might be in the form of gutters to divert water from the area; or it might require placing of rip rap or other protective material.

2. If, upon inspection, some of the exposed piles are found to be badly deteriorated, it will be necessary to repair them before filling the void, as described above.
    (a) If the piles are timber or if they are steel, but there is no room to work to effect a repair by plating, then one type of repair would be as follows:
        (1) Cut out the deteriorated portion of the piles from footing bottom to sound piling.
        (2) Pour new concrete from footing bottom to 6" below the new top of pile elevation using Class I concrete.
        (3) In topping out this new concrete, maintain a hydrostatic head in the new concrete at the interface between the fresh concrete and the old footing. Also, make every effort to eliminate voids at that interface.
        (4) If the number of deteriorated piles is large it will be necessary to phase the above type of repair so that there is sufficient support for the structure at all times.
        (5) Fill the void as described in Case B 1 above.
    (b) The piles may be repaired by plating if the deteriorated piles are steel, not too numerous, and there is sufficient working room to weld. Loss of section is this case should be less than 50%.

The webs and flanges of the piles can be strengthened by welding new steel plates extending far enough above and below the deteriorated area to develop the full load carried by the pile.

When the welding is completed, all the exposed piles should be given a heavy protective coating of a suitable material. Fill the void as described in Case B 1 above.

4.530 Footings

4.531 Description: Except in the older bridges, the footings are rarely seen since they are usually located entirely below the grade line.

The type of failures that occur when the footings are above grade and subject to the action of weather and water are the following:

a. Deterioration of the concrete resulting in the rounding off of the footing projection and spalling of the exposed faces of the footing.
b. Severe deterioration at the bullnose of a pier footing due to ice, debris and chemical laden water. These elements can also result in deterioration along the sides of a footing.
c. A footing may be cracked transversely due to uneven settlement of the pier or abutment. This will invariably be accompanied by a crack continuing up through the pier or abutment.

4.532 Objective: Repair all cases of footing deterioration to preserve the load carrying capacity.

4.533 Repair Methods

Cases (a) & (b):

1. In the case of footings in water, the water will have to be kept clear of the work area by means of diversion channels, cofferdams of sand bags or sheet piling as required, and by pumping if necessary.
2. Chip away the deteriorated concrete until sound concrete is reached. Clean away all loose material with air blast or other means.
3. If it is necessary to install reinforcing bar anchors and rods, they should be drilled and installed now.
4. Construct the form to restore the footing and dimensions as much as possible to its original shape.
5. If it is intended to use patented compounds or neat cement paste for bonding, this should be applied just prior to pouring the new concrete into the forms.
6. Mix and pour the new concrete using a 1-2-4 mix and 2½" maximum slump. Vibrate the new concrete thoroughly to ensure a dense pour and good bond.
7. After the new concrete has cured at least 3 days, remove the forms and the cofferdam and restore the stream channel to its proper course.
8. In some cases, where shotcrete is to be used extensively on other parts of the structure, the above described repairs may be affected using the shotcrete method as described in Section 4.543.

CASE (c):
Where there is a crack in the footing it is advisable to seal the crack to prevent the intrusion of silt, debris, and water (which could result in deterioration due to ice formation).

1. V-out the crack at the surface approximately 2-3 in. in width using small pneumatic chisels.
2. Thoroughly flush out and blow out the crack using high pressure air and water.
3. Secure some sort of retaining form over the vertical portion of the crack on the face of the footing.
4. Thoroughly wet the surfaces of the crack by pouring liberal quantities of water into it. Then pour the crack full with a cement and fine sand grout in a 1-2 mix which will run freely.
5. Clean out the V'd portion at the surface after the grout has partially set. Then apply bonding compound or neat cement paste as a bonding agent to the surfaces of the Vee and fill the Vee with a stiff 1-2 mortar of cement and concrete sand.

4.540 Abutments and Piers

4.541 Description: The repair problems usually encountered in the abutments and piers of a bridge are as follows:

1. Settlement or movement
2. Vertical cracking (Differential Settlement)
3. Surface deterioration
4. Deterioration at the water line
5. Deterioration of pier caps and tops of abutments

1. Settlement as used here describes settling or movement of the pier or abutment as a whole. It may be a tipping movement in any direction or the concrete mass may remain vertical and settle or move in the direction of applied pressure. The important thing to determine in correcting this type of problem is whether the pier or abutment is still moving or whether the situation has stabilized and movement has ceased.

2. Vertical cracking may result when one portion of a pier or abutment under load settles while the remaining portion does not.

3. Surface deterioration, as in all concrete elements of a structure, may be the result of chemical attack, poor aggregates, poor concrete, freeze-thaw damage or various combinations of these. The damage is usually in the form of spalling, scaling, pop-outs or sloughing off of corners and architectural effects. The depth of the deterioration may vary from superficial to 8" or more usually depending on how long the concrete has been subject to attack.

4. Deterioration at the water line is peculiar to piers or abutments in contact with a stream or river. It takes the form of a cavity in the concrete extending some distance above and below the average flow line of the stream. It usually occurs on the upstream face and along the sides of the pier for all or part of its length. This deterioration probably results also from a combination of causes mentioned in 3 above plus the abrasive action of ice, debris, and water.

5. Deterioration of pier caps and tops of abutment. This is a very common occurrence on structures and the damage can be quite extensive. It is usually a direct result of leaky joint mechanisms which are all too numerous and very difficult to remedy. Most highways are heavily salted for snow and ice control. The resulting brine solution finds its way through the leaky joint mechanism and falls onto the top of the pier cap or abutment below. Frequently there is an accumulation of sand and dirt on the concrete which has also found its way through the joint. The brine is absorbed in this debris from which it seeps out slowly causing maximum damage to the concrete.

4.542 Objective: To maintain abutments and piers in a condition that will preserve the load carrying capacity of the structure.

4.543 Repair Methods:

1. Settlement or Movement
   It is not practically possible or feasible to restore an entire pier or abutment to its design location. The first thing that must be done is to determine whether (a) movement has ceased; (b) movement has been arrested by the action of structural members: or (c) movement is continuing.

   In the second or third case above the continuing movement must be stopped before any correctional action may be taken. If the pier or abutment is pile supported it may be necessary to drive additional piles and somehow tie them to the structure to gain additional support.

   If it is an earth-bearing foundation the needed support can usually be gained by underpinning, by loading in the proper location with dumped rip rap, or by a combination of these.

   Once movement has ceased, steps can then be taken to restore the superstructure of the bridge to its proper position. Depending on the direction of the original movement or settlement one or more of the following corrective actions would have to be taken:
   (a) Remove and replace backwall.
   (b) Jack the superstructure and restore it to proper elevation by pouring concrete lifts at the bridge seats or shimming with steel.
   (c) Reset the bearings and rockers.
   (d) Jack the superstructure longitudinally. (In jacking, careful consideration should be given to member stresses and the Bridge Maintenance Engineer should be consulted prior to the jacking operations.)
   (e) Check and adjust expansion mechanisms and seal joints.

2. Vertical Cracking (Differential Settlement)
   Everything outlined in Section 4.543 (1) above would also apply to the repair of this type of failure.

   In addition it will be necessary to thoroughly clean out, fill and seal all cracks in the pier or abutment. This can be done as outlined under Section 4.533 Case (c).

   An alternate method of sealing the cracks after thoroughly cleaning them is to use some of the commercially available pressure grouting equipment.

3. Surface Deterioration

   The first step in the repair of surface deterioration, or any other type of deterioration in concrete, is to completely remove all unsound concrete using various types of air tools. No satisfactory repair can be made until there is clean, sound concrete to which the new concrete may be bonded. The edges of the cut out area should be undercut on the deeper patches to help retain the new material.

   Bonding - The method of bonding the new concrete to the old will depend upon the depth and volume of the repair and also upon whether or not the shotcrete method of repair is used.

   For surface repairs, using formed concrete, one of the many patented bonding agents may be used without any additional mechanical bonding. If used in strict accordance with the manufacturer recommendations, on clean, sound concrete, these materials give excellent results.

   A grout of neat cement paste can also be used as an effective bonding agent if an epoxy compound is not available. This might also be used where the form for the concrete is so constrictive that the epoxy material cannot be applied effectively. The open area can be sloshed liberally with the grout just prior to pouring the concrete.

   Shotcrete - Briefly stated shotcrete is a means of pneumatically projecting a sand, cement mortar to rebuild a properly prepared area where deteriorated concrete has been removed.

   No further attempt will be made to describe the Shotcrete method of concrete repair, instead reference is directed to the American Concrete Institutes Recommended Practice for Shotcrete (ACI 506-66). Generally, the deterioration must be quite extensive on a structure to justify moving and setting up the necessary plant and equipment required for shotcrete work. Most of the work should also be of a type which is not well suited to the conventional methods of forming and pouring; such as isolated vertical and overhead surfaces.

   When the shotcrete method of repair is used no bonding agent is necessary except when the depth of patch exceeds 3". In this case, hook anchors are secured to the existing concrete on about 12" centers and 2" x 2" wire mesh is hooked and wired to the anchors. This anchoring system must be repeated for each 3" of depth of shotcrete installed.

   It is recommended that wherever the repair is readily adaptable to the method of forming and pouring concrete then that method should be used. This is because shotcrete tends to be wasteful of cement and requires much greater skill to obtain a good product.

   When the concrete is reinforced, surface deterioration will frequently reach to the first layer of steel reinforcement. In this event removal of concrete should continue to a point 1½" to 2" behind the layer of steel. This will provide an excellent anchor for the new concrete or shotcrete. If removal stopped at the plane of reinforcement a cleavage plane will be very apt to develop at this interface between the old and new concrete.

4. Deterioration at the Water Line

   The repair problem here is very similar to the surface deterioration problem except that there is the additional necessity of controlling the stream flow so that the work can be done in the dry.

It is sometimes possible, where the stream level fluctuates sufficiently and remains at low level for a long enough period, to perform the work during periods of low flow. On a stream whose flow is regulated by a dam, it may be possible to secure the cooperation of the authority controlling the dam and thus obtain a lowered water level.

Once the water is controlled, the repair of the damaged concrete would follow the usual methods. Shotcrete can be used to good advantage in some cases since it eases the problem of getting the concrete to the repair area.

5. Deterioration of Pier Caps and Tops of Abutments
This damage and the methods for repairing it are also similar to those described in Section 3 above. The depth and extent of damage to these areas is apt to be greater than that on other surfaces due to their proximity to the leaking joints and due to the presence of dirt and debris on them.

4.550 Backwalls: The backwalls of a structure are generally subject to the following types of distress:
1. Deterioration of concrete due to salt leakage through deck joints and pounding by traffic.
2. Shearing of the wall due to pressure from the approach pavement.
3. Contact with the structural steel due to excessive movement of the steel or the abutment. This sometimes results in cracked concrete in the backwall.

4.551 Objective: To maintain the backwalls of structures in a safe and efficient condition so that there is no danger to traffic over the structure and no leakage of fill through the wall.

4.552 Standard: In order to keep the work load for Bridge Repair Crews within practical limits, backwall repairs should be put off until one or all of the following conditions prevail:
1. A hole develops in the pavement surface at the backwall.
2. The expansion mechanism breaks loose from its anchorage in the backwall.
3. Earth or gravel fill leaks through the cracked or sheared backwall in such quantities as to be judged a serious condition.

4.553 Material: 1:2:4: concrete made from cement and aggregates meeting New York State Standard Specifications. Bonding compound. 1" diam. reinforcing bars. Form lumber and nails including dimension lumber, ship-lap and plywood. 4'x10'x¾" steel plates as required to maintain traffic.

4.554 Method:

1. Backwall work can be performed with a minimum hindrance to traffic by using 4'x10'x¾" steel plates. Traffic is restricted to one lane during working hours. At the end of the work day, the gap in the one lane of pavement is bridged over by one of the steel plates. This permits full use of all lanes during the non-working hours. The plates may be recessed into the pavement, if it is bituminous, or simply placed on the pavement surface with a fillet of winter mix or bituminized shoulder gravel at the edges.

2. The deteriorated or damaged portions of the old backwall must be removed using pavement breakers and other air tools as necessary. The top surface of the remaining concrete, after removal of the bad concrete is completed, should be as nearly level as possible longitudinally as well as transversely.

3. Drill and set 1" dia. rebar dowels on 16" centers. These can be set with portland cement mortar grout or epoxy mortar grout. The dowels should be embedded about 12" deep and should extend to within 3" of the top of the finished wall.
4. The structure side of the backwall must be formed to fit the original configuration of the wall. On the other side only a small amount of form should be required at the top of the wall. Sometimes the surface of the backfill can be maintained in good enough condition to serve as the back side of the form. Forms can be braced from the bridge superstructure.

5. Immediately before pouring concrete, the forms should be thoroughly cleaned out and all dust blown off the old concrete surfaces. Bonding compound should then be applied to the old concrete. After pouring, check to be sure that expansion mechanisms are properly positioned before concrete sets.

6. After the concrete is poured and finished, the steel plates are replaced and left in position until the concrete cures, usually 5 to 7 days. Plates are then removed, forms stripped, any necessary earth fills made and the blacktop pavement restored.

4.560 Bridge Seats: The failures that occur in bridge seats are in most cases the direct result of failures of other elements of the structure. Following are the most common types of failures in bridge seats:

1. Deterioration of the concrete - Usually the result of salt leakage through joints or around the approach corners of the structure.
2. Cracking or splitting of the pedestal - Usually caused by the "freezing" of a movable bearing either on the pedestal or on the opposite end of the beam which the pedestal supports.

4.561 Objective: To maintain the bridge seats and pedestals in a satisfactory condition to safely and adequately support the superstructure of the bridge.

4.562 Standard:

1. When the start of deterioration is observed on a bridge seat or pedestal the leaking joint or improper highway drainage should be corrected immediately.
2. Similarly, if a cracked pedestal is found, an attempt should be made, as soon as possible, to free the faulty bearings which are causing it.

These measures should slow down or prevent the worsening of distress in the bridge seats.

3. Repairs to the bridge seat should be made as early as possible after discovery. Timing will of course depend on the nature and priority of other scheduled repair jobs.

When either deterioration, splitting or cracking reaches a point where the bridge seat is in danger of being unable to properly support its load, it must be repaired immediately.

4.563 Materials: The following materials will be needed: Cement and aggregates complying with New York State specifications, form lumber, steel ties and reinforcing, bonding compound and form oil. If pneumatically projected concrete is used, all of the associated equipment will be required. It is well to have penetrating oil and lubricant available for bearings. It may also be necessary to provide sandblasting equipment for cleaning the bearings and bearing plates.

4.564 Method

4.5641 Repair of Deteriorated Concrete in Bridge Seats:

1. The first step, as always, is to remove *all* deteriorated concrete stopping only when sound concrete is reached.
2. In accomplishing step (1), it may develop that the poor concrete extends back under the bearing plate. If this happens the load carried by the bridge seat must be temporarily supported by jacking and blocking. Once the load is off the seat, all deteriorated concrete including that under the bearing plate can be removed.
3. Rebuilding of the bridge seats with shotcrete should be limited to those cases where deterioration extends either very slightly or not at all underneath the bearing plate.
4. When deterioration extends completely under or substantially under the bearing plate the seats should be rebuilt by forming and pouring concrete. The plate should be carefully set at its proper elevation. The new concrete can then be poured up to the plate. Care must be taken to eliminate voids in the new concrete under the plate.
   After the concrete in the new seat has cured for 10 to 14 days, the load can be transferred to it.
5. Approximately 30 days after placing the new concrete or shotcrete it should be coated with linseed oil and mineral spirits. This must be followed by a second coat when dry and then scheduled for a coating every other year thereafter. (See Section 4.332-A)

4.5642 Repair of Cracked or Split Bridge Seats:

1. In some cases the damage will be so great that there will be no alternative but to temporarily transfer the load from the seat then remove and rebuild it. This repair method would be the same as Section 4 and 5 of 4.5641.
2. If the crack, or split in the bridge seat is ½ inch wide or under, and the pieces are not vertically displaced with respect to each other, another method can be used. This is the method of steel stitching which is very fully described in one of the reference books listed in the appendix (Deterioration Maintenance and Repair of Structures, by S. Johnson). (Also see Section 4.632-C)
   A very adequate repair can be made in this way, provided that the "frozen" bearing or other failure which caused the seat to crack in the first place, can be eliminated.
   Another important feature of this type of repair is that the crack be carefully sealed. This will prevent entrance of debris and water which would further enlarge the crack in the course of many freeze-thaw cycles.
3. In certain cases the repair can be made without stitching by simply filling the crack with cement mortar or epoxy mortar after thoroughly gouging and cleaning the crack.

4.570 Wingwalls: The most common types of deterioration or failure that occur in the wingwalls of a structure are the following:

1. Settlement - This may be the result from either settlement or erosion of the earth foundation material.
2. Tipping or Overturning - This is usually caused by excessive earth pressures on the wall, undermining of the wall or a combination of the two.
3. Vertical Cracking
4. Deterioration of the Concrete

4.571 Objective: To maintain the wingwalls on a structure so that they will adequately protect the abutments, support the approach pavements and present a pleasing appearance.

4.572 Standard:

1. The necessity of repairing failures of the the tipping or overturning type is dependent upon the amount of movement and upon whether the movement is progressive. If the amount of movement is sizable, and is continuing, repairs should be done immediately.
   If the amount of movement has been relatively slight and has stabilized, steps should be taken as soon as possible to reseal any joint or joints that have opened as a result of the movement. Realignment of the wall surfaces in this case can be put off as lower priority work.
2. Vertical cracking should be repaired as soon as possible to prevent intrusion of water and earth into the crack.
3. Repair of deteriorated concrete is usually a matter of aesthetic appearance except when it is severe enough to render the wall structurally inadequate or causes loss of height sufficient to result in inadequate support of the backslopes. In the latter two cases repairs should be made as soon as possible.

4.753 Materials: Same as those listed under 4.563 with the possible addition of steel or timber sheet piling and heavy, dumped rip rap.

4.574 Method

4.5741 Settlement: A determination must first be made as to whether or not settlement of the wingwall is still progressing.
1. If settlement has ceased the repair will consist of resealing all open joints and restoring the surfaces of the wall to the original elevation and alignment. The concrete work will be similar to that described under other sections of this manual as regards to removal, bonding, forming or shotcrete, curing, etc.
2. If settlement is progressing it will be necessary to consult with the Bureau of Soil Mechanics to determine the cause and possible corrective measures. Some of the options might be: (a) Stabilize the foundation soil chemically; (b) alter the footing dimensions to provide greater support; (c) monitor the settlement, if it is not excessive, to determine if natural stabilization will eventually be reached. When stabilization is achieved, repair the wingwall as described in Case 1 above.

4.5742 Tipping or Overturning: In wingwall failures of this type the first step will also be to determine whether or not movement is continuing.
1. If movement has ceased the repairs will be similar to those outlined in Case 1 of 4.5741. However, if undermining of the footing is involved it will be necessary to repair this as outlined in Section 4.510 of this Section.
2. If movement of the wingwall is progressing it will first be necessary to stabilize it. This can be done in one or more of the following ways. In some cases it may be advisable to consult the Bureau of Soil Mechanics.
   a. Where undermining is involved, repair this first according to Section 4.510 of this manual.
   b. Where channel geometry will permit, the lower portion of the wall can be loaded with heavy dumped rip rap. In some cases this will be sufficient to offset the excessive earth pressure on the rear of the wall.
   c. If the fill behind the wall consists of unstable soil, remove it and replace with free draining, backfill material meeting New York State Standard Specifications.

   Once the wall is stabilized all joints should be resealed and mating surfaces may be rebuilt so that they conform to their original alignment. This work would be detailed as outlined in Section 4.5741 of this Section.

4.5743 Vertical Cracking and Deterioration of Concrete: Repair methods for these types of failures will be similar to those described under Section 4.543 (2).

4.600 SUPERSTRUCTURE MAINTENANCE AND REPAIR

4.610 Approach: The approach to the maintenance and repair of bridge superstructures, as with all other maintenance work, should follow a logical pattern of problem analysis.

In order to properly analyze a superstructure maintenance or repair problem the following general procedure should be used as a guide.
1. The deterioration must be located.
2. The cause of the deterioration must be determined.
3. The strength of the deteriorated structure should be evaluated.
4. The need for immediate or future maintenance and repair work should be established.
5. The maintenance and repair procedure should be selected and implemented.

During the implementation of the repair procedure, if good results are to be obtained, it is extremely important that the specifications and plans be followed completely, carefully and exactly in every detail.

4.620 Steel Superstructures

Standard: To maintain all steel superstructures in a condition, as nearly as possible to their original condition, free of corrosion and other forms of deterioration and without loss of strength.

4.621 Basic Types and Causes of Deterioration of Structural Steel Superstructures: In the discussion to follow it will be assumed that the design has been prepared with sufficient care that defects due to overstress are not a problem. The following items are the most prevalent causes of deterioration in steel structures.

- A. Corrosion - This is by far the most wide spread form of steel deterioration and the most problematic to the maintenance forces. Although corrosion is a complex chemical or electrochemical reaction it can simply be stated as a process that converts the metallic iron into an oxide or other compound.
  The results of corrosive action are a loss in cross sectional area of the member and thus a reduction in load carrying capacity.

- B. Abrasion - This form of deterioration results from the movement of two parts that are in contact with each other. This type of deterioration can be readily identified by the worn, smooth appearance of the abraded surface.

- C. Loosening of Connections - This type of problem is most generally connected with truss structures. Bolts and rivets used in connections on steel structures subject to shock or impact loadings tend to work loose in time. This loosening of the connections induces slip in the joints, causes distortion of the structure, creates areas of extreme stress concentration and increase the vulnerability of the structure to fatigue failure.

- D. Fatigue is a situation that results when a structural member is subjected to repetitive or fluctuating loads which are at or below the usual allowable design values.
  Fatigue failures are preceded by small hairline cracks oriented perpendicular to the lines of stress. *These cracks if undetected can result in collapse without warning.*

E. Impact - Impact failures result from damage caused by moving objects such as traffic. Usually impact damage is characterized by local distortion of the affected members.

4.622 Cleaning of Structural Steel Superstructures: The corrosion of structural steel will be greatly accelerated if dirt and debris is allowed to accumulate on the steel. The accumulation of dirt and debris retains rain or wash water and maintains this moisture in contact with the steel surface.

Standard: Annually, in the spring after the winter snow and ice season, wash and clean thoroughly all dirt and debris from the surfaces of the structural steel superstructure.

Procedure: The cleaning process shall be accomplished by flushing the steel with water. Those areas with heavy accumulations of dirt and debris, shall be thoroughly cleaned by brushing and/or scraping. The water shall be applied under pressure utilizing a pump and hose. When the structure being cleaned is a stream crossing, the water may be pumped directly from the stream. For bridges that do not cross over waterways, the source of water shall be obtained from a portable water tank.

Truss structures should be given particular attention in the annual cleaning program with special attention to the more inaccessible areas at the panel points and bearings.

4.623 Spot Painting of Structural Steel Superstructures: The isolated areas of exposed structural steel, where paint has failed, will be protected from further deterioration by the application of a protective coating of paint. The accomplishment of an annual spot painting program will greatly increase the time interval between complete painting projects.

Standard: Annually, after completion of the structural steel cleaning program apply at spot locations of exposed steel one coat of dull orange primer and two coats of finish paint.

Procedure: The spot locations of exposed structural steel found as a result of the annual cleaning program shall be thoroughly cleaned by wire brushing, scraping and chipping. When the steel has been completely cleaned of all rust and dirt, one coat of dull orange primer shall be applied to the cleaned surface. The dull orange primer shall be allowed to dry completely to a hardened surface. When the primer has dried, a first coat of finish paint shall be applied and allowed to dry thoroughly. The project should then be completed by applying a second coat of finish paint.

4.624 Repair of Corroded Steel Members: After cleaning areas showing a high incidence of corrosion a careful examination of the steel should be made in order to determine the amount of metal loss that has taken place. If the examination and analysis shows that sufficient metal has been lost to reduce the load carrying capabilities of the member then additional plating should be designed to replace the lost metal thus restoring the member to its original strength.

Standard: Install plating or doublers on all members found to have significant metal loss resulting in a loss of strength below the original design limits.

Procedure: Clean thoroughly the area of corrosion and make necessary measurements to determine the amount of metal loss. Measurements can be made directly with rulers and calipers or with more sophisticated electronic equipment such as ultrasonic measuring devices.

Based upon the degree of metal loss that has occurred, the material that remains available for load carrying can be determined. If the analysis shows that there is insufficient member strength available for carrying the design or posted loadings the situaion should immediately be remedied by the installation of plating or doublers.

The installation of plating or doublers should be carried out with considerable care and follow the procedures dictated by new construction methods. The existing steel should be cleaned completely of all dirt, rust and loose metal. The new steel should be ground to fit in order to provide good contact with the existing member. The plating or doubler section should be seal welded to the existing member and the finished section should be prime coated with dull orange primer and then receive two coats of finish paint.

NOTE: When designing the plating or doubler section, it should be realized that the problem was created by a high incidence of corrosion. Therefore, it is advisable to provide additional section (cross sectional area) in the plating or doubler section to allow for future corrosion. The repaired section should also receive regular inspections in order to detect the attack of corrosive elements and the need for repainting. It is advisable to check overall design with Structures Division before proceeding.

Of course, if at all possible, the source of corrosion should be removed. For example, a leaking deck joint or leakage along the curb line should be sealed.

Some typical examples of the use of plating or doublers in the repair of deteriorated members are shown below:

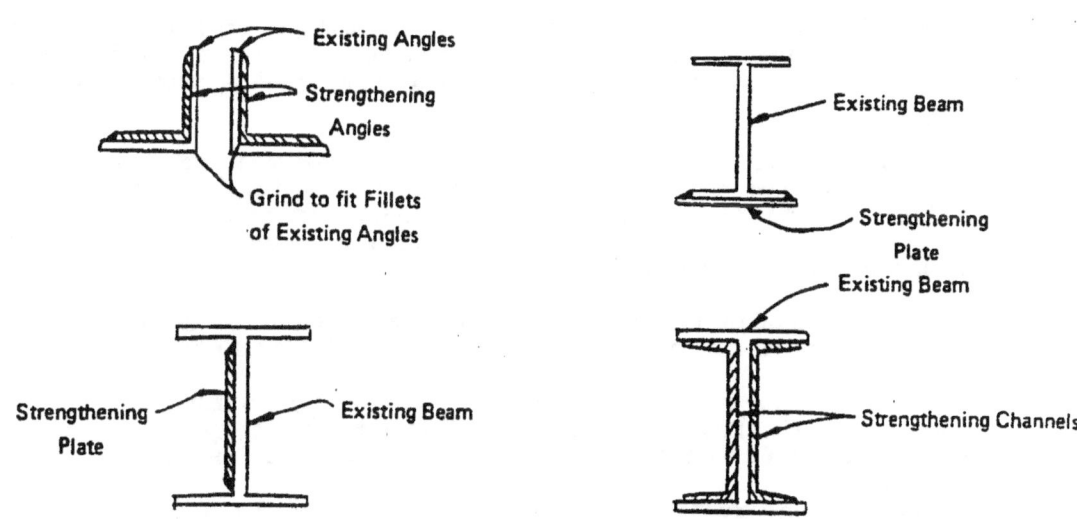

4.625 Replacement of Deteriorated Members: After cleaning areas showing a high incidence of corrosion and making a careful analysis of the degree of metal loss and resultant loss of strength it may be determined that there is insufficient usable section remaining and a complete replacement of the member will be required.

Standard: Remove and replace with a new member those members found to be deteriorated beyond the point of having sufficient usable load carrying capacity.

Procedure: Clean thoroughly the corroded member and make necessary measurements to determine the usable section remaining for load carrying. Measurements can be made directly with rulers and calipers or with more sophisticated electronic equipment such as ultrasonic measuring devices.

Based upon the degree of metal loss that has taken place the load carrying capacity of the member may be determined. If analysis indicates that the load carrying capacity has fallen below the design or posted requirement and that there is insufficient material remaining to receive plating or doublers, then the complete member replacement is required.

The installation of the new member should be carried out with considerable care and follow the procedures dictated by new construction methods. If the member is connected to the structural system by rivets, the rivets should be carefully removed and replaced with high strength bolts. Also, in selecting the section for the replacement member, consideration should be given to providing sacrificial metal (additional cross sectional area) to compensate for future corrosion.

After installation of the new member, it should be primed with one coat of dull orange primer and then receive two coats of finish paint.

The replacement member should receive regular inspections in order to detect the attack of corrosive elements and the need for repainting.

Of course, if at all possible, the source of corrosion should be removed. For example, a leaking deck joint or leakage along the curb lines should be corrected.

4.626 Encasement of Members Subject to Corrosion: When a structural member, because of its location in the structural system, is particularly subject to corrosive action, it is sometimes advisable to encase the member. If additional weight and bulk can be tolerated on the member, concrete may be used.

Thought should be given to the use of noncorrosive metals, reinforced bituminous coatings or plastics especially when weight and bulk are a problem.

Standard: Structural members subject to highly corrosive elements shall be provided with an external protective coating of a noncorrosive material. Consideration should be given to using concrete, noncorrosive metals, reinforced bituminous coverings, plastics or other acceptable noncorrosive material.

Procedure: Structural members continually subject to corrosive elements, where the application of paint does not produce adequate protection, should be thoroughly cleaned by wire brushing, scraping, chipping or sand blasting. In the event that the member is severely corroded it shall be replaced in accordance with Section 4.625 except that the new member shall not be primed or painted.

Upon completion of the cleaning of the existing member or the installation of the new member, the member shall be encased with a corrosion resistant material.

If concrete will be the encasement material, the encasement process shall use pneumaticaly projected concrete. The pneumatically projected concrete shall be applied in accordance with the American Concrete Institute Code for Shotcreting (ACI 506-66).

If another noncorrosive material is used, the application shall be in accordance with the manufacturers specifications.

4.627 Repair of Riveted and Bolted Joints: Bridge superstructures incorporating riveted or bolted joints as part of the structural system are subject to loosening of connections. This loosening of the connections induces slip in the joints, causes distortion and increases the vulnerability of the structure to fatigue failure.

Standard: Make periodic inspections of riveted and bolted connections to assure that all rivets and bolts are maintained in a tight condition and the joints are not allowed to slip.

Procedure: Riveted connections should be checked by striking the individual rivet heads with a ball peen hammer which has a steel shaft. Those rivets that have retained the proper tightness will give off a sharp, distinct ringing sound. Those rivets of questionable tightness will produce a dull sound.

Rivets that are deemed to be loose should be replaced. The replacement of the defective rivets should be accomplished by cutting the rivet heads off and removing the shank. Care shall be exercised not to damage the adjacent metal and if necessary the rivet shanks should be removed by drilling.

After the defective rivet has been removed a high strength bolt should be installed and tightened by the turn-of-nut method. The turn-of-nut method of obtaining bolt tension requires that the bolt be made "snug tight". Snug tight shall be defined as the tightness attained by a few impacts on an impact wrench or the full effort of a man using an ordinary spud wrench. The bolt shall then be tightened additionally by the applicable amount of nut rotation specified below:

NUT ROTATION FROM SNUG TIGHT CONDITION
Disposition of Outer Faces of Bolted Parts

Both faces normal to bolt axis or one face normal to axis and other face sloped 1:20 (bevel washer not used)		Both faces sloped 1:20 from normal to bolt axis (bevel washers not used)
Bolt length not exceeding 8 diameters or 8 inches	Bolt length exceeding 8 diameters or 8 inches	For all lengths of bolts
½ turn	2/3 turn	¾ turn

NOTE: Bolt lengths are measured from underside of head to extreme end of point.

A bolted connection shall be examined for loose bolts by checking the nuts. If the nuts are found to be loose they should be replaced rather than retorqued. The replacement bolt should be tightened in accordance with the turn-of-the nut method outlined above.

Concrete Superstructure

Basic Types of Deterioration of Concrete Superstructures: Reinforced concrete superstructures are subject to three primary types of deterioration:

A. Cracking
B. Spalling
C. Disintegration

When cracking is found to be present on a bridge superstructure it does not necessarily indicate a serious problem. It must be realized that in concrete construction some cracking is to be expected. In the analysis of the cracked concrete it is more important to determine whether the cracks are active or dormant.

Dormant cracks generally result from construction operations or drying shrinkage and will not proceed beyond the point at which they are originally found.

In order to determine whether the cracks are active or dormant tell tales should be used to establish the growth, if at all, and the rate of growth. Two examples of a means of checking crack growth are illustrated below:

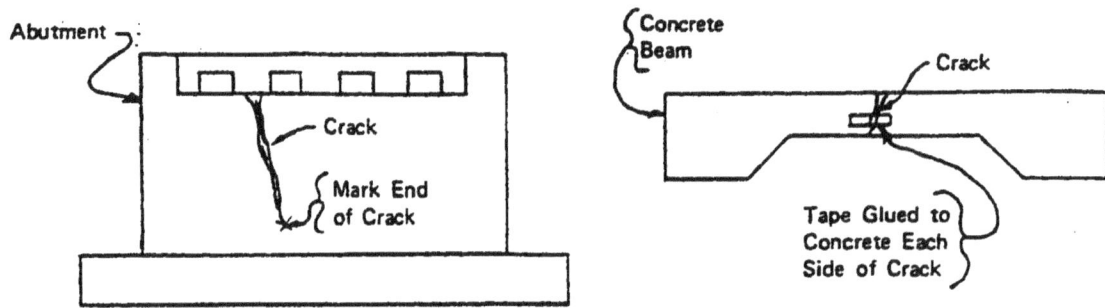

The period of measurement should span over a minimum of six months, preferably one year. If, over the measurement period, no discernable movement takes place, the cracks can be classified as dormant. If, however, noticeable movement has occurred, the the cracks are to be considered active and corrective measures should be instituted to prevent further deterioration.

Spalled and disintegrated areas of concrete generally indicate a more serious condition than areas of cracking. Spalling and disintegration are accompanied with a loss in section (cross sectional area) and consequently indicate loss of strength.

The area of deterioration should receive immediate inspection and repair. The repair procedure developed should take into account that there probably has been a loss in strength and compensate for this fact.

4.632 Repairing Cracks in Concrete Superstructures: Concrete superstructures that are found to have areas of active cracking should undergo immediate repair before serious damage results.

Standard: Inspect annually all concrete superstructures for areas of cracking and determine the nature of the cracks, whether they are active or dormant. For structures with cases of active cracking a method of repair should be developed and implemented.

Procedure: Depending on the nature and extent of the cracks, different approaches can be developed. Some of the more common are listed below: (Whenever possible, Structures Division and Materials Bureau should be contacted for special expertise and latest developments of materials and techniques.)

A. Epoxies

Cracks in concrete may be bonded by the injection of epoxy bonding compounds under pressure. The most common technique is to drill into the crack from the face of the concrete at several locations. The crack is then flushed with water and allowed to dry thoroughly. The face of the crack is then surface sealed between injection points and the epoxy compound is injected into the crack until it runs out of the adjacent sections of the crack or the surface seals begin to bulge.

This is by far the best solution to the problem of cracks in concrete. However, it must be realized that if the cause of the cracking is not removed, rendering the cracks dormant, there will undoubtedly be additional cracking developing elsewhere in the structure.

B. Routing and Sealing
This method requires the enlargement of the crack along its exposed face and filling and sealing it with a suitable material.

The routing and sealing technique is only recommended for dormant cracks. If the cracks are active, the cause of cracking should be determined and the cause removed.

C. Repair of Cracks by Stitching
This process will restore the tensile strength to the concrete. Basically, stitching requires the drilling of holes on both sides of the crack. Care should be taken to stagger the holes so that all stress is not transferred to a single plane in the concrete.

Rods, bent in a shape similar to stirrups, are gouted into the holes and provide a means of transferring stress across the crack.

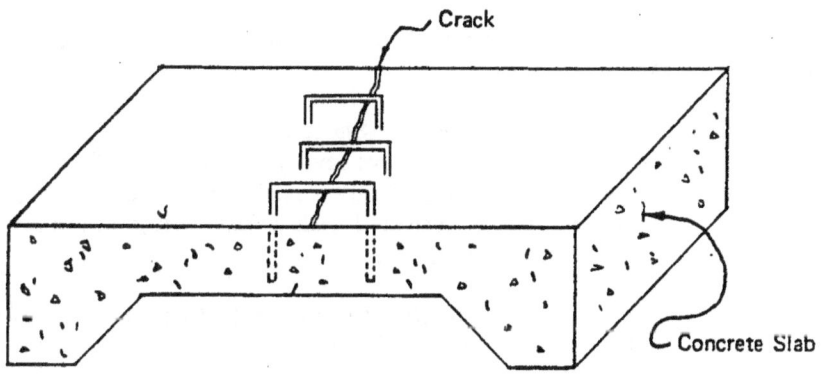

D. External Stressing
This procedure works particularly well for beams that have failure cracks along the tension area.

It is required that anchors be affixed to the sides of the beam below the neutral axis. These anchors serve as attachments for tie rods that are inserted and placed under tension thereby restoring and/or adding load carrying capacity to the structure.

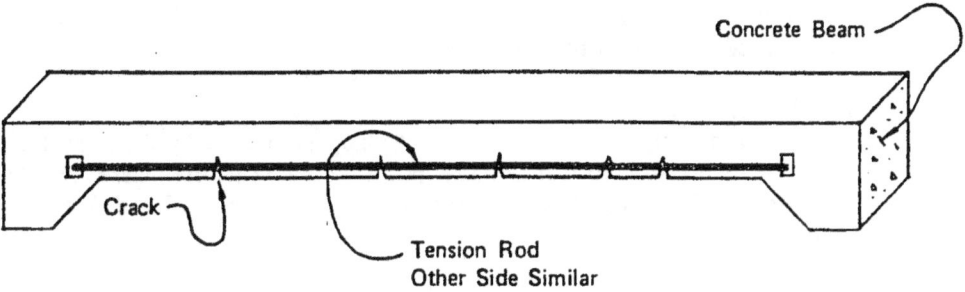

4.633 Repairing Spalled and Disintegrated Concrete: As mentioned previously, spalled or disintegrated concrete areas generally indicate a potential for more serious failure than areas of cracking.

Therefore, these areas should receive immediate analysis, and based upon the results of the analysis, repairs should be implemented.

Standard: Remove all areas of unsound concrete that have spalled or disintegrated and replace same with new concrete.

Procedure: Areas of spalled or disintegrated concrete shall be repaired by removing all unsound concrete. The unsound concrete shall be removed by chipping hammers or other mechanical means.

Sound concrete can be determined generally, as a rule of thumb, by striking the concrete surface with a mason's hammer. Those areas of sound concrete will produce a sharp ringing sound. Those areas of unsound concrete will produce a dull, hollow sound when struck with the hammer.

After all unsound concrete has been removed, new concrete shall be placed by one of the following methods:

1. Pneumatically Projected Concrete (Shotcrete)
   This is the application of successive layers of a mixture of cement, sand and water under pressure. To provide increased bonding the area to which the shotcrete is to be applied is covered with welded wire mesh (6 x 6 x No. 10) with provisions for a two-inch cover.

   The specifications of the American Concrete Institute Standard Practice for Shotcreting (ACI 506-66) should be carefully followed in order to assure the best possible results.

2. Pressure Grouting
   This requires the placement of formwork surrounding the area to be repaired. Also, if accessible, the area to be patched should be coated with a bonding agent such as epoxy or other material with similar characteristics.

   The forms should be provided with holes where the concrete can enter and vent holes for the release of air and which also indicate when the forms are filled.

   A high slump concrete is then pumped into the forms under pressure until the forms are completely filled as indicated by concrete pushing out of the vent holes. For shallow patches, say 1½" to 2½" in depth, an epoxy grout can be used in place of the concrete.

3. Forming and Pouring
   This method is the standard method of placing concrete by forming the area to be patched and conventionally pouring the concrete. Care should be exercised in the placement to assure that all the voids are filled. Vibrating is recommended.

   Also, the surface area of the patch should be coated with an acceptable bonding agent such as one of the epoxies.

4.640 Maintenance and Repair of Bridge Bearings

General Comments: As mentioned previously in the definition of terms, the primary purpose of the bridge bearing is to transmit the entire loading of the superstructure, both dead loads and live loads, to the bridge substructure.

The bearings also provide for longitudinal movement due to changes in temperature, i.e., expansion and contraction, and rotational movement due to deflection.

The neglect of these elements of the bridge structure can lead to very serious consequences. The bridge bearing that is not properly performing its function can resses into the structure that will result in loss of load carrying capacity and reduce the usable life of the bridge.

Cleaning and Spot Painting of Bridge Bearings: Bridge bearings should receive careful analysis during the annual bridge inspection program for defects, non-functioning parts and areas of corrosion.

4.6421 Standard: Annually clean and spot paint the fixed and expansion bearings on each bridge structure.

Procedure: Thoroughly clean each bearing by flushing with high pressure water, scraping and wire brushing. If the bearing has areas of excessive corrosion, sand blasting may be in order.

Once thoroughly cleaned, the areas of bare metal or excessive paint loss should be prime coated with dull orange primer. When the primer is completely dry, the bearings should receive two coats of finish paint.

Bearing Realignment: Many times bearings will become misaligned due to the rotational settlement of the bridge abutment or pier. Also, pavement creep in the adjacent highway may push the backwall and superstructure causing excessive movement of the bearing rocker and base plate. This movement of the bearing results in cracking and destruction of the bridge pedestals and bridge seats.

Standard: Annually inspect bearing rockers, base plates and anchor bolts for excessive movement and misalignment. Realign rockers, and base plates and restore or replace anchor bolts for all bearings found to have suffered excessive movement.

Procedure: Inspect the bridge bearings and when movement beyond design limits has occurred make necessary measurements to determine the degree of this movement. The measurements should be analyzed and a determination made as to the nature and extent of the corrective procedures.

If analysis dictates, the bearing should be realigned by jacking the superstructure and reseating the base plate and anchor bolts. Extreme care should be taken in the design of the jacking procedure as generally high loads will be encountered.

If the existing bearing is comprised of a roller nest then consideration should be given to replacing the roller nest with some other suitable bearing configuration.

DECK ELEMENTS & WEARING COURSE MAINTENANCE

Definitions - Deterioration of Decks, wearing surfaces, curbs, and sidewalks is prevalent due to extensive use of de-icing chemicals during winter months. Implementation of corrective measures should be done as soon as defects are discovered because of the structural importance of the deck, the importance of the sidewalk to pedestrian safety and the importance of the wearing course to the riding quality of the bridge.

The following types of deck construction are most common in New York State:

  a. Structural deck used as the wearing surface (monolithic construction)
  b. Reinforced concrete deck supports a separately cast concrete wearing surface. A membrane water proofing is sometimes used to protect the deck.
  c. Structural decks which carry an asphalt wearing surface. Epoxies or emulsified asphalt sealers are used to protect the deck.
  d. Precast concrete decks with asphalt or concrete wearing surfaces.

Water proofing of the deck is aimed at preventing salt, which chemically destroys concrete, from entering the deck.

Sidewalks and curbs are generally separate pours, with a water proofing membrane applied to the deck prior to sidewalk and/or curb construction.

Joints where contraction and expansion occur are most vulnerable to deterioration becuase adequate sealing is difficult.

4.720 Repairs to Bridge Decks: Deck deterioration begins on the surface producing poor riding conditions and then progresses deeper into the deck, decreasing its load-carrying capacity with subsequent damage and failure. Loss of strength becomes noticeably detrimental when the bond fails between the reinforcing steel and concrete through the action of de-icing chemicals.

4.721 Objective: To restore sound concrete where deterioration is present, thereby maintaining full deck strength and producing a smooth riding surface.

4.722 Standard: Deck repairs should be made on all structures where decay is present to the following extent:

  a. At least 30% of the deck surface is cracked and has pot holes.
  b. Reinforcing steel is exposed where pot holes have developed.

4.723 Material: A number of materials are available for concrete deck repair. Many of these are highly specialized both in application and placement procedures. These highly specialized materials should be used in conjunction with the manufacturer or other sources of expertise until our own personnel acquire necessary experience. The following materials have become commonly used:

  a. Epoxy Grout - This is a two-component mix to be applied to the old concrete surface. Upon hardening, it serves as a bonding compound between the new and old concrete.

  b. Concrete - The mix should consist of State-approved materials. A minimum of 6% air entrainment should be developed by use of an adequate additive to increase resistance to freezing and thawing. Accelerators prove helpful where deck repairs are made to structures carrying a high volume of traffic. The accelerators facilitate the speed or the repair work and reduce the time required for the maintenance and protection of traffic.

4.724 Method: Repairs should begin with the removal of all disintegrated concrete. Saw cuts should be made around decayed areas prior to chipping. After bad concrete is removed, the existing surface should be thoroughly cleaned by blowing or in extremes cases sand blasting. Epoxy grout should then be applied. New concrete should be poured before the epoxy sets to insure a good bond.

Another method of repair which may be employed is by pneumatically projecting concrete (shotcrete). "Ready mix" or "transit mix" concrete may speed up operations where large deck areas are to be repaired.

4.730 Repairs to Concrete Wearing Surfaces: The objective, standards, method and materials described under deck repairs should apply. In cases where either all of, or a large portion of the concrete wearing surface is in deplorable condition, it should be entirely removed and replaced with a new cement concrete or asphalt wearing surface. If deck damage is discovered, corrective action should also be taken. Also, deck drains should be installed prior to placing the new wearing surface and in accordance with the detail on the following page.

4.740 Replacement of Asphalt Wearing Surfaces: Freezing of water trapped between deck and wearing surface causes destructive action to asphalt overlays.

4.741 Objective: To replace a cracked and raveled asphalt wearing surface with a smooth, water tight asphalt overlay which restores good riding qualities.

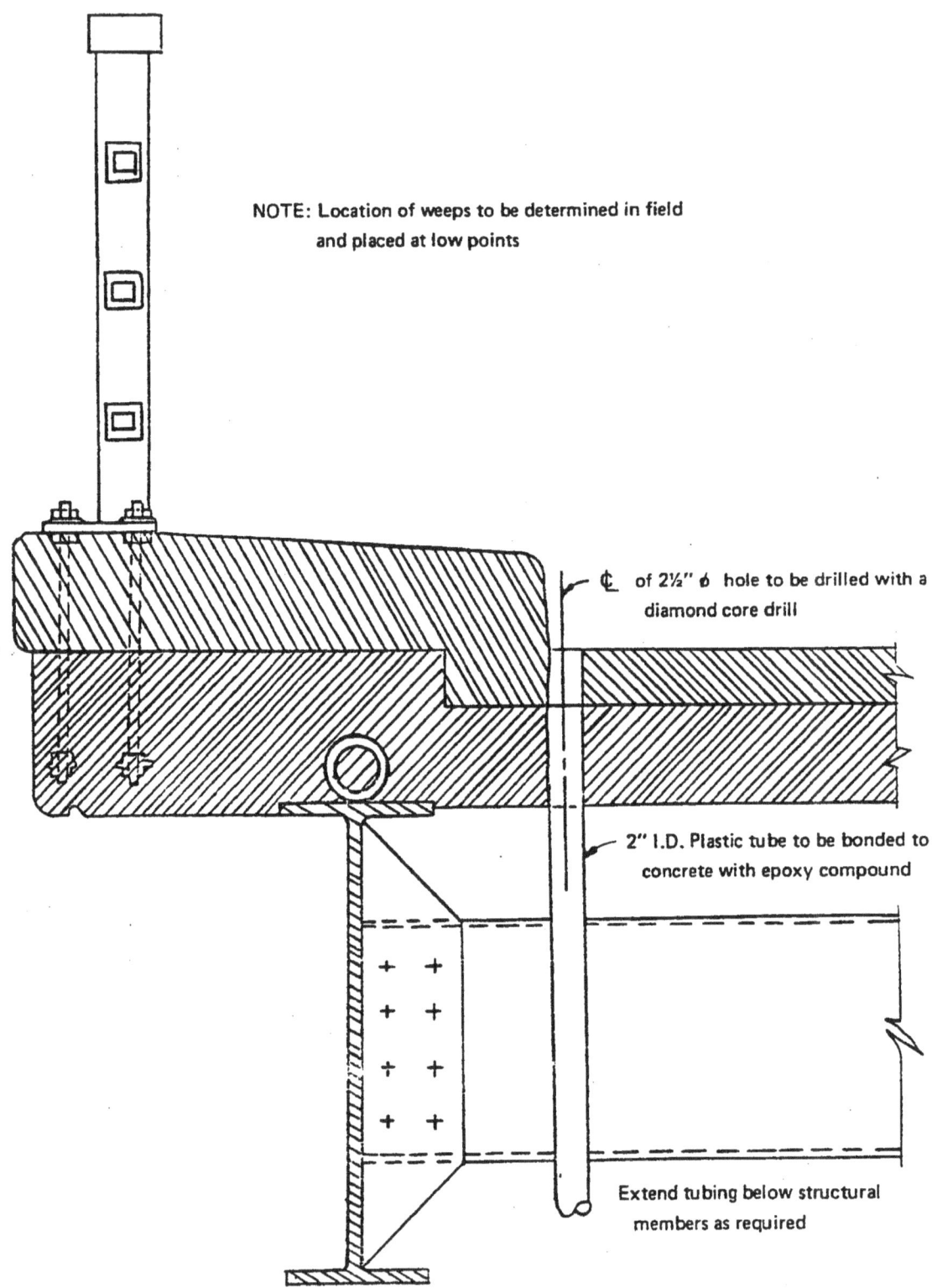

TYPICAL DECK DRAIN INSTALLATION

4.742 Standard: An asphalt wearing surface should be replaced wherever cracking is prevalent and deck is exposed, or whenever deck repairs are needed. A recommended frequency of replacement is once every ten to fifteen years.

4.743 Method: Old overlays should be scarified, removed and the deck surface thoroughly cleaned. Any deck repairs required should be performed while there is no overlay. Prior to the application of the sealer, the deck surface should be cleaned by air pressure and in extreme cases sand blasted. All foreign material should be removed. The sealer should then be applied and allowed to set. Where emulsified asphalt is used as a sealer, it should be chipped and allowed to cure a minimum of seven days before surfacing with armor coat. Where appropriate a waterproof membrane can be installed.

4.750 Repairs to Curbs and Sidewalks: Sidewalks tend to become dangerous to the pedestrian user when they become disintegrated and cracked. Anchorages for steel railings become weakened creating a safety hazard for the driver as well.

4.751 Objective: To restore the original sidewalk and curb section to its original condition.

4.752 Standard: Any sidewalk should be repaired that show deterioration over 25% or more of its surface. Concrete curbs should be restored when reinforcement becomes visible in deteriorated areas. All sand and salt should be cleaned once a year during the early spring. A linseed oil treatment of one coat should be made once a year. Metal curb protection plates should be cleaned of rust and scale and painted every five years.

4.753 Materials: Concrete sidewalks should be repaired with materials described under "Deck Repairs". If it is deemed feasible, due to the extent of disintegration, to replace the entire sidewalk, a waterproofing membrane should be applied to seal deck surface. Sidewalk approaches should be reconstructed wherever cracked and wherever settlement has taken place.

4.754 Method: Repairs to these elements could be made with either gunite or cast-in-place concrete. The most practicable method should be employed and will be determined by the extent of corrective work required. Good judgment is to be used and the final decision made by the Bridge Maintenance Engineer.

Wherever railing anchorages are affected by poor concrete, they should be re-established by recasting the deteriorated areas. Railings should be removed while these repairs are in progress and reset upon completion. While the railings are removed care should be taken for the adequate protection of pedestrian and vehicular traffic.

The final step in these repairs should be a three-coat application of linseed oil as described under "Materials".

4.760 Replacement of Damaged Railing: Railings are frequently damaged by vehicle accidents. If an entire section of railing is demolished, emergency measures should be taken to protect the traveling public by setting up a temporary barricade with cable. Drums should be placed along the damaged area to alert the traveling public of the existence of a dangerous situation. Permanent repairs should be made as early as possible by reinstalling new railing conforming in type to the existing railing. If damage is limited to slight bending or breaking, repairs may only be welding and straightening of members by heat treatment. When heat straightening, care must be taken to avoid embrittlement of metal which makes rail unsafe.

Concrete parapets are heavy and if damaged should be replaced with standard steel railing. An exception to this rule is the concrete safety shape similar to "Jersey" barrier, which should be retained. A good time to do this is in conjunction with other required repairs to be made to a bridge. Again, good judgment is required in programming these replacements. Decisions should be made by the Bridge Maintenance Engineer.

4.770 Repairs to Joints: Joint failures are very detrimental to other elements in their vicinity since their main function is to allow for expansion. Also, inadequate sealing allows water to pass through, resulting in rusting of the superstructure steel and deterioration of bridge seats. A contributing factor to joint failures is the collection of incompressibles in the surface of the joint.

4.771 Objective: To restore the proper function of the joint by corrective repairs and adequate sealing.

4.772 Standard: Joints should be cleaned at least four times a year to keep them free of foreign materials which may impair their function. Corrective action should be taken wherever there is evidence of improper function (cracked headers, disintegrating wearing surface near the joints, broken finger plates, disintegrated seal systems, etc.). It should take priority in all bridge repair programs because of the poor riding conditions that result and the subsequent costly damage to other superstructure and substructure elements of the bridge.

4.773 Material: Following is a list of required materials with recommended quality standards.

    a. Concrete - Requirements should be as described under Section 501 and Section 701.
    b. Epoxy Grout - Requirements should be as described under Section 721.
    c. Bituminous Joint Material - Material should conform to specifications for 705-07.
    d. Joint Filler - Material should conform to specifications for 705.
    e. White Pigmented Curing Compound - Materials should conform to specifications for 711-05.

Other materials which may be required are structural steel, sealers, adhesives, and asphalt which should be purchased from an approved supplier.

4.774 Method: Repairs which pertain to replacement of deteriorated concrete along joints should be made as described in Section 4.720. Wherever existing headers are loose or disintegrated, they should be entirely removed and recast. A recommended minimum thickness is 3½" and width of 12". It may be necessary to raise the grade of the bridge by means of an armor coat overlay to obtain this thickness. If this is necessary, approval should be obtained from the Deputy Chief Engineer (Structures) prior to adding the extra dead load. Epoxy grout (M29G) may be used to bond the headers to the deck. Bituminous joint material may be used as the form for both sides of the joint. The last steps are to clean the joint thoroughly and fill with an approved joint sealer.

Damaged armorings in sliding plate or finger plate joints may be repaired by welding or studding. Where the plate is badly rusted or damaged, it should be replaced. Poor deck concrete should be repaired when the armoring is removed since it probably caused the failure by entrapping water.

4.800 PAINTING

4.810 General Principles: Painting of structural steel serves two important functions:

1. Preservation of the structural integrity of the steel by preventing the attack of corrosive elements.
2. Provides a pleasing appearance to the traveling public.

Paint protects by interposing a barrier film between the corrodible steel and the corrosive environment. It is effective only as long as there are no pinholes, breaks, or weaknesses in it. At such places, corrosion will start and if not discovered and sealed by spot repairs, will proceed by prying and undercutting and will progressively destroy the entire paint system. This means that regular inspection and spot repair are essential to prolong the life of the coating.

Paint systems gradually fail under prolonged exposure to sunlight, heat, freezing, and chloride salts used for de-icing highways.

AASHO recognizes 5 degrees of film failure or rusting which require different methods of cleaning for painting:

Condition	Treatment
A. Nonrusting - Surface unsightly or rotted. Paint is sound, adhering and not too thick to be detrimental.	Solvent cleaning if necessary. Apply one finish coat.
B. Same as A, but paint eroded to show undercoats.	Solvent cleaning if necessary. Apply one intermediate and one finish coat.
C. Slight rusting localized area less than 25%.	Spot clean, remove all defective paint and spot coat. Apply one or two cover-all coats as required. (See A & B)
D. 25% to 40% rusting in localized areas.	Same as C.
E. Over 40% rusting.	Remove all defective paint and spot coat. Apply prime, intermediate and finish coat over all.

4.811 Corrosion: Corrosion is the destruction of metal by chemical or electrochemical reaction with its environment. Iron and steel corrode in the presence of *both* oxygen and water. Corrosion usually does not take place in the absence of either of these. Corrosion is negligible when the relative humidity is below 60%, however, water with oxygen dissolved in it may be highly corrosive.

Rust can exist in many forms, but the only stable form is the orange-brown variety; the highest oxidation product of iron. There are dark brown varieties and even black rust scale (also commonly experienced as mill scale). Any of these darker forms of rust are iron oxide in an unstable state of oxidation which, by slow combination with oxygen and water, will gradually increase in volume, lose adhesion to the steel, and finally attain the stable orange-brown form. Then, even though they are initially adherent, these darker forms of rust and mill scale should be considered potentially loose residue and be removed.

4.820 Surface Preparation: The importance of properly cleaning steel preparatory to painting cannot be overemphasized. The very best paint applied to an unprepared surface could not only prove to be a complete waste of time and money but also could cause additional expense for removal of the paint from the structure. There is no point in painting a structure unless it is properly cleaned and prepared for painting. The methods used depend upon the condition of the surfaces prior to painting.

4.821 Objective: The removal from the surface of the steel all contaminants which directly affect the ability of the paint to protect and decorate the steel, namely:

1. Grease, oil, dust, old paint, moisture, old tar base paint.
2. Rust and mill scale.
3. Visible and invisible rust stimulants.

4.822 Standard: No paint should be applied over a surface which evidences grime, oil, excessive chalking, blistering, or a loose, scaly, flaking condition. No area should be cleaned so far in advance that it cannot be painted before rusting begins.

Grease, oil, dirt and moisture should be removed with clean petroleum solvents, such as mineral spirits, applied with clean rags in such a manner that the oil substance is actually removed and not simply diluted or spread out over a greater area.

Areas that have been exposed to salt and other de-icing materials should be scrubbed with detergents using a wet short bristle brush, flushed with clear, clean water and allowed to dry thoroughly before painting. All loose or non-adherent paint should be removed. Thick edges of remaining old paint shall be feathered so that the repainted surface will have a smooth appearance. The remaining old paint should have sufficient adhesion so that it cannot be lifted as a layer by inserting the blade of a dull putty knife under it.

Special attention should be given to those areas which are difficult to clean and paint such as members of trusses. All points of refuse and moisture collection should be thoroughly cleaned and flame dried, where practical, before painting.

4.823 Methods: The various methods are given under the headings of mechanical cleaning and chemical cleaning. In selecting the method or methods to be used on a particular structure, consideration should be given to the anchor pattern left after cleaning which may be so rough that peaks are formed which are impossible to protect with paint. Sharp ridges, burrs, or cuts may be left in the surface of the metal by means of mechanical cleaning equipment and it is difficult to obtain adequate paint thickness over these irregularities.

Generally, solvent cleaning to remove oil, grease or other soluble contaminants should be the first step in any surface preparation.

Mechanical Cleaning:

4.8231 Hand Cleaning: As a general rule, hand cleaning is employed only when power-operated equipment is not available, where the job is inaccessible to power tools, or where the job is too small to warrant bringing in power tools. Tools needed are wire brushes, scrapers, chisels, knives, chipping hammers, and emery or sandpaper. In close areas, the tool should be shaped so that it can enter the areas that are to be cleaned.

Rust scale forms in layers and it is removed first, usually by impact from hand chipping hammers. Where rust scale has progressed to the point where the thickness of the metal has been corroded so that only a thin section remains, extreme care must be used in removing rust scale by impact to prevent the heavy sledge from puncturing the metal.

Next, all loose and non-adherent rust, loose mill scale, and loose or non-adherent paint is removed by a suitable combination of scraping and wire-brushing. The method of cleaning depends upon the nature of the surface, loose voluminous rust is easily removed by a combination of scraping with thin blade scrapers and then wire-brushing the surface. Tightly adherent rust is removed generally with the heavy type of scraper.

After cleaning is completed, the surface is brushed, swept and dusted and blown off with compressed air to remove all loose matter. Painting should proceed as soon as possible after the hand cleaning operation although it is not as critical as in the case of sand blasting where virgin metal is exposed.

The steel wire of the wire brushes should have sufficient rigidty to clean the surface, should be kept free of excess foreign matter, and should be discarded when they are not longer effective because of loss of bristles or bad bending of bristles.

Scrapers may be of any design and should be made of tool steel and tempered. They should be kept sharp to be effective and should be operated in such a manner that no burrs or sharp ridges are left on the surface and no sharp cuts are made into the steel.

4.8232 Power Tool Cleaning: The methods and equipment employed in hand cleaning are interpreted in the design of power tools such as large rotary wire brushes, chipping hammers, descalers and rotary scalers. Safety goggles should be worn when doing this type of work.

Wire brushes come in a variety of designs for every possible use. The speed of the machine is governed by the size of the brush, grinding wheel or disc used; the greater the diameter the slower the speed.

It is very important that too high speed is not used or the brush is not kept on one spot for too long as detrimental burnishing of the surface may occur. Under such circumstances, the surface is smooth and develops a polished, glossy appearance, it provides a very poor anchor for paint. As rotary power wire brushes are particularly notorious for spreading oil and grease over the surface, solvent cleaning is essential to remove them before power wire brushing. Power wire brushing removes only loose rust and scale and is not satisfactory for the removal of tight scale, paint or for the cleaning of severely corroded structures, particularly riveted work.

Power operated impact tools such as *scaling hammers* and *chipping hammers* can be either electrically or pneumatically powered. Rotary impact *tools* employ centrifugal force to throw the cutters or hammers against the surface to be cleaned at high speed. These impact tools are suitable for removing heavy deposits of rust scale, mill scale, thick old paint, weld flux, slag and other brittle material. In some cases, it may be necessary to wire brush the surface after using impact tools. The chisel may be of different shapes and materials but should be kept in a sharp condition, otherwise it will drive rust and scale into the surface. Scalers operate on an impact principal also but the piston also acts as the impact tool. A hammer piston is a circular shaft with the cutting end shaped somewhat like a star chisel. These scalers are available with 1, 2 or 3 pistons operating in one tool. Great care must be exercised in using these tools because of the tendency to cut into the surface excessively, removing sound metal, and leaving sharp burrs where the paint will fail prematurely. The cutting action of the sharp chisel is valuable for shaping sharp edges to a rounded or less sharp surface so that the paint will not have a tendency to pull away, and also, to remove imperfections from the surface. These tools may be used to remove some tight mill scale and surface rusting, but in general practice, this is not desirable in view of the gouging of metal which then must be removed to do a thorough job.

Grinders and sanders can also be used but usually are very expensive for large areas. The abrasive grit size used must be properly selected. Too coarse an abrasive will create a deep anchor that is unsuitable for good paint performance; too fine an abrasive causes early clogging of the grinding wheel or sanding disc, thus making the process inefficient. After power cleaning operations are completed, dust and other loose matter shall be removed from the surface as noted under "Hand Cleaning" - Section 4.8231.

4.8233 Flame Cleaning: Metal scrapers are used to remove rust scale and foreign materials. The surfaces are then cleaned and dehydrated by flame, wire brushed and wiped to remove loose scale, rust, dirt, old paint and similar matter. The operation consists of sweeping an oxyacetylene flame (or propane, gasoline, etc.) from 2 to 12 inches wide over successive small areas to be cleaned. The speed with which the flame passes over the steel should be such so as not to fuse any scale or foreign matter with the surface and without overheating or otherwise injuring the steel. On old paint, several flame passes are necessary with intermittent scraping and wire brushing to remove the softened paint. After the wire brushing is completed, the surfaces are wiped clean and immediately painted while the temperature of the steel is above that of the surrounding atmosphere, but not so hot as to harm the paint.

4.8234 Sandblast Cleaning: Sandblast cleaning consists of abrading the surface through the high velocity impact of silica sand (or some other abrasive). Rust, mill scale, and old paint are removed along with some of the base metal in this type operation, leaving an etched surface that provides a good anchor for the paint to adhere to. The components of an efficient sandblasting operation are discussed in the following paragraphs.

Compressed Air Supply - This is the most critical part of the operation because work will be done in direct proportion to the volume and pressure of air passing through the nozzle. Volumes of 81 CFM to 338 CFM at a pressure of 90 to 100 lbs. are required. Blasting on steel plate should be done in the 90 to 100 PSI range while on masonry or glass a range of 40 to 50 PSI is appropriate. The larger the compressor, the larger the nozzle it can operate and the faster the job will be completed. Sandblasting is one of the most difficult jobs a compressor can perform because it requires a constant high volume, high pressure air stream for hours at a time and as a result, only the best compressor should be used for this purpose. Rotary type compressors are best because they can supply the air without heating it up and with the oil removed which is not true of the piston type compressor. The compressor should be kept as close to the sandblast machine as possible, but placed in such a position that prevailing winds will keep the dust away from the compressor. Allow a compressor 10 to 15 minutes to warm up before starting to blast. Some typical figures relating nozzle diameter, nozzle pressure, CFM and sand use/hour are given in the table as follows:

Nozzle Dia. (Inches)	\<td colspan=7\>Nozzle Pressure							
	40	50	60	70	80	90	100	
1/8	10.	11.3	13.2	15.1	17.	18.5	20.25	CFM
	69.	84.	97.	110.	127.	140.	154.	Sand/Hr.
3/16	22.	26.	30.	33.	38.	41.	45.	CFM
	160.	188.	214.	245.	270.	298.	330.	Sand/Hr.
1/4	41.	47.	54.	61.	68.	74.	81.	CFM
	276.	336.	390.	443.	510.	560.	618.	Sand/Hr.
5/16	65.	77.	89.	101.	113.	126.	137.	CFM
	495.	585.	688.	755.	840.	925.	1015.	Sand/Hr.
3/8	91.	108.	126.	143.	161.	173.	196.	CFM
	710.	835.	955.	1080.	1200.	1315.	1440.	Sand/Hr.
7/16	124.	147.	170.	194.	217.	240.	254.	CFM
	840.	1120.	1290.	1470.	1640.	1810.	1980.	Sand/Hr.
1/2	165.	195.	224.	252.	280.	309.	338.	CFM
	1230.	1450.	1670.	1890.	2100.	2320.	2530.	Sand/Hr.

Air Supply Hose - It is desirable to have a large diameter air line (1¼" minimum) from the compressor to the sandblast machine to cut down on friction loss through the hose. It should be attached to the bull hose outlet on the compressor, not the small valve manifold found on most compressors.

Sandblast Machine - The machines currently in use are of the direct pressure type which means that the sand supply is held under pressure. The size of the machine determines only how often it has to be refilled. As noted previously, the compressor size determines the size nozzle that can be used and the amount of sand used. The machines are equipped with hand holes to allow for inspection of the inside of the machine and to allow the operator to remove any foreign object that may have fallen in the machine, such as part of the sand bag, pieces of wood, rock, etc. Newer models are equipped with a remote control Deadman valve which allows the operator himself to shut off the machine at the nozzle rather than have the pot tender turn off as is necessary with the older models.

The sand metering valve is the heart of the sandblast machine because it controls the amount of abrasives that will be fed to the nozzle. Regulation of the sand control valve to provide the proper flow of sand to the nozzle is usually done by first opening the valve to its full open position, and then bringing the handle towards the closed position until the exact right mixture is available at the nozzle without cutting down production. (The sand can barely be seen leaving the nozzle.) If the sand coming out of the nozzle is spitting or feeding erratically, this is usually caused by an improper adjustment of the sand control valve and adjusting it should eliminate the condition. If the condition persists, it is frequently an indication of moisture in the sandblast machine and hoses, at which point an efficient self-dumping moisture separator should be installed.

Sand Blast Hose - Rule of thumb is that the inside diameter of the hose should be 3 to 4 times the orifice diameter of the nozzle. Care should be given to store the hose in a dry area. In use, the hose should be laid out in as straight a line as possible avoiding all radical 90 degree bends. If you have to curve the hose around an object, do it with a long curve as sharp bends and curves will create rapid wear on the tube of the hose causing a blow out at the bend. (Use as short a hose as possible).

Sandblast Nozzle - The selection of the proper nozzle for the work to be done is of prime importance. It governs the material requirements and the production that is obtained. The efficiency of the nozzle depends upon its shape and size in addition to the distance that it is held from the work. The further the nozzle is held from the work, the less the velocity of the particles when they strike the surface, and therefore, the less work they do on the surface.

The orifice size is designated by the diameter of the nozzle at its smallest point in 16ths of an inch (i.e., a No. 4 nozzle is 4/16" or ¼"). As noted previously, the maximum diameter that can be used is determined by the capacity of the compressor, and the largest possible nozzle to fit the available air supply should be used. Work will be done in direct proportion to the volume of air pushed through the nozzle at high speed. There are several different lengths of nozzles available. A short nozzle (3") is sufficient for an easy to clean surface but if the surface is extremely difficult to clean, such as rust, mill scale, prior coatings, etc., a long nozzle (4½" to 8¾" depending on orifice size) should be used. In blasting inaccessible areas, sometimes nozzles shorter than 3" will have to be used so that they can be worked around in behind beams or other structural members.

Nozzle linings are constructed of different materials with wide differences in their useful life.

Ceramic nozzles	1 to 2 hours	Cost approximately $.35
Cast Iron nozzles	6 to 8 hours	
Tungston Carbide	300 hours	
Norbide	750 to 1000 hours	Cost up to $150.00

The 1,000 lb. sandblast machines purchased for the bridge crews in 1967 had both ceramic nozzles and norbide nozzles (No. 4 and No. 5 straight bore 3" long). The ceramic and cast iron nozzles should not be used because their rapid wear destroys the blast pattern, overtaxes the compressor and uses exorbitant amounts of abrasive per sq. foot cleaned. A fairly new development is the venturi shaped nozzle which doubles the outlet velocity of the sand using the same air supply. Because of the increased outlet velocity, the control of the sand is more efficient than in a straight bore nozzle, and as a result, you have almost equal impact over the entire surface of the pattern instead of a high concentration in the center. The nozzle lining is quite brittle so any shock to the outer jacket will fracture the inner lining. Wrenches should not be used to attach or remove the nozzle from the holder. Be sure that there is a new washer behind the nozzle each day to protect the liner and jacket from the abrasive. Slipping a small piece of hose over the jacket will protect the nozzle against cracking.

In removing rust and mill scale, the proper attitude of the nozzle is between 80 degrees and 90 degrees to the surface being cleaned. A similar downward angle will help to direct the dust sway from the operator's helmet and insure better visibility. If loose paint, or other easy to remove coatings are being knocked off, a greater angle to the nozzle will speed up the job, as the air will work under the material and break it loose.

Blasting Hoods or Helmets - For most blasting operations, an air fed helmet or hood should be used which provides for a separate supply of air to the operator to be sure that no dust can enter his respiratory tract and cause silicosis. The eye plate should be replaced periodically once it starts to frost over.

4.8235 Chemical Cleaning

4.8235 Solvent Wiping: Solvent wiping is the least efficient of the chemical removal methods. Solvents employed cover a wide range of materials such as mineral spirits, naptha, coal tar solvents, alcohols, ethers, mixed alcoholic ether compounds such as the Cellosolves and Carbitols, petroleum fractions, chlorinated hydrocarbons and many others. Petroleum base mineral spirits, with a minimum flash point of 100 degrees F. or "Stoddard Solvent" should be used under normal conditions. Their use allows the subsequently applied paint film to wet the metal surface, forming a good bond with the metal. It is generally used as an auxiliary method for removing gross soil prior to a more effective cleaning method. The solvent soon becomes contaminated with the removed soil and thus after a short time merely redeposits oil on the surface. In order to be effective, therefore, clean solvent and clean rags must constantly be employed and this necessitates the use of large quantities of solvent and rags.

All solvents are potentially hazardous and they should be used under such conditions that their concentration in the air being breathed by the workmen is low enough for safety. This usually is not a problem as long as there is at least a slight breeze.

4.8236 Alkali Cleaning: It is more efficient, cheaper and less hazardous than solvent cleaning. Alkaline cleaners are dissolved in water and used at high temperatures. They clean by saponifying (turning into soap) certain oils and greases and their surface active components wash away other types of contaminants so that removal is by detergency or saponification rather than by solvency. After the soil has been displaced, it may be emulsified throughout the body of the cleaner, or may be partially or wholly saponified by the cleaner with the formation of water soluble soaps. The most effective alkaline cleaners must be blends of alkalies and other products to improve such properties as buffering action (ability to retain a given degree of alkalinity of PH), rinsibility, wetting and emulsifying action, detergent properties, etc. Heat improves the activity of the cleaner, improves the effectiveness, and increases the solubility of the surface contaminants. Strong solutions may be particularly effective in removing paint because the alkali saponifies the dry paint vehicle. Since the soaps that are formed are soluble in water, the contaminants are more easily removed by rinsing with water after saponification, and the adhesive nature of the old paint is reduced by chemical action.

Caution should be used in handling alkali cleaners and men should wear rubber gloves, rubber aprons and goggles when brushing and scrubbing the cleaner on the structure. Trisodium phosphate is a commonly used alkali in the proprietary products that are available. They should be used and diluted as recommended by the manufacturer (usually ½ oz. to 2 oz./gal. of water). Thorough rinsing with water is required to remove residues of alkalies. The water should be hot or under pressure, preferably both.

Following this, the surfaces should be passivated by rinsing with an acidic wash containing about 0.1% by weight of chromic acid, or sodium dichromate or potassium dichromate, to overcome the harmful effect of traces of alkali on paint adhesion. This passivating rinse may be applied by brushing or spraying. Respirators should be worn if the rinse is sprayed on. After rinsing, the steel should be allowed to dry completely before painting is started.

4.8237 Steam Cleaning: It can be used to remove heavy soil deposited on top of existing paint, especially from locations that would be difficult or impossible to solvent wipe and improved quality of cleaning. It is not a substitute for sandblasting, and in some cases must be augmented by wire brushing or spot sandblasting. The gross soil is readily removed by the combined action of high temperature and high velocity of the wet steam and should be augmented with the detergent action of alkali cleaners. A typical cleaner is composed of 45% Sodium Metasilicate, 43% Sodium Sesquisilicate, 10% Sodium Tetraphosphate and 2% Nacconal. For most projects 0.5% by weight of this cleaning powder at the nozzle is sufficient.

Structures on which the paint has weathered to the point that the finish coat appears chalky can be economically repainted by steam cleaning and applying a fresh finish coat of paint.

Equipment required is a steam generator capable of supplying steam or hot water to the nozzle at a temperature of approximately 300 degrees F, and 150 to 200 PSI. Steam should be directed against the surface to be cleaned by either a round or fan shaped nozzle. The fan shaped nozzle is best for broad surfaces while the round nozzle is better for the smaller inaccessible areas. If some scouring is required to remove grime, a nozzle fitted with a fiber brush is available. The operator should hold the nozzle within 6 inches of the surface and tilted in the direction of travel. The surface should first be wetted to allow the cleaning compound to loosen foreign matter which is later removed by a cleaning pass. The time interval between passes should be regulated according to the degree of dirt accumulations but it is usually sufficient to go twice over an area that is conveniently reached from one position. The speed of pass over an area is about the same as used for spray painting and it should not be held in one spot too long as it is quite easy to "cook" the sound paint. If an area has been properly cleaned it will feel firm and somewhat tacky, but not slick or grimy. In most cases, properly cleaned areas can be verified by sight. Excessive deposits of compound on sections which do not properly drain should be flushed off with water. Always work from the top down and try to leave the cleaned area as dry as possible.

It is important that the concentration of detergent does not exceed 0.75% because it will then tend to remove sound paint. In repainting a bridge that requires both spot sandblasting and steam cleaning, the steam cleaning should be done first because it will expose areas of unsound paint and the blasted areas would rust very rapidly if steam were applied to them. There should be a lapse of several days between steam cleaning a structure and painting to allow the surface to dry.

4.830 Paint Application: While surface preparation is probably the most critical and most important factor which governs the performance of paints, improper paint application may result in paint failure, even over blast-cleaned surfaces.

4.831 Objective: To apply uniform thickness paint films to properly prepared surfaces to prolong the useful life and appearance of the structure.

4.832 Standard: The 3 coat paint system in current use has a normal life expectancy of 8 to 12 years, therefore every structure should receive a complete finish coat on a cycle of 8 to 12 years depending on the type of environment that it is in. In order to achieve this, it is necessary to spot paint as signs of rust appear on an annual basis (see 4.623). Highway grade separation structures are usually of the composite I-beam types and are on display to the people traveling under them. The exposed face of fascia beams are subject to weathering by the sun, salt spray, rain, etc., and should be painted about midway in the cycle (5 years) for complete painting so that the structure presents a pleasing appearance at all times. For high structures and those over large bodies of water, the bridge maintenance engineer should prepare plans to have the necessary painting done by contract. Also, if the Regional Crews can't do all the necessary painting, plans should be prepared so the work can be done by contract.

4.833 Materials: All paint used on structural steel shall conform to the requirements of the current construction specifications of the New York State Department of Transportation. These paints will be sampled, tested, and accepted prior to shipment as specified in Materials Method No. 6. Paint that has been accepted will be received in containers with two security seals. The red seal indicates it has been sampled and the green one indicates that it has been accepted. This paint can be used as soon as it is received as long as the two seals are intact.

A brief summary of the paints currently specified and the uses for each follows:

M18CA - Dull Orange Primer for prime coat over bare metal. Should be used in preference to red lead which settles making remixing difficult or impossible, or **M18B - Maroon Primer,** which the paint companies find very difficult to formulate.

M18G - Gray Paint is the first field coat.

M18HS - Sage Green is the final field coat.

M18J - Ready Mixed Aluminum Paint can also be used. Type I for the first coat and Type II for the final coat although the M18G and M18HS are preferred.

M18TA - Textured Concrete Finish Paint should be used on exposed concrete surfaces, which have been shotcreted, to give them a uniform appearance. Where these paints have to be thinned for spray painting it is recommended that mineral spirits or turpentine be used.

The normal spreading rate for all the above paints (except M18TA) is in the range of 400 to 500 square feet per gallon so as to provide wet film thickness of 3.2 to 4.0 mils. Every paint crew should make use of a wet paint thickness gauge to check the rate of application. Stir paint thoroughly before application, taking care to remove any skin that may have formed in the container before mixing.

4.834 Method: The two methods that are commonly used are application with either brush or spray gun. For both methods, paint should be applied only under favorable weather conditions which are:

A. Relative humidity less than 85% or when moisture is not condensing on the surface to be painted. If when a small area of the surface is moistened with a damp cloth so as to apply a clearly defined, thin film of water and if this film evaporates within 15 minutes, the surface shall be considered safe to paint from the standpoint of continued condensation at that particular time.

B. Air temperature of 40 degrees or above and no likelihood of change in weather conditions within two hours after application which would result in the form of rain, snow, condensation, etc. Paint must be protected from freezing until it has dried. Because drying time increases as the temperature decreases, the time between successive coats should be lengthened in cold weather.

4.8341 Brush Application: Brushing of primer coats is recommended, because it flows on easily and results in better adhesion to the surface than spraying, it works the paint into cracks and crevices and also works the surface dirt into the paint where it can do the least harm.

Do not dip the brush deep in the paint as this results in overloading the bristles and in filling the "heel" with paint. Even undried paint may be difficult to remove. A brush with a "heel" full of dry paint loses much of its flexibility and shape.

All crevices, such as around rivet heads, sharp angles, projections and other areas where early failure tends to occur, are first traced or striped (at least 1" from the edge); then, after the stripe coat has dried to the touch, the entire surface is coated without attempt to "lay-off" the paint in one direction; lastly, runs are picked up and the paint is laid off in one direction so as to leave a uniform film, free from runs, sags or brush marks caused by not "feathering" or blending one lap into another. Brushes should be round or oval in shape, springy, and frequently cleaned. A sheepskin dauber can be used to paint the inside of enclosed parts and pipes.

4.8342 Spray Application: For rapidity in painting large areas, the easiest method to use is a spray gun. Most spray guns have a choice of nozzles which permits the spraying of a wide range of materials. Sometimes thinning is required but it should be kept to a minimum.

The spray pattern should be adjusted to correspond with the size and shape of the surface being painted. The quantity of paint being delivered to the gun should be adjusted to correspond with production speed by adjusting the tank pressure and maintaining a ratio of tank pressure to gun pressure that will give maximum atomization of the paint particles with the least vaporization of the thinner. Too high an air pressure at the gun will cause the painted surface to appear dry and grainy. Too low an air pressure will result in the painted surface appearing too heavy and too wet. Paint pressure is generally adjusted so that when the trigger of the gun is fully open without any atomizing air turned on, the paint will form a stream from the gun which will shoot out about 4 or 5 feet before falling vertically. Atomizing air pressure is then adjusted as required to properly atomize the paint: it should be kept as low as possible.

The spray gun should be held perpendicular to the surface to be coated and about 8" away. The gun should be steadily moved through a deliberate pattern that permits overlapping of the previous pass by 50% and at a speed that will leave a full, uniform coat. Overspray should be held to a minimum. To obtain maximum efficiency and a minimum of trouble, keep the equipment clean. Dirt and incorrect adjustment will result in variable spray patterns, runs, sags, and uneven coats. At the end of each day, or when completing a job, clean the gun thoroughly even though this requires disassembly. The manufacturer's recommendations should be followed.

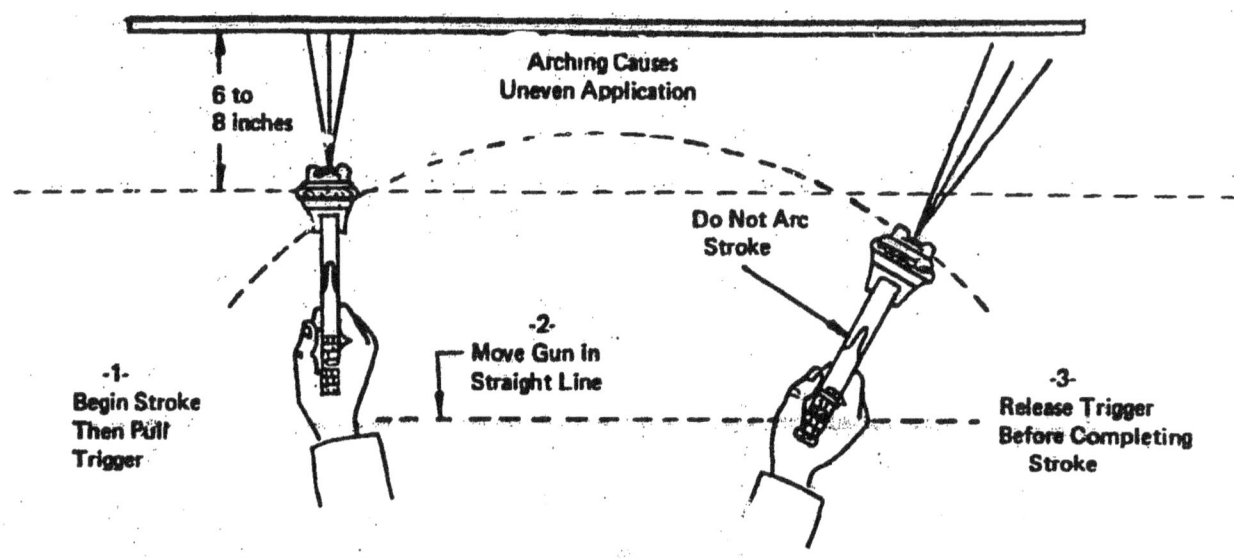

SHOWING PROPER METHOD OF MAKING SPRAY GUN STROKE

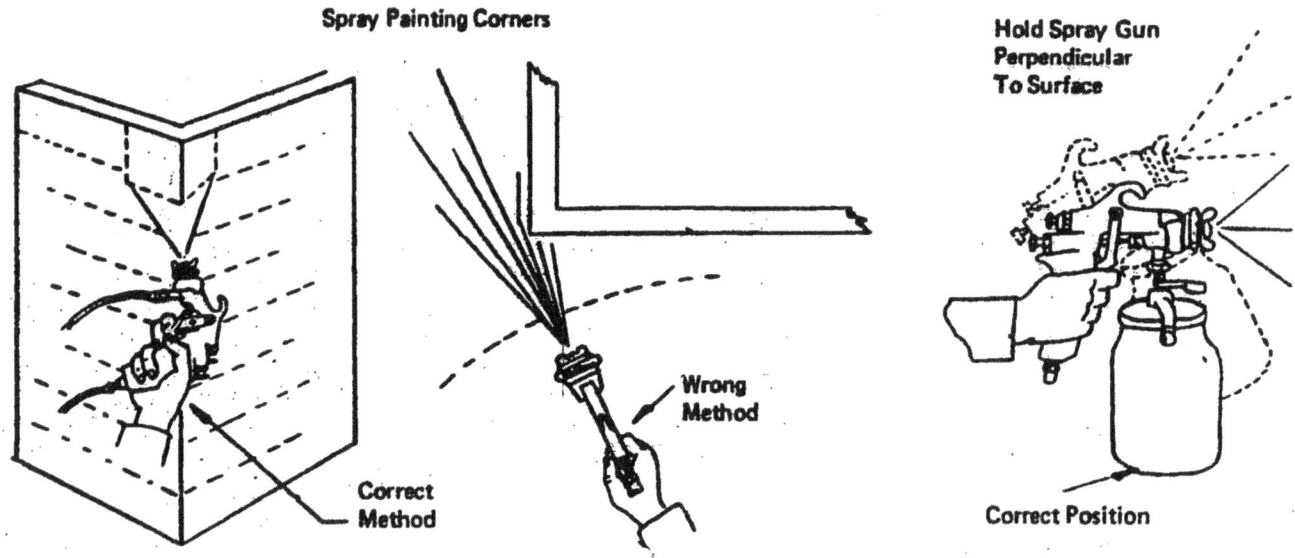

FUNDAMENTALS OF GOOD SPRAYING TECHNIQUE

Illustrations courtesy of
Steel Structures Painting Council

www.ingramcontent.com/pod-product-compliance
Lightning Source LLC
Chambersburg PA
CBHW081814300426